Courting Islam

Courting Islam

US-British Engagement with Islam since the European Colonial Period

Sean Oliver-Dee

LEXINGTON BOOKS
Lanham • Boulder • New York • London

Published by Lexington Books
An imprint of The Rowman & Littlefield Publishing Group, Inc.
4501 Forbes Boulevard, Suite 200, Lanham, Maryland 20706
www.rowman.com

6 Tinworth Street, London SE11 5AL, United Kingdom

Copyright © 2020 The Rowman & Littlefield Publishing Group, Inc.

All rights reserved. No part of this book may be reproduced in any form or by any electronic or mechanical means, including information storage and retrieval systems, without written permission from the publisher, except by a reviewer who may quote passages in a review.

British Library Cataloguing in Publication Information Available

Library of Congress Cataloging-in-Publication Data Available

ISBN 978-1-4985-0505-5 (cloth)
ISBN 978-1-4985-0506-2 (electronic)

To my wife, our children,
and the
many family and friends whose support remains invaluable to me.

Contents

Introduction		1
1	Islam, Muslims, and the Anglo-American Milieu	21
2	Views from the Top	39
3	Foreign Affairs	57
4	Economics	79
5	Public Activism: Cartoons and Mosque-Building	95
6	Proselytizing and Conversion	113
7	Education	127
8	Radicalism	147
Conclusion		165
Bibliography		173
Index		193
About the Author		195

Introduction

The relationship between "the West" and Muslims over the past two centuries is both an important subject and one which has been hampered by the wider political and cultural debates which have characterized the public spaces of both America and Britain over the last decade. The culture war being fought out on both sides of the Atlantic has meant that balanced discussions about the long-term relationship between what might be described as the culture of the North Atlantic and the cultures of the so-called Muslim world are almost impossible to find.[1] The subject is too fraught with sensitivities on all sides in the post-9/11 era. Yet, it is a subject which needs discussion. The manifestation of fears of cultural change in Western Europe and North America have become important political forces and these political forces have been catalyzed in large part by the perception of the growing presence of apparently radicalized Muslim communities.

In this polarized atmosphere, sides have been drawn between those who highlight perceived incompatibilities between the North Atlantic cultures and Muslim cultures and those who emphasize their believed compatibility. In such debates, much time is spent in trying to attain the moral high ground and, from there, dictate what policies or actions should flow from what eventually becomes the dominant narrative.

How, therefore, can this subject be discussed without falling into the pattern described here?

The first fact to acknowledge is that the necessity of having such a debate is testament to the fact that historically, there are reasons to believe that the US-British and Islamic cultures have not always coexisted peaceably. But that, secondly, while tensions and conflicts have existed, those struggles have also not been the sole manifestations of those interactions.

In the context of the competing narratives alluded to already, therefore, both sides of the argument have material upon which to draw their narratives.[2] As such, there is the possibility that both sides will "cancel one another out" and that the debate will eventually subside because neither perspective is either strong enough or weak enough to permit a consensus to emerge.

This book seeks to offer a different way forward in this arena by exploring one aspect of that historical engagement: Anglo-American governmental experiences with Islam and Muslims. In taking this approach this book is seeking to take one element of Western–Muslim encounters and to seek to explain what impression of the faith of Islam and Muslims has been left in the collective consciousness of two Western governments: America and Britain. As such they provide case studies of how the experiences of governments in the West have shaped their views of Muslims and Islam. In focusing on experiences rather than simply perceptions, it seeks to understand what perceptions about Muslims and Islam within government circles might be, and where those perceptions have their origins.

It needs to be made clear that this book is therefore not seeking to assess generalized Western perceptions of Islam. To make any kind of assessment of that kind, analysis of other Western governments would need to be included, along with public polling data and writings by media publications for all the countries concerned. This book does not seek to do that and instead takes one facet of the West: the American and British governments and explores their experiences with the people and states who profess to follow the faith labeled "Islam." In so doing, it will hopefully provide some analysis of what perceptions there are of Islam in these two governments and where they have come from.

Anglo-American governmental relationships with Islam and Muslims since the dawn of the Enlightenment era have been complex and often contradictory. Yet, they are relationships that have been one of the core strategic connections that have been instrumental in shaping a number of the key globally significant events over the past two centuries—events whose implications are still being worked through.

Both sides need to work together as members of the wider international community in areas of common concern such as climate change, organized crime, trafficking, and terrorism. They also need to cooperate in areas of mutual benefit such as resourcing (oil and minerals) and trade. And, while these needs will evolve and shift with time (such as with the growing self-reliance of US oil production over the past decade), those relationships still remain important.

But why choose Britain and America together for this study? Perhaps another state partnership such as France and Britain, or France and America, or Germany and America might also have been appropriate?

The answer lies in the relative commonality of culture which acts first as a control in relation to shedding light onto whether the perspectives of one country are also seen in the other country's relationship, thereby helping to understand whether the issue was specific to the one country, based on particular historical or cultural circumstance or common to both, which would suggest that the problem was deeper than one binary relationship. Second, Britain and America share a common political cultural and linguistic heritage which has been the basis of the so-called Special Relationship over the decades since the Second World War. Furthermore, both countries have not had the interruption of invasion. This has permitted both to develop free from the sudden cultural upheaval which conquest brings. They are also close economic and security partners, although both also pursue their own interests. The website of the US Embassy in London summarizes the relationship thus:

> The United States has no closer ally than the United Kingdom, and British foreign policy emphasizes close coordination with the United States. Bilateral cooperation reflects the common language, ideals, and democratic practices of the two nations. Relations were strengthened by the United Kingdom's alliance with the United States during both World Wars, in the Korean conflict, in the Persian Gulf War, in Operation Iraqi Freedom, and in Afghanistan, as well as through its role as a founding member of the North Atlantic Treaty Organization (NATO). The United Kingdom and the United States continually consult on foreign policy issues and global problems and share major foreign and security policy objectives.[3]

As a diplomatic mission the website is going to be saying positive things about the US-British relationship. But, without turning a blind eye to the multiple conflicts and tensions after the War of Independence such as the War of 1812 and, more recently, the Suez Crisis in 1956, a close working relationship between the two has been the overwhelming narrative of at least the past century.[4]

The other principal reason for choosing these two countries to focus upon is that, for Muslims, the United States (principally) and Britain embody the West. For that reason, although the French, Germans, Australians, Canadians, and others are all part of the West and have their own perspectives on interactions with Islam and Muslims, it is Britain and America which are talked about (negatively) when anti-Western sentiments are being expressed. Therefore, while this book is an analysis of American and British perceptions of Islam based upon their experiences, it is also a wider vehicle for the exploration of whether there is any truth to the charge that the West is out to destroy Islam.[5] An accusation which, as will be seen in the book, has been leveled at "the West" for over a century.

METHODOLOGY

In taking on this subject there are a number of potential pitfalls, the most serious of which is the temptation to blame one side or other and to choose incidents which evidence that narrative. Being aware of this, this author has sought to ensure that a range of subject areas will be covered so that, for example, engagements in foreign relations do not become the dominant narrative over issues at home in Britain and America. These incidents and the correspondence they prompted will offer insights into the perceptions and considerations of the officials and politicians upon which this book's analysis is based. However, this does not purport to be an exhaustive engagement with all events and issues over the period. Instead, a series of issues has been discussed which, taken together, provide an evidence base for the patterns of perception which emerge. A rationale for those incidents not discussed is that they would take up a huge amount of space given the range of engagements which have taken place and, rather than attempting to discuss each one which would lead to a somewhat surface treatment of each incident, I have decided to discuss a few seminal issues in more detail within the differing subject areas.

Another methodological point which needs to be made is that, by the very act of discussing reactions to specific incidents and issues, this book does not aspire to producing a long and detailed narrative of all interactions between Muslims and US-British governments. Instead, it provides some relevant wide-angle contextualization but spends the majority of its time on an analysis of the attitudes and perceptions the correspondence throws into relief.

The final methodological note to be made is that, although the book is generally chronological, this is not a deliberate element of the framework of the book's structure. Seeking to confine the book to a specific narrative structure proved to be too much of a constraint on the thematic focus which lies at the heart of the book. So, while the book does generally adhere to a chronological structure, there will be moments where, of necessity, it does stray from that.

PROPOSITION

The central proposition of this book is that the experiences of American and British governments with differing aspects of policy engagement and cultural interaction have taught them that while Islam and Muslims can be useful instruments and valuable allies, they are also a significant threat. This is of course an unnuanced statement and, as shall be seen, there has also been a recognition that differing denominations and ideologies within Islam offer both grounds for optimism and grounds for concern. Yet, the correspondence shows that these concerns have played and continue to play a secondary role compared to the broader, and ultimately decisive, fact that for a host of strategic and economic reasons, both countries need the goodwill and cooperation of Muslims and Muslim-majority states.

SETTING THE SCENE

Changing Political Philosophy

A book of this nature and subject needs to acknowledge at least one fundamental fact: that in seeking to understand the complex interactions and multifaceted relationship that developed between the Anglo-American sphere and that of Muslim peoples and states it is impossible to define a settled Anglo-American view of Islam and Muslims. There might be consistent themes, or streams of thinking, but talking in terms of a settled American, or British, or Anglo-American viewpoint is impossible as the perspectives of British and American officials and Muslims (of any denomination or sect) evolve fundamentally over the period this book covers.

For example, political philosophy in the United States and United Kingdom has seen an important shift from Enlightenment to postmodernism which has seen the growing dominance of liberalism, poststructuralism, and social constructivism as theoretical constructs replacing entrenched realism. As part of that shift, cosmopolitanism has become the default position of the Western political elites, including in the United States and Britain.[6] Of course, each country's policymaking culture has its particularities which nuances the brand of Cosmopolitanism found from country to country. But the fundamentally utopian vision envisaged by Kant's *To Perpetual Peace: A Philosophical Sketch* (1795) and refined over the course of the next two centuries before being brought into modern neoliberalism through the work of Keohane and Nye has become a constant philosophical bedrock across the Western policymaking world until the challenge posed by Steve Bannon's Economic Nationalism.[7] Of course, the seminal work of John Rawls in this field cannot be overstated, but he will not be discussed until later in this chapter because his views on religion have recently been reevaluated in a way that could, rather than placing him firmly within the liberal camp as has been generally accepted, put him instead in the post-secular camp.

The importance of this shift in thinking cannot be overstated when seeking to understand the US-British engagement with Islam.

The past two centuries have witnessed this internal philosophical shift at the same time as internal geopolitical and ethno-cultural shifts have also occurred that are inextricably linked to the changing global environment. In crude philosophical or ideological terms this could be construed as the move from Realism to varying strains of liberalism and Constructivism, as well as, recently, the growing preeminence of Post-secular theories.

The end of the Cold War brought an opportunity for a New World Order based around liberal, Cosmopolitan theories and ethics. The longed-for Covenant of Peace which Kant envisioned back in the depths of the Napoleonic Wars, it seemed, became an achievable aspiration, rather than a distant utopian vision.[8] The spread of democracy and therefore (so Fukayama and other theorists believe) the foundation of global peace would be inevitable, whether, in the short term, obstacles arose or not.[9] Even the 9/11 attacks have not shaken that core fundamental belief because the cosmopolitan conception of the essential universality of fundamental human values has encouraged Western political elites to push past the impact of global jihadism and to push even harder toward the utopian vision of Kant and latterly, Norman Angell.[10]

In terms of US-British and Islamic engagement, this thinking has helped transform policymaker's thinking about Islam and Muslims from the Realist-based model of civilizational competition and limited cooperation to one of inclusivism and integration. The post–Second World War evolution of mass global migration has also been a factor in this shift in thinking, but its impact should not be too overstated, certainly in relation to Britain at least. For, during the period of the Empire, the size, geographical spread, and positions of power and influence that characterized the imperial Muslim communities meant that the language of cooperation and inclusivity were fundamental pillars of imperial stability. In that sense, the development of cosmopolitanism in the British milieu represents far more of a natural continuity than it does for US policymakers, as shall be seen in chapters 3 and 4.

Away from International Relations theories, the growing importance of Post-secular theory across Europe, including the UK, has also helped to make the internal political and academic shift from a postmodern policymaking culture to new territory in which Western political philosophical norms are being fused with non-Western ones, notably Muslim. The very fact of this process alone helps to shift the nature of perception on how Islam and Muslims are viewed in government circles. Calhoun, Juegensmeyer, and van Antwerpen captured this shift and explained it in terms of the growing prevalence of the views of Weber and Habermas who both allowed greater space for the presence of religion in the policymaking and public space as part of a secular settlement and an acknowledgment of the growth of religion globally.[11] Central to this viewpoint is the principle that the claims of faith must be treated respectfully, alongside those of secular reason and in this, Muslim political thinking has been increasingly researched and referenced in an attempt to broaden the religio-cultural scope of intellectual enquiry. Post-secularization therefore has sought to paint secularization as another form of religious settlement in which secularists absorb the language, culture, and practice of religion without naming them as such and, in turn, religion develops increasingly sophisticated rationalist streams of thought.

In the United States, where neoconservativism took root despite the theoretical separation of faith and state, a slightly different narrative has played out in relation to secularization and post-secularization. Since the end of the Cold War, the dynamic has become more strongly focused around the shifting ideological viewpoints of the two principal parties with the Democrats moving toward a more secular (with post-secular elements) stance and the Republicans increasingly retrenching toward neoconservatism.[12]

Nevertheless, a post-secular narrative has developed on both sides of the Atlantic, in part, because of the number of high-profile cases concerning religious freedom issues (often in relation to religious conscience versus gay rights) which have brought the place of religion in public life back into focus in the everyday. Outside of the legal negotiation, Minority World governments have come to realize that religious NGOs are often both better informed and more widely networked within many global regions than the traditional web of embassies and diplomatic networks and have therefore sought to use international religious networks as sources of information and diplomacy in relevant situations.[13] It is important to note that these developments are taking place independently of more high-profile debates such as the place and role of the Church of England in the UK and jihadism across both countries. This partnership between state and faith, especially the Church of England with its established status, has been manifested most clearly perhaps in the Building Bridges and Near Neighbors streams of work which have been carried out by the Church of England with the prompting (and funding in the case of Near Neighbors) of successive British governments.[14]

Yet this openness to partnership with religious NGOs does not necessarily reflect an openness to the place of religion in political life and authority more broadly. This observation was brought into sharp focus with the controversy surrounding the former leader of the Liberal Democrat Party in the UK, Tim Farron, who resigned his position following the 2017 British General Election saying that, while he believed that classic liberalism was entirely compatible with his Christian beliefs, modern liberalism had evolved in a way which had alienated Christian viewpoints.[15]

And it is here that a discussion of the viewpoints on John Rawls should be rightly placed, for this most influential of Liberal Political theorists has often been viewed as hostile to the place of religion in public life: certainly a surface reading of his *Theory of Justice* (1974) would suggest that Rawls would have been far more content with the removal of religion from the policymaking world. But evidence of his views as recently articulated in Tom Bailey and Valentina Gentile's *Rawls and Religion* (2014), a recent reevaluation of his work, instead suggests that Rawls was actually more closely allied to the post-secularists than might previously have been thought.[16]

In their Introduction Bailey and Gentile characterize Rawls's views on the religious-government nexus as critical to the development of liberal political life.

> He [Rawls], envisions consensus over political authority as emerging internally and dynamically from citizens' various religious and other moral worldviews, such that religions and engagement with them are crucial to his conception of liberal political life.[17]

This assertion becomes the basis for the reevaluation which forms much of the book in which they seek to revise previous understandings of what Rawls meant by the terms "respect" and "consensus" and discussing Rawls's approach to the accommodation of illiberal religious views. All this discussion eventually turns back to an evaluation of liberalism from the perspective of religion.

The core of the book is a discussion of Rawls's delineation between public reason and comprehensive doctrine as pathways to a political conception of justice which should be founded and established upon overlapping consensus. These terms are conceptualized as the relationship between religion or worldview (comprehensive doctrine) and common defensible ethics and concepts which are shared by citizens (public reason). The overlapping consensus is therefore what emerges from the interaction of the first two elements leading to a body of law which is based in that cultural discourse. For Rawls, therefore, religious adherents need to be able to transmit the relevant elements of their comprehensive doctrines into concepts which can be absorbed (or at least discussed) in the wider public domain. In doing so they will participate fully in the process of liberal democracy. Moreover, were they not to do so, the entire concept of liberal democracy would be at risk because of an important element of the foundations upon which overlapping consensus (and therefore, the law) would not be laid. This, then, is the core of reasonableness as understood in the Rawlsian sense.

It is for this reason that Rawls, after initially agreeing with the Laïcité Exclusivist theory, rejected it after seeing the impact of such figures as Martin Luther King Jr., whose faith directly inspired his political activism.[18] Bailey and Gentile sum up Rawls's revised position on religion (or comprehensive doctrine) thus: "reasons which reflect citizens' comprehensive doctrines may be employed in public deliberations and decision-making, as long as supporting reasons which reflect citizens' shared conception of political authority can be provided 'in due course.'"[19] Yet this apparently open invitation to religious adherents to contribute to the development of the overlapping consensus is tempered with the non-privileging of faith, whether Christian, Muslim, or other, in the public sphere.

As we shall see, this caveat is vitally important in understanding where the thinking lies at the base of many of the frustrations and concerns felt by Muslims in the policymaking sphere. While, for Christians, the loss of privilege for the faith which adherents are coming to terms with on both sides of the Atlantic is a source of confusion and frustration. This book is not concerned with the Christian perspective, only with the perspective of the US and British governments who have been absorbing the liberal, and increasingly post-secular, political ideologies developed by Rawls and others. But the increasing dominance of this thinking as the period under discussion has continued helps to understand the fundamental idea that, when coming to Islam (or any other faith), this book will not therefore be discussing a homogeneous or fixed view, but a number of views derived from a multitude of personalities with their own perspectives and, vitally, a shifting policymaking culture.

The question might therefore reasonably be asked, can this book achieve its stated aim in the context it has presented in this chapter? The answer to which is yes, but in order to do so, it will need to return to this discussion of shifting political culture in the conclusions in order to frame its observations.

So, before moving into a discussion of the specific events, national, international, and individual, which have helped to frame the British and American government's views on Islam and Muslims, it is worthwhile looking back at the longer historical accounts of US and British interactions with Muslims before the period under discussion in order to get a sense of the long-term perceptions of Islam that had already built up for both governments and cultures. For in so doing, we acknowledge that viewpoints are not generated in a vacuum and that, therefore, the views of the officials and politicians on both sides of the Atlantic being discussed here already had some roots before being watered by their own experiences.

Changing Cultural Context

Constitutionally, the United States is well known for operating its separation of church and state. Within that, the First Amendment protects religious freedom and stipulates that the government will not establish any one religion as the state religion. However, while this position reflects a desire among the drafters of the US constitution to reject any formal state religion, Alexis de Tocqueville's sharp observations about the cultural place of faith in America reflect the place that Christianity traditionally had in the country up until the mid-twentieth century. "When I first arrived in the United States, it was the religious aspect of the country that first struck my eyes." He added later, "Religion still has great sway over the people here."[20]

That Christian culture began to shift in the period of the 1960s when, as Kevin McCaffree describes it, there was "a profound generational shift away from orthodox Christian religiosity, church attendance and daily prayer."[21] It is a dynamic which has continued at differing paces in differing parts of the United States ever since.[22]

In the context of the arrival of large-scale Muslim (and other non-Christian faiths) in America, therefore, the impact of Islam on North America has become increasingly felt at a time when the whole continent is in the throes of a struggle about the place of religion in its culture. Connected with this has been the beginnings of a form of postcolonial questioning about the nature of America's role in the world where its old certainty of "mission" is being significantly eroded.

The United States has suffered internationally through its invasion of Iraq and Afghanistan and has been roundly condemned for its actions in relation to Extraordinary Rendition. That said, according to the IMF and the World Bank, the United States remains the most wealthy single nation on earth with a GDP 7 trillion dollars bigger than that of China, the next largest economy.[23] With that wealth comes considerable global influence even if the days when it was able to dictate policy internationally appear to be over.[24]

At the same time as the public place of institutional religion and faith in Europe and the United States are in protracted change, European and North American societies are going through enormous social upheaval.

Polls conducted over several decades by the Pew Research Center on social attitudes within the United States have revealed that the country is experiencing similar patterns of social change to those experienced in Europe and other Minority World states: particularly telling is the data on attitudes to marriage and the family where the "Millennial Generation" (MG) are 46 percent married as compared to "Generation X" (GX) of whom 57 percent were married.[25] It is an America which is a little younger proportionally than the Generation X (MGs make up 45 percent of the population as compared to GXs who made up 40.5 percent). Furthermore, it is an America in which the role of women has changed dramatically from the "Silent" generation to the MG, with only 25 percent not in employment as compared to 58 percent in 1966. Perhaps not surprisingly, therefore, another national poll taken by Gallup indicates that Americans have lower expectations for the future than their parents' generation did with 57 percent of Americans of the "MG" believing that they would have a better life.[26] This was down from GX who had polled the same question at 75 percent in 1995. However, the wave of classic American optimism does not appear to have entirely died, for over 60 percent of Americans believe that their financial situation is likely to have improved by next year.[27]

The impact of the culture war has been profound in many aspects of life in America.[28] It has been raging in the United States since the counterculture of the 1960s but was really driven into public consciousness with the presidential candidacy of Patrick Buchanan in the 1992 presidential campaign. When, at the Republican National Convention in Houston, he proclaimed that the cultural war was "as critical to the kind of nation we will one day be as was the Cold War itself."[29] It is a "war" which encompasses both how America wants to understand itself and how it wants to understand its role on the international stage. Consequently, narratives which highlight the evils of racism and slavery vie with those who highlight the spread of democracy and the triumph over Soviet Russia. It is a battle which is being fought out in new media; outlets such as *The Young Turks* pitch their progressivism against the conservatism of *The Daily Wire*. Among Millennials and Post-millennials, it is these YouTube, Patreon, and Instagram accounts where such competing narratives are fought out. In this context, the financial crisis and, latterly, the election of Donald Trump have helped to bring to the surface the cultural divide which had been developing in the United States over decades. It is a battle which is impacting all areas of public life: politics, media, and even museums and art galleries.[30]

Independent of, but not disconnected from, the culture war, there have been profound changes in attitude toward sex and sexuality across both the United States and Britain, as well as attitudes toward abortion. What is more directly relevant, however, is the changes in attitudes toward other races and cultures which have also taken place across both countries. Of course, this has been more profoundly pronounced in relation to segregation in the Southern United States but across both countries, an expectation of multicultural living, particularly in urban areas, has become normative.[31]

In Britain the British Social Attitudes surveys and the data held at the Office of National Statistics have become vital sources of analysis in tracking the shifts taking place in culture and politics. Many publications have already analyzed the findings, but there is one area of change which is of particular relevance to this book which is worthwhile drawing out.

Nothing embodies the changing nature of British culture than the debate which has taken place over the definition of, and perceived need for, Fundamental British Values.

The term "Fundamental British Values" had first been used by the coalition government in 2011 when, in response to Lord Carlisle's review of counter-terrorism policy, the coalition sought to bring forward a raft of policies which addressed the problem of government funding going to groups who, though nonviolent, espoused an ideology which provided fertile ground for jihadism to bloom. Yet, Fundamental British Values was a new phrase which tried to capture a sense of commonality and belonging for the increasingly ethnically diverse citizens of the UK.

This all too apparent lack of community and sense of "togetherness" had been developing over decades. In this context, the attacks by jihadists simply forced an awkward discussion about what being British meant in the world of dissolving borders and mass migration. Incidents such as the Tottenham riots in the 1980s (when some African and Caribbean background people protested violently against ongoing racial harassment) highlighted the lack of collective connection among differing elements of the British population. A growing sense of frustration among the British political establishment was manifested in then government minister Norman Tebbitt's complaint about the fact that, during cricket matches between England and her former colonies, immigrants from those former colonies seemed to be supporting their homeland, rather than their adopted country. Consequently, Tebbitt argued that in order to be considered properly British, a person needed to support English (or British) sports teams. It was a comment which became laughingly known as the "Tebbitt Test."[32] But away from this rather superficial discussion, the introduction of Citizenship classes into the newly created National Curriculum in 1987 highlighted that citizenship now had to be taught, rather than inculcated, through the home and local communities.

Unfortunately, it was a concern that was impossible to debate in the context of a nation which was struggling with accusations of institutional racism and an overwhelming sense of guilt about the UK's recent colonial past. So there was no proper discussion of it during the Thatcher-Major Conservative government's time in office, and while this embarrassed silence settled over the political classes, European integration began to gather pace. Three years later a new government swept to a landslide victory. Tony Blair and his New Labor government sought to find a different answer to the unanswered conundrum of finding a new language of commonality and belonging which was not perceived to have racial connotations.

On March 28, 2000, Tony Blair made a speech on "True Britishness." In it he argued that "True Britishness" lay "in our values, not unchanging institutions."[33] He went on to add, "standing up for our country means . . . standing up for the core British values of fair play, creativity, tolerance, and an outward-looking approach to a world."[34] Blair had been much influenced by a lecture given by historian Linda Colley at Downing Street in 1999 in which she argued for a vision of twenty-first-century Britishness which was based around the concept of the citizen nation rather than an obsession with identity. This theme was reiterated post 7/7 when Tony Blair and his successor, Gordon Brown, continued to talk in terms of a Britishness that was based upon common values and was outward-looking, rather than based upon any one ethnic identity. They were given backing by scholars such as Tariq Modood who proposed the concept of multicultural citizenship.[35]

The debate about multiculturalism was really an attempt to create the space for diversity but, as *The Casey Review* reported (2016), multiculturalism ran up against segregationist desires and could not provide the tools to counter them.

Casey's remarks highlighted the shift which had taken place in the political landscape from New Labor and Multiculturalism in the wake of the continued terrorist attacks in the UK, the "foreign fighter" phenomenon, and a series of surveys which appeared to show a desire toward separatism among some Muslim groups. Casey's findings drew criticism from some quarters such as the Stand Up to Racism group who argued that the report did nothing by way of encouraging strategies for combatting racist and Islamophobic attacks.[36] But these criticisms were relatively isolated as compared to the broader consensus about the core of the review's findings. Indeed, the Cantle-Kaufmann report (2016) evidenced an increasing polarization and separation among all communities.[37] Those findings, coupled with a reemerging national pride (undefined), reset the public landscape for a debate about being British which shifted away from common citizenship toward a desire to create a sense of belonging rather than simply affiliation. In this context Brexit was a symptom rather than a catalyst.[38]

Linda Colley in her book *Britons* (1992) argued that it was not simply economic differences which separated the British from the French in the minds of the British at that time, but it was also religious: the Protestant British against the Catholic French. Protestantism, particularly the established Church of England, was an essential ingredient of belonging.[39] In this context it is therefore important to note the findings of the September 2018 British Social Attitudes survey, which asked a question about religious affiliation. The survey found that, for the first time, those identifying as members of the Church of England dropped below half the population (48%).[40] Yet, as the statistics earlier evidenced, the sense of pride in being British has actually been growing rather than dropping. In the light of these numbers, therefore, it seems reasonable to suggest that the definition of being "British" is shifting away from the old Protestant-centered paradigm.

The historic lack of significant immigration to Britain itself meant that questions about Fundamental British Values were discussed in the context of Empire, rather than those within the borders. In the Empire, Britain had shown itself to generally make very few demands of adhering to British values, other than opposing (indeed seeking to remove) what it saw as appalling cultural practices such as sati (widow burning).[41] Questions about integration or assimilation during the imperial period therefore did not arise in the British home context for "The other" was remote and distant, negating any reason to discuss absorbing competing visions of cultural norms.

In the same period as these shifts in public attitude and cultural norms have been taking place, public concern in both countries about Islam has been growing.

One facet of this concern has been demographic and the potential for cultural change that could take place if the trend of ethnic white birthrate drops while nonwhite birthrate increases continues. Although this concern is not specific to Islam in one sense, the potential effect upon what has been known ethereally as the British way of life has been encapsulated for some in what has been portrayed as "Islamic otherness."[42]

These concerns have been given academic substantiation in the work of Eric Kaufmann's "Second Demographic Transition Theory" which has been developed further in the recent *Whiteshift: Populism, Immigration and the Future of White Majorities*. Kaufmann's theory was based upon a lengthy study of twenty years mapping the demographic patterns of religious and nonreligious groups. His results clearly showed that in general, religious people have more children than nonreligious ones. Furthermore, other studies have shown that Muslims appear to be out-birthing any other religious group.[43]

So, while there would not be a general awareness of Kaufmann's theory, the findings of polls both in the United States and United Kingdom would strongly suggest that public perception of the demographic shift, coupled with the dynamics outlined earlier has been a motivational factor in the policy shifts and political changes which shall be discussed further in the rest of the book.[44]

RELEVANT LITERATURE

Many scholars have made contributions to the field of Muslim engagement with the Anglo-American milieu. Some have dealt with sociopolitical issues and others with specific subject or geographical areas such as identity, the Middle East, Pakistan, or terrorism.

Iftikhar Malik's *Islam and Modernity: Muslims in Europe and the United States* explores the nature of Muslim communities on both sides of the Atlantic, seeking to understand the struggles they have, both internal and external. The book seeks to set the War on Terror in a historical context, arguing that what is currently happening is, in effect, the latest in a series of Western wars against Islam which date back to the Ottoman period. Malik's perspective and analysis are insightful of the Muslim perspective of victimhood that courses strongly through many Muslim narratives concerning the West.

Courting Islam turns the picture around and looks at how British and American governments have tried to understand Islam, and work with Muslims over many decades for a multitude of strategic reasons.

Humayun Ansari's *The Infidel Within: Muslims in Britain Since 1800* and Sophia Gilliat-Ray's *Muslims in Britain* both give broadstroke narratives of Muslim presence in the UK. They delve into Muslim communities in order to tell their stories from the perspective of those communities. As such they deal both with internal community struggles, as well as intra-community ones, painting a picture of a set of people who have successfully rooted, despite a series of obstacles. Ansari's narrative is politically focused, whereas Gilliat-Ray takes a closer look at sociological issues in greater detail.

Kambiz GhaneaBassiri's *A History of Islam in America* covers much of the same ground as that which I cover here. However, whereas GhaneaBassiri is focused largely on the internal narrative of the growing prominence of a minority group, my narrative is focused upon delving into the story behind the governmental perspective which GhaneaBassiri covers more briefly. In that sense, GhaneaBassiri does for Islam in the United States what Ansari does for Islam in the United Kingdom. GhaneaBassiri's historical approach is complemented by an anthropological survey reported in Akbar Ahmed's *Journey into America: The Challenge of Islam*, which focuses on questions of identity for both Muslims and non-Muslims in America. It is based upon 2,000 interviews which took place across the United States over 2008 and it seeks to provide a snapshot of how Islam fits into the broader questions of identity which Americans are increasingly asking in the post-9/11 world.

Jane Smith's *Islam in America* takes a sociological approach. Although dated, its observations and analysis remain valuable, particularly as it provides a snapshot of the state of affairs in the United States before the events of 9/11.

Tahir Abbas's (ed) *Muslim Britain: Communities Under* details the effects of the fear and suspicion undergone by Muslims in the UK as a result of international terrorist activities. In a similar, though more positive, vein, Asthma Gull Hasan's *American Muslims: The New Generation (2nd Ed)* seeks to open the non-Muslim to currents within Muslim communities in the West. Moreover, Ron Geaves, Theodore Gabriel, Yvonne Haddad, and Jane Smiths's *Islam in the West Post 9/11* is written as a documentary record of the experiences of Muslims and practicing Islam in the era of Extraordinary Rendition and the new Conter-Terrorist strategy, shortend to CONTEST. This collection of essays broadens the story out to the whole of the West and includes some important developments in Christian-Muslim relations.

All of these books have made a valuable contribution in helping to understand the issues and concerns of Muslims in the UK and America.

Courting Islam turns the lens around and explores the perception of Muslim communities in the United States and United Kingdom, and Muslim-majority states from the perspective of the successive British and American governments. It analyzes how Muslims have been perceived by government officials who have dealt with them and their issues over the two centuries.

STRUCTURE

In order to understand the complexity and long-standing nature of the transatlantic governmental engagement with Islam over the course of more than two centuries, we will need to begin with a history of Islam in America. There are quite a number of histories of British-Islamic engagement already published and, as far less attention has been given to Islam and Muslims in America it seemed appropriate to spend a little time on the Muslim-American experience rather than doing a general history of Islam in both states. This initial overview of Muslims in America will highlight the presence of Islam in tiny numbers on the continent from the earliest years of its development and seek to show how the presence of Muslims in the United States has become more and more significant, not necessarily from a demographic perspective but from a geostrategic perspective.

Subsequent chapters explore the range and depth of transatlantic and Islamic engagements by focusing on different aspects of government policymaking in relation to Muslims, as well as Muslim attitudes toward those Anglo-American interactions. Each chapter in turn will explore the value and perspectives on the interactions exhibited by all sides with a view to building up a broad, complex picture of the impressions created by those interactions on both sides. Those interactions cover a range of domestic, diaspora, and international issues, including economics, foreign policy, birth and death, education, and the manifestation of faith in the public space over the whole of the period under discussion.

NOTES

1. This is discussed in Andrew Hartman, *A History of the Culture Wars: A War for the Soul of America*. Chicago: University of Chicago Press, 2015. See also David Goodhart, *The Road to Somewhere: The New Tribes Shaping British Politics*. London: Penguin, 2017.

2. See, for example, Mohammad Samei (2010) "Neo Orientalism? The Relationship between the West and Islam in Our Globalized World," *Third World Quarterly* Vol. 31, Iss. 7, pp. 1145–1160; Sumita Mukherjee and Sadia Zulfiqar (eds), *Islam and*

the West: A Love Story? Cambridge: Cambridge Scholars Publishing, 2015; Plamen Makariev (ed), *Islamic and Christian Cultures: Conflict or Dialogue*. Washington DC: The Council for Research in Values and Philosophy, 2001; Gema Munoz, *Islam, Modernism and the West: Cultural and Political Relations at the End of the Millennium*. London: I.B. Tauris, 1999; Andrew Kirk, *Civilizations in Conflict? Islam, the West and Christian Faith*. Oxford: Regnum Books International, 2011.

3. Anon (No Date) "History of the Special Relationship," https://uk.usembassy.gov/our-relationship/policy-history/.

4. Kathleen Burke's books *Old World, New World*. London: Abacus, 2009, and Kathleen Burk, *Lion and the Eagle: The Interaction of the British and American Empires 1783–1972*. London, New York: Bloomsbury Press, 2018 both discuss the complexity of the relationship in detail.

5. This narrative is engaged with in Ed Husain, *The House of Islam: A Global History*. London: Bloomsbury, 2018. See also Raza Raja's thoughtful article "Why Are Conspiracy Theories So Rife in the Muslim World," *The Huffington Post*, July 7, 2017.

6. In *Superhubs* Sandra Navidi describes how the current international consensus was developed through the personal relationships formed at key institutions and places: the Massachusetts Institute of Technology, Goldman Sachs, the World Economic Forum, the Clinton Global Initiative, and the Four Seasons restaurant in New York. See Sandra Navidi, *Superhubs: How the Financial Elite and Their Networks Rule Our World*. New York: Nicholas Brealey Publishing, 2017, pp. 83–84.

7. Robert Keohane and Joseph Nye, *Power and Interdependence*, 4th edn. Boston: Longman, 2011.

8. There is an important discussion of post-Cold War liberal thinking in the chapter entitled "A Victory or Crisis of Liberalism," in Georg Sorensen (ed), *Rethinking the New World Order*, London: Palgrave MacMillan, 2016.

9. See, for example, Francis Fukayama (1989) "The End of History," *The National Interest* Vol. 16, pp. 3–18.

10. Norman Angell, *The Great Illusion*. Originally published 1910, Republished and updated 1933. Ithaca (NY): Cornell University Press, 2011.

11. See Craig Calhoun, Mark Juergensmeyer, and Jonathan van Antwerpen (eds), *Rethinking Secularism*. Oxford, New York: OUP, 2011.

12. There has been significant academic engagement with the place of religion in American policymaking and political life and more recently, the growing (and more apparent) divide between the two main political parties in relation to faith and state. See Edward L. Cleary and Allen D. Hertzke (eds), *Representing God at the Statehouse: Religion and Politics in the American States*. Lanham (MD): Rowman & Littlefield, 2006; Sue Crawford and Laura Olson (eds), *Christian Clergy in American Politics*. Baltimore (MD): The John Hopkins University Press, 2001; Kenneth Wald and Allison Calhoun-Brown, *Religion and Politics in the United States*, 5th edn. Lanham (MD): Rowman & Littlefield, 2010; Laura R. Olson, "Mainline Protestant Washington Offices and the Political Lives of Clergy," in Robert Wuthnow and John H. Evans (eds), *The Quiet Hand of God: Faith-Based Activism and the Public Role of Mainline Protestantism*. Berkeley (CA): University of California Press, 2002, pp.

54–79; Laura Olson and Edward Jelen, *The Religious Dimension of Political Behaviour. A Critical Analysis and Annotated Bibliography*. Westport (CT): Greenwood Press, 1998; Laura Olson, *Filled with Spirit and Power. Protestant Clergy in Politics*. Albany (NY): State University of New York Press, 2000; John Green, *The Faith Factor: How Religion Influences American Elections*. Westport (CT): Praeger, 2007; Geoffrey Layman, *The Great Divide: Religious and Cultural Conflict in American Party Politics*. New York: Columbia University Press, 2001.

13. See Timothy Blewett, Adrian Hyde-Price and Wyn Rees, *British Foreign Policy and the Anglican Church: Christian Engagement with the Contemporary World*. Aldershot: Ashgate Publishing, 2011; Jan Beyers, Rainer Eising and William Maloney (2008) "Researching Interest Group Politics in Europe and Elsewhere: Much We Study, Little We Know?" *West European Politics* Vol. 31, Iss. 6, pp. 1103–1128; Pieter Bouwen (2002) "Corporate Lobbying in the European Union: The Logic of Access," *Journal of European Public Policy* Vol. 9, Iss. 3, pp. 365–390; David Coen and Jeremy Richardson (eds), *Lobbying the European Union: Institutions, Actors and Issues*. Oxford, New York: OUP, 2009.

14. There is a brief summary of the work of Building Bridges at https://nifcon.anglicancommunion.org/inter-faith-in-action/dialogues/building-bridges.aspx. See also Michael Ipgrave (2005) "Anglican Approaches to Christian Muslim Dialogue," *Journal of Anglican Studies* Vol. 3, Iss. 2, pp. 219–236. For a discussion of Near Neighbors, see Julia Ipgrave, "Inter Religious Relations and the English Model of Church Establishment in Nation and Parish," in Wolfram Welbe, Katajun Amirpur, Anna Kors and Dorthe Vieregge (eds), *Religions and Dialogue: International Approaches*. Munster, New York: Waxman, 2014. See also Johannes Quak and Cora Schuh (eds), *Religious Indifference: New Perspectives from Studies on Secularization and Nonreligion*. Cham: Springer, 2017, pp.73–79.

15. The text of Tim Farron's resignation speech can be found at https://www.huffingtonpost.co.uk/entry/tim-farron-quits-as-lib-dem-leader_uk_594171ece4b003d5948ccbd2.

16. Tom Bailey and Valentina Gentile (eds), *Rawls and Religion*. New York: Columbia University Press, 2014.

17. Ibid., p. 2.

18. Ibid., p. 77.

19. Ibid., p. 4.

20. See James Shleifer (2014) "Tocqueville, Religion and *Democracy in America*: Some Essential Questions," *American Political Thought* Vol. 3, Iss. 2, p. 256.

21. Kevin McCaffree, *The Secular Landscape: The Decline of Religion in America*. New York: Palgrave Macmillan, 2017. p. 3.

22. Jean Twenge's Chapter Five: "Irreligious: Losing My Religion (and Spirituality)," in *iGen: Why Today's Super-Connected Kids Are Growing Up Less Rebellious, More Tolerant, Less Happy—and Completely Unprepared for Adulthood*. New York, London: Atria Books, 2017, contains an illuminating analysis of the psychology and perceptions of today's American teenagers.

23. GDP list of countries for the year 2018 can be found on the World Bank Database: https://data.worldbank.org/indicator/ny.gdp.mktp.cd?name_desc=true.

24. Joseph Nye (2010) "The Future of American Power: Dominance and Decline in Perspective," *Foreign Affairs* Vol. 89, Iss. 6, pp. 2–12 discusses the possible potential for US global influence into the future. This article was the core of Nye's later book: *Is the American Century Over?* Cambridge: Polity Press, 2015.

25. All the statistics here are taken from the Pew Research Center website from the surveys last taken in February 2019: http://www.pewsocialtrends.org.

26. As reported in the *Atlanta Journal* September 7, 2011.

27. See the Pew Social Trends site at Footnote 25. Interestingly, the survey found that Hispanics and Afro-Americans were generally more optimistic than "whites," although the definition of "white" itself now includes Hispanics in the last US census.

28. The context and course of the culture war are brilliantly analyzed in Hartman, *A History of the Culture Wars*.

29. Ibid., p. 1.

30. See Kevin Coffee (2008) "Cultural Inclusion, Exclusion and the Formative Role of Museums," *Museum Management and Curatorship* Vol. 23, Iss. 3, pp. 261–279; Kate Mcleod, "The Role Museums Play in Social Activism," www.americansforthearts.org, August 2, 2017.

31. Data on ethnic diversity, including inter-racial relationships, in the United States can be found at https://www.census.gov/ quickfacts/fact/table/US/IPE120217, July 1, 2018, and for the United Kingdom at https://www.ethnicity-facts-figures.service.gov.uk/uk-population-by-ethnicity/national-and-regional-populations/regional-ethnic-diversity/latest, August 1, 2018.

32. It is interesting to note that a similar debate was triggered in America when Mexican-Americans booed the US soccer team when Mexico and the United States played each other in 1998. See Samuel Huntington, *Who Are We? America's Great Debate*. New York: Free Press, 2004. p. 14.

33. The text can be found at https://www.theguardian.com/uk/2000/mar/28/british identity.tonyblair.

34. Ibid.

35. See, for example, Modood's article "Multiculturalism and Nation Building Go Hand in Hand," *The Guardian*, May 23, 2007.

36. As reported in Lizzie Dearden, "Theresa May's Government Condemned for Driving 'More Austerity and More Racism' after the Integration Review," *The Independent*, December 6, 2016.

37. Ted Cantle and Eric Kaufmann, "Is Segregation Increasing in the UK?" http://tedcantle.co.uk/wp-content/uploads/2013/03/099-Is-Segregation-Increasing-in-the-UK-Cantle-and-Kaufmann-Open-Democracy-Nov-2016.pdf.

38. Polling done in 2003 and 2013 found that those who said they were "somewhat proud" to be British increased from 39 percent in 2003 to 47 percent in 2013. See http://www.bsa.natcen.ac.uk/media/38109/proud-to-be-british-data.pdf.

39. Linda Colley, *Britons: Forging the Nation, 1707–1837*. New Haven, London: Yale University Press, 1992, pp. 23–33.

40. See http://www.natcen.ac.uk/news-media/press-releases/2018/september/church-of-england-numbers-at-record-low/, September 7, 2018.

41. Lawrence James, *Raj: The Making and Unmaking of British India*. London: Abacus, 1997. p. 226.

42. In her 2016 article, Denise Carter analyzes the "othering" of Islam in her qualitative study (2016) "(De)constructing Difference: A Qualitative Review of the 'Othering' of Muslim Communities, Extremism, Soft Harms and Twitter Analytics," *Journal of Behavioral Sciences of Terrorism and Political Aggression* Vol. 9, Iss. 1, pp. 21–36.

43. Eric Kaufmann, *Shall the Religious Inherit the Earth? Demography and Politics in the 21st Century*. London: Profile Books, 2010; *Whiteshift: Populism, Immigration and the Future of White Majorities*. London: Penguin, 2019.

44. Polling data on both sides of the Atlantic presents a clear picture of growing unease with large-scale Muslim presence. Perhaps the clearest example in the UK (which also covered mainland Europe) was Chatham House's 2017 survey "What Do Europeans Think about Muslim Immigration?" by Matthew Godwin and Thomas Raines. Published February 7, 2017. https://www.chathamhouse.org/expert/comment/what-do-europeans-think-about-muslim-immigration. For American attitudes, see, for example, the Pew Center's "Republicans Prefer Blunt Talk on Islamic Extremism, Democrats Prefer Caution," February 3, 2016. http://www.pewforum.org/2016/02/03/republicans-prefer-blunt-talk-about-islamic-extremism-democrats-favor-caution/.

Chapter 1

Islam, Muslims, and the Anglo-American Milieu

This chapter provides three interconnected elements of contextualization for the principal discussion. It offers a brief, long-lens view of Muslim interactions with America and Britain. Subsequent chapters will provide specific contextual overviews relating to engagement with Islam and Muslims in home and foreign affairs over the twentieth and twenty-first centuries. This has been done in order to break up what otherwise would have been one extremely long chapter which attempted to contain all the necessary contextual historical detail in one place.

In organizing the material in this manner it could reasonably be argued that I am obstructing continuity in the narrative. This is unavoidable, but I hope that the disruption will not impinge on the broad narrative and analysis of the book.

ISLAM AND AMERICA

Islam in the United States

An accurate historical account of the history of Islam in America is very hard to render due to the "Christianization" of Muslim names that many of the early Muslim immigrants appear to have adopted. Nevertheless, the historical account which follows sketches a broad picture of the key dynamics and themes which were a feature of the Muslim experience in the New World up to the period which is the focus of this book. Of necessity, it omits details that would be present in a fuller rendition of this story; however, the history given here serves to draw out some of the key dynamics that speak to the discussion later in the book.

Records suggest that one Anthony Jansen van Vaes was the first Muslim to settle in the New World in what is now New York City around 1630.[1] Van Vaes was originally from Fez in Morocco, a Dutch colony at the time, as was New York (New Amsterdam then). Yet, while van Vaes is recorded as the first settler, there is some suggestion that several Arab and African-Muslim slaves were part of the Conquistadores: notably one Estevanico de Dorantes who traveled with Cabeza de Vaca's expedition through Mexico in 1527. That said, information on Estevanico, or indeed many of the other Muslims who were reputed to have traveled to the United States at this time, has proved impossible to verify by historians.

What therefore can be said with a degree of certainty though is that van Vaes was the first free Muslim to settle in America. And, while, van Vaes appears to have been a rather isolated settler among free people, in terms of his background, by the War of Independence, there were significant numbers of Muslim African slaves in the New World. Historians Gomez and Austin among others present convincing evidence in the form of bills of sale, as well as posters requesting the capture of runaway slaves, which show that thousands of African-Muslim slaves existed in North America by the end of the eighteenth and early nineteenth centuries. Some of these escaped slaves appear to have sought refuge with Native American tribes, but there is no evidence that proselytizing and conversion resulted.[2] Many of the African-Muslim slaves came to be in the colonies as a result of being captured and sold by fellow Muslims during the jihadi wars of Usman Dan Fodio. Kambiz GhaneaBassiri suggests that many of the slaves were sold as revenge for not converting to the Salafi Islam that Dan Fodio was propagating.[3] Indeed, many of the Christian slaves that were also sold to the transatlantic traders appear to have been victims of the same dynamic, although in their case, the selling was in revenge for nonconversion.

John Azumah though offers a different viewpoint on who the jihadis believed could be sold into slavery: proposing that the jihadists deliberately chose not to convert the Christians in order to make them eligible for slavery along with those Muslims who would not convert to their form of Islam.[4]

Whatever the truth, it is clear that significant numbers of Muslims existed within the African slave population up to and through the American Civil War. After its conclusion, an 1870 amendment to the 1790 Naturalization Act added Africans to the remit of citizenship that had previously been limited to "free white persons" by stating that citizens of "African nativity and African descent" could be citizens of the United States.[5] At the same time, Arab Christians and Muslims challenged the definition of "white" in order that they too might become fully fledged citizens. However the numbers of Arabs, Muslims, or otherwise were so small as to make little dent on the national consciousness and their advocacy met with only varying degrees of success depending upon the individual state.[6]

Up to the late nineteenth century, therefore, any exposure to Islam among US citizens and officials was limited to overseas and any interaction with slaves (or former slaves). The main exception to this general rule was the growing Muslim communities which were developing around the manufacturing industries in Illinois and Michigan, along with the nascent community growing in the melting pot of cultures and ethnicities that were to be found in New York.[7] The vast majority of these communities were part of the large migrations from the Ottoman Province of Greater Syria, of whom the majority were Christians.

The earliest official figures on Muslims in the United States come from the 1920s. Since many Muslims were still changing their names to Christianize them during this period, the accuracy of these figures cannot be confirmed. What is interesting is that, in reply to a query from a missionary to the United States in 1920 concerning numbers and placement of Muslims, the US Census department estimated that there were thousands of Muslims and that their principal concentrations were in Milwaukee, Chicago, Pittsburgh, Cleveland, Akron, New York, Philadelphia, Baltimore, Boston, and Worcester.[8] In this period the largest ethnic Muslim group were the Syrian and Lebanese who had been escaping heavy Ottoman taxation, although far more Christians from the same area had been migrating than Muslims.[9] Other than these, a sizeable minority also came from Turkey itself, while Kurds and Bosnians also made the trip to the New World in search of work.[10] Many Syrians, Lebanese, and others had been lured by the Ford Motor Company in Detroit who had offered $5 a day for work in the factory. It is estimated that around 8 percent of the Ford workforce was Muslim.[11] Tiny numbers of South Asian (mostly Punjabi) Muslims also began to migrate in the 1930s, most of which went to California and settled as farmers.

This increasing influx of migrants from former Ottoman and other imperial lands contributed to the establishment of the Asian Barred Zone by Congress which specifically banned immigration from Asian lands to the United States.[12] This legislation was supplemented by the Immigration Act 1924, which used a quota system to favor European immigration. Perhaps stimulated by this growing population, the first US incarnations of Islam were born in this period: the Moorish Science Temple, under Noble Drew Ali, and the Nation of Islam (NoI), founded by Fard Mohammed. That said, there appears to have been little adherence to the practice of faith among these early settlers as this extract from an open letter by an Ahmadiyya missionary shows:

> I beg to be excused to say that in the majority of cases you are Moslems in name only—Islam not playing a practical part in your everyday life. Nay, even your names are generally no more Moslem because you have adopted American names.[13]

For most of the Muslims living in the United States at the time, the guiding principle for the practice of their faith was to be found in Q67, (al-Mulk) which explained the situation of Muslims in terms of Allah's Providence, and of eventual judgment to come for slavers.[14] Therefore it is clear that they had not simply absorbed into the culture around them without forgetting where they had come from, for it seems that a lot of money was sent back to their homelands. Furthermore, a large percentage of the immigrants remained temporarily, not bringing over family, or even marrying locally but rather choosing to reside for a time and then heading back to their former country.[15] That said, once the trend to remain in the United States began to increase in the 1930s, the overwhelming early dynamic of the family was to send the children back to Syria for their schooling and to marry within the Syrian community only. This changed after the Second World War: a study of 128 Palestinian Muslims in Detroit in 1947 found that 7 married outside the community. By 1966, a further study of Arab American Muslims in Detroit showed that 50 percent of the children of Syrian immigrants had married outside of the community and by the third generation, none had married Muslims.[16]

However, while this dynamic was apparently diluting any concept of Islamic identity in the United States, the Second World War itself marked a significant turning point in the way that the United States as a whole defined itself, for no longer did it see itself as specifically Protestant white European but rather as a defender of certain values which were nonethnically specific. By way of example, the Uniting Islamic Society of America was formed in 1943 in Philadelphia: it sought to encourage African American interest in Islam by showing its compatibility with the values that the United States and its allies were fighting for at the time while reflecting the hypocrisy of segregation within US society.

Following the war, seeing the way the wind was blowing, Muslim communities quickly began to seek a national voice, especially as the United States as a global power was now intimately involved in many of the Muslim heartlands.[17] In this they were encouraged by the speech of President Eisenhower in 1957 when opening the Islamic Center of Washington, for he made it clear that Islam had a place in the United States so long as it was in keeping with America's civil religion. These encouraging signals prompted the founding of a number of national Muslim organizations. Among the early national organizations was the Federation of Islamic Organizations of the United States and Canada (FIOUSC), which was the idea of Abdullah Igram. Igram had served as an officer in the Second World War and set up the FIOUSC to counter what he saw as the misinformation about Islam that was being peddled in America, and also to promote what he understood to be the essential compatibility of Islamic values with American ones. The FIOUSC set up its first convention at Cedar Rapids in

1952, which was attended by around 400. Its specific aim was to counter negative propaganda about Islam and to "to see Islam and America's 'Civil Religion' intertwined."[18] At an advocacy level, it also successfully petitioned to have an "I" for "Islam" included among the options for a soldier's dog tags.[19] Aside from this, however, its national profile was limited and it achieved little else.

At the same time, the first serious attempts at daw'ah were applied with the Islamic Mission to America (IMA), under the guidance of the Caribbean immigrant Daoud Ahmed Faisal. The movement was multiethnic, including two Pakistanis and Faisal's Iranian wife. It published *al-Islam: The Religion of Humanity* in 1950 as a missional tract. The movement didn't last long, but it was three members of IMA that went on to form the Dar ul-Islam movement, which sought to bring sharia to the United States and was strongly influenced by Maududi. According to McCloud, it was the

> most influential African American Islamic philosophy amongst Sunni African American Muslims.[20]

As far as the wider public consciousness was concerned, though, Islam came to prominence through the investigation of the activities of the NoI, particularly the PBS documentary *The Hate That Hate Produced*, screened in 1959. This exposure for the NoI positioned it, and Islam, more widely as the religion of liberation for many African Americans and, even though Malcolm X left the NoI in 1964 because of its tangential relationship with mainstream Sunni thinking, he continued to be a spokesperson for equality issues.[21] As shall be seen in chapter 8, the US government considered the NoI to be a radical organization and the basis for that perception will be explored in that chapter.

However, it wasn't simply the NoI that brought Islam in US public consciousness; a number of jazz musicians had already converted in the 1940s and 1950s. The reasons for conversions like this appear to lie less with a devotion to faith and instead an interest in stepping outside of the class and race structure. Dizzie Gillespie said in his autobiography that

> they had no idea of black consciousness: all they were trying to do was to escape the "stigma" of being colored.[22]

While Islam itself was entering the public consciousness more completely in the late 1950s, a significant instrument of change was arriving in the form of rapidly increasing numbers of Muslim students. Their increase was a direct result of the changes in the immigration laws that took place in 1956 (permitting more non-European students) and, more significantly, in 1965, with the *Immigration Act* (also known as the *Hart-Cellar Act*), which permitted far more non-European immigration into the United States, initially as students, then as permanent residents.²³ Most of the Muslim students were coming from Egypt, Iran, Pakistan, and Turkey and it was their arrival which prompted the inauguration of the Muslim Student's Association of America and Canada (MSA) in 1963 at the University of Illinois. The founding members were also members of the Jama'at i-Islami in Pakistan and the Muslim Brotherhood: the character and nature of the MSA were therefore informed by the Salafi principles that embodied both those organizations.²⁴

The energy brought by the MSA and the FIA, coupled with the stimulation of greater numbers and the heightened awareness of Islam that had come through the NoI (which was in the process of coming into mainstream Sunni Islam in the late 1960s and 1970s), produced an unprecedented period of mosque-building, as well as the development of many new associations. That said, it is argued by Bassiri and Poston that many of the immigrants were not radicalized insofar as they were generally socially high class and coming into good jobs. This fits ill with the sense of the nature of the MSA that he and Poston both picture and it further implies that such people cannot be radicals; both assumptions are somewhat open to question.²⁵

Islam and US Foreign Affairs

Two overseas engagements particularly brought America into their earliest contacts with Islam internationally: their colonial struggles in the Philippines and the Barbary Wars.

In common with European vessels, American trading ships sailing across the Atlantic and into the Mediterranean became targets of the Barbary pirates operating from the North African provinces of the Ottoman Empire even before the United States had gained its independence. During the independence struggle the US ships were protected by the French but with independence that ceased. Relatively unprotected as they were, therefore, they became easy prey and it is estimated that 1.1 million European-American people were captured and sold as slaves in the markets of the Saharan coast.²⁶ Initially the United States sent envoys to barter with the North African Muslims which met with some success: Morocco signed a treaty in June 1786 which ended all piracy against US shipping; however, Algeria proved a far harder negotiator, and it was not until 1795 that 115 captured US sailors were released at a cost of over $1 million. The price for the ongoing freedom of American ships to sail in the Mediterranean free from capture continued to go up to the point that, when Thomas Jefferson took the presidency in 1801, the Pasha of Tripoli demanded $3.2 million (equivalent in 2018) for allowing US sailors their freedom. Jefferson refused and the Pasha declared war. The war raged for four years until the capture by the United States of the city of Derna in 1805 forced the Pasha to sue for peace. The resulting treaty did not end the problem and subsequent wars were fought by the Europeans, along with the United States, until the Barbary Coast pirates were eventually defeated.

When the United States took over the Philippines from Spanish control in the late nineteenth century the Sultan of the Moro was assured by the United States that the protectorate status that the Moros had under the Spanish would continue under the new US leadership. The Bates Treaty guaranteed the independence of the sultanate but, once the war with the Filipinos in the north of the islands was concluded in 1901, the United States invaded citing continuing piracy by Moro peoples against US ships as the cause. After much fighting, Moro land was annexed, the sultan deposed, and the Carpenter Treaty was imposed in 1915.[27]

Both of these international engagements presented the United States with a vision of Muslims as "criminal" peoples, not to be trusted. In the context of these engagements, and with only a minute experience of American-Muslim engagement until after the Second World War, such an impression was perhaps unsurprising and even entirely reasonable.

So with limited interaction with Muslim rulers and states (and frequently unhealthy ones when they did occur), the perception of Islam in US government circles that were brought into the deeper and wider engagement with Islam which occurred over the course of the twentieth and twenty-first centuries came from a negative starting point. This, as shall be seen in the following chapter, was reflected in the views of Islam found at the very top of the US government in the early years of its existence before a dramatic shift in attitude (at least publicly) took place.

ISLAM AND BRITAIN

Islam in the UK

The history of Islam in Britain is indelibly mixed up with the colonialism of the eighteenth to the twentieth centuries when much of British expansionism came at the expense of the Muslim nawabs and sultans who had been the rulers in South Asia, Southeast Asia, and the Middle East, where much of the imperial territory was established. Yet Britain's interaction with Muslims predated colonial expansion by several centuries.

England, Scotland, Wales, and Ireland were part of the European trading networks that flourished through the Middle Ages in spite of the wars and disease which also ravaged the continent during that period.[28] For that reason, there was a consciousness of Islam particularly among the educated and upper classes which came from individual Muslim traders who came to

British shores, as well as from British traders who went to the Mediterranean basin and brought back tales of the "Mohametans" that they encountered. Evidence of the extent of British awareness of Islam through these encounters in this period is microscopic. But Chaucer's referencing of scholars in Muslim world, such as Mashallah, the Jewish astronomer at the Abbasid court in "The Squire's Tale" in his seminal work *The Canterbury Tales* (published 1386) provides evidence of the awareness of the existence of Islam, and engagement with its scholarship among British intellectuals at the very least.[29]

Nail Matar provides evidence of growing engagement between British people and Muslims primarily abroad but also within the borders of the UK, describing conversions both to and from Islam, discussions in churches and coffee houses, as well as growing concern about the activities of the Barbary pirates.[30] Indeed it was frustrations with the activities of these pirates that brought the English diplomat from the Stuart court, Sir Thomas Roe, to Istanbul in 1621. The seven years he spent in the capital of the Ottoman Empire included the tumultuous year of 1622, when Sultan Osman II was toppled and murdered. Thomas Roe's presence in this place, at this time, along with his previous post at the court of the Mughal emperor Jahangir gave him an almost unique insight into the two most powerful Muslim courts of the time.[31] It is therefore a pity that his activity lies outside of the scope of this book, especially as he was only the second English ambassador to the Ottoman court (as diplomatic relations had only been officially opened for less than half a century).

The increased exploration of sailors such as Sir Francis Drake and John Davis opened up observations on Islamic societies, rituals, and customs to a growing audience through the printing press. The breadth and depth of these interactions also increased as trading enclaves were established in Asia Minor, the Levant, and South and Southeast Asia.[32]

In his book *The Infidel Within: Muslims in Britain since 1800*, Humayun Ansari tracks the development of increasing Muslim communities in the UK from the early colonial period onward. As he outlines the establishment and growth of significant Muslim communities in a number of Britain's industrial centers he describes a primarily economically driven immigration which was also influenced by global events such as the First World War. He summarizes:

> In practice, Muslim movement to Britain went through peaks, troughs and disjuncture's caused by the material and ideological circumstances of individual migrants and the societies from which they came.[33]

This fascinating phrase leaves more questions than it gives answers, but some sense of the range and depth of Muslim engagement with Britain and the British over the centuries is encapsulated by it. It is hoped that this book will help to unpack that phrase further, but it is worth highlighting that Ansari's enigmatic summary hints at two dynamics which are worthwhile bearing in mind in relation to contextualizing the discussion in this book. First, that there is no sense that Muslims coming to Britain have been fleeing persecution. Muslims have been voluntary, economic migrants rather than refugees fleeing persecution unlike, say the Huguenots of the sixteenth century or the Jews of the late nineteenth, early twentieth century. Second, that some Muslim communities have come to Britain specifically for the spreading of their brand of Islam. Such as the migration of members of the Tablighi Jama'at to the UK after the Second World War (or Sufi missionaries to the United States in the late nineteenth century). No barriers to their open emigration for these purposes were expressed by the British government. This is an important point, for, as shall be seen later in the book when proselytizing and conversion are discussed, attitudes to Christian missions among Muslims by British and US governments were enigmatic at best.

The British engagement with Muslims and Islam was therefore long and complex but really only began to become more continuous, proximal, and strategically important during the period of imperial development. As such, Britain's most rigorous engagement with Islam and Muslims really only occurred in a similar time frame to that of the United States. The difference, however, was the strength of Britain's overseas engagement with Islam as opposed to America's limited engagement with Islam up to the twentieth century.

Islam and British Foreign Affairs

British and Irish noblemen, including King Richard I, had encountered Islam through their participation in the Crusades against the Muslims in the Middle East since the twelfth century. This interaction was by no means limited to the elites as men, women, and children from all levels of society participated in the Crusades. Clearly this was a negative engagement with Islam in the sense of the fighting that took place and there is no evidence of conversion to Islam among those who went to Palestine.[34] But, while Islam as a faith was not embraced, it is clear that there was substantial interest in the scientific knowledge available in the region. It was noted earlier that Chaucer had been aware enough of Muslim scientific engagement to have included it in his *Canterbury Tales*. And, while this cultural observation (rather than interaction) demonstrates an awareness of Islam even in Britain, a land remote from the immediate proximity of Muslim political power and culture, formal government-to-government interaction was minimal throughout the Middle Ages. The notable exception to this lack of government-to-government engagement was a delegation sent to the English king Henry III from the

Caliph Ala ud-Din in 1238 requesting military assistance against the burgeoning Mongol threat to the Muslim Empire.[35]

A more sustained engagement with Islam began in the Tudor period with embassies traveling both from and to the Ottoman court, particularly in the reign of Elizabeth I when she requested assistance from Sultan Murad III against the Spanish Armada in 1588.[36] This was one among a number of diplomatic exchanges which took place between Elizabeth and Muslim diplomats through her reign as the politics of the Reformation and the expansionism of Britain brought British ships and merchants into contact with Muslim (principally Ottoman) subjects. This ongoing interaction continued to Elizabeth's death, just before which a plan was evidently being hatched between her and the Moroccan ambassador, al-Mansur, to jointly attack Spanish territories in the Americas.[37]

The Stuarts, from James I on, substantially reduced their contact with the Ottomans and other Muslim leaders, mostly because they had domestic considerations paramount in their minds, even though overseas expansionism continued. However, at this time that expansion mainly went West, toward the Americas, and even though the East India Company had been developing its toehold in the subcontinent, the venture did not become diplomatically or territorially significant until the eighteenth century. Nevertheless, as British merchants joined the mercantile traffic in increasing numbers over the course of the seventeenth and eighteenth centuries, they, like the Americans, came into contact with the Barbary pirates—an occurrence which became so irksome and commonplace that it found its way into popular literature, such as in Lord Byron's poem "The Corsair" (1815).[38]

By the late Hanoverian period, especially once the Battle of Plessey (1756) had been won, and America had been lost, British interaction with Islam became continuous and multifaceted.

From the moment that the British Empire began to expand into areas hitherto dominated by Muslim leadership, successive politicians, officials, and senior executives understood that securing and maintaining these territorial gains required strategic alliances with local Muslim nobles, merchants, and the population at large. It was a policy which was not exclusive to Muslims (in India Hindu "zamindars"—local landowners—were the backbone of British power in country), but because the areas of expansion in the Middle East, Asia, and Africa had frequently been under Muslim imperial rule (such as the Ottoman Empire or Mughal Empire), it was Muslim princes, nobles, and merchants who tended to be the power brokers, whether it be in politics or trade.

Yet this partnership between the British rulers and Muslim elites was not an easy or particularly happy one.

An example of this uneasiness in interaction can be found in the events and results which flowed from the 1857 Rebellion (or First War of Independence).

For the British believed that it was Muslim princes who were the prime movers in the rebellion. On the Muslim side, the rebellion was, in large part, the result of growing concerns about the belief that the British were seeking to not just rule India but to facilitate the conversion of all Indians to Christianity and to change Indian culture through education, infrastructure, and governance.

There was reason for both sides to believe the perceptions they had. William Dalrymple notes that when the British captured Delhi in September 1857, the journalist for the *Times* who was taken to see the now-captured emperor Bahadur Shah II was told that it was the emperor and those around him who had plotted the rebellion.[39] Indeed, in his 1873 tract on the rebellion, the writer Syed Ahmed Khan Bahadurk felt the need to make a vehement case against Indian Muslims being the perpetrators of the rebellion. Something he would not have felt the need of if the narrative of Indian Muslim's perceived culpability had not taken root in British consciousness.[40] This suspicion by the British of Muslim perceived propensity for revolt was deepened through the Mahdi Rebellion in Sudan of the 1880s and 1890s. As we will see in the following chapter which reviews perceptions of Islam and Muslims by presidents and prime ministers, the Mahdi Revolt was one among a number of events which helped shape Winston Churchill's perceptions of Muslims.

On the British side therefore there was, from their perspective, concrete evidence to back their belief in a Muslim tendency toward religiously inspired revolt or warfare more broadly. But what about Muslim suspicions of British motives?

In his book *Empire: The British Imperial Experience from 1765 to the Present*, the British historian Denis Judd makes the following comment about Christianity and the British Empire:

> Although the British did not, in general, propagate the Christian faith with the zeal and ruthlessness of, say, the Spanish Conquistadors in Latin America, their insistence on the benevolence, justice and evolutionary potential of British imperial rule was, in effect, an alternative religion.[41]

Judd's contention therefore is that it was the British understanding of "Democracy" and their broader perception of the superiority of the "Civilization" being offered by the British governance that was paramount rather than the promulgation of Christianity per se. The fact that British "Civilization" was not wholly divisible from Christianity was tacitly acknowledged although not embraced by all. But, as the eminent Marxist historian Eric Hobsbawm observed, the embrace of democratic liberalism as a gospel to be spread through the Empire was increasingly developed over the imperial period.

> Before about 1865, it was possible to see the encounter between British and other cultures in terms of a dialogue. But, by the time of the New Imperialism in the late nineteenth century, the balance had changed.[42]

This evangelical zeal for the liberal democratic gospel was assisted by the activities of Christian missionaries of the nineteenth century who, as Judd puts it, advanced Christianity and liberal democracy hand in hand:

> Beyond the bounds of officialdom, but often acting as the advanced guards of European civilization, British missionaries also played an important part in both criticizing the sexual and social activities of local populations and encouraging restraint on the part of Europeans living amongst indigenous people.[43]

This close relationship between conceptions of "Civilizational gospel" and Christian message did not mean that the British government, or even local British officials, saw Christian missions as a "good" undertaking. Yet there was an expectation within British mission circles that British government officials (or the East India Company) were important to have onside and so, even in the late eighteenth century, before the British government took direct rule of India, and before what became known as the Scramble for Africa, British evangelicals pursued public advocacy for government support for Christian mission in Asia.

In his book *Religion versus Empire?* Andrew Porter highlights that, from the earliest years of missionary activity in India, and later in Africa, Protestant missionaries had an expectation of necessary engagement with government agency.

> There was to be no escape for the missions from encounter and engagement with, even dependence on, governments, whether imperial or colonial. At first however, neither side sensed where events were leading and neither state nor mission societies wanted dealings with each other.[44]

This nervousness from government officials was a step removed from the open antagonism toward Christian mission in their territories, for, as John Darwin argues,

> They [Company Officials] were equally nervous of offending local religious belief or lending open support to Christian missions despite their suspicion that Islam (for example) was intellectually bankrupt and Hinduism a medley of superstition and ignorance.[45]

It was concern about giving offense and the potential for social unrest that could attend it which entrenched the East India Company's opposition to permitting Christian missionaries into India. The evangelist William Carey was impeded and frustrated in his attempts to get to India in order to proselytize specifically because the East India Company was afraid of the potential unrest that might be unleashed should conversion occur.[46] For that reason, when senior Indian Home Administration official and Evangelical Christian, George Grant, proposed what became known as the Pious Clause in 1793 he was strongly resisted, on the grounds of not only the potential trouble and social unrest which might result from missionary activity but also the acknowledged increase in educational awareness which missions activity would also bring. Sir Stephen Lushington, a former senior Company director, was one among a number who opposed the Pious Clause (which included provision for the Company to not only allow but financially support missionary activity) on the grounds of potential social unrest and belief that the increased education which attended Christian missionary activity might cause the peoples of India to throw off Company rule. Lushington had had in mind the recent (for that time) revolution in the United States,[47] as well as the rebellion in Jamaica stimulated by Baptist missionaries, particularly Sam Sharpe.[48]

Grant's and the Clapham Sect's advocacy did not succeed in 1793, despite the success of Grant's pamphlet *Observations on the State of Society among the Asiatic Subjects of Great Britain, Particularly with Respect to Morals, and on the Means to Improve It* (1792). This argument for the happiness, general welfare, and moral improvement of peoples under imperial rule was extraordinarily influential and indeed was one of the decisive factors in opening the door for missionaries to enter India with the East India Company charter renewal of 1813.[49]

The argument of that tract was revolutionary insofar as it put the onus of perceived failures in imperial possessions not, as had previously been argued, on the back of rulers, or poor economic conditions but on the faith which underpinned the culture (in this case Hinduism). As such it flew in the face of the prevailing attitudes in the aristocratic and middle classes, who had been fascinated by Hinduism.

Yet, while Company officials were opposed to Christian missionary ventures on the subcontinent, they appeared eager to enact social and cultural change through education and the law. And it is in this that Grant's advocacy had perhaps unintended consequences, for in making the case for the believed barbarism of other faiths, the public debate which opened the door to missions work in East India Company territories perhaps influenced the officials of the East India Company themselves, for it is noticeable that educational and invasive legal-cultural programs emerged during this period. It is as if the missionary zeal of the evangelicals was transferred into the civil society zeal of the liberals. As such, it could be argued that the winning of the Pious Clause debate contributed directly to the simmering resentment which boiled over into the Indian Rebellion/First War of Independence of 1857–1858. For, as Nicholas Dirks argues, even though East India Company officials opposed Christian missions,

> members of the upper reaches of Hindu and Muslim society saw things a little differently. Through the agency of the East India Company, the British had toppled Indian rulers, dispossessed landlords and seemed to encourage attacks on the indigenous religious and cultural order. The proselytizing of evangelical Christian missionaries, and the reforming assault on local religious practices such as sati . . . in conjunction with other social and economic reforms, had all seemed to be part of the Company's programme to subvert the Indian tradition. / The governor-generalship of Lord Dalhousie, between 1848 and 1856, intensified resentments that had been building up for many years.[50]

The Indian Rebellion was blamed on arrogant British behavior and fears among both Muslims and Hindus of the increasing missionary zeal of the British.[51] Whether this is true or other factors such as simple competition for political power in the region among differing groups is not for discussion here, but there can be little doubt that the fears of the potential for social unrest which could arise from mission activity expressed a century ago would appear to have been realized in the 1857–1858 war.

For Muslims, therefore, the roles of the East India Company, the British government, and Christian missionaries were bound up together as entities dedicated to the undermining, even destruction, of the faith in the subcontinent. The perception of the connection between them was clearly understood by the British government who took direct control of East India Company lands on the subcontinent for, it is telling that, when Queen Victoria issued her "Proclamation" as Empress of India in 1858 her pronouncement included a commitment to religious freedom, which, unlike post–Second World War definitions, was fundamentally a commitment to keep Muslims and Hindus free from proselytization by Christian missionaries.

SUMMARY

Both diplomatically and culturally, Britain generally, and British officials specifically, came into the period under discussion with a wider experience of Muslims than those of American officials. Their perceptions were not only based upon the everyday interaction of diplomacy, a burgeoning fascination with "the Orient" but also, perhaps crucially, on the experiences of the revolts that have been alluded to. However, for the Americans, Islam was not immediate in the sense that the numbers of Muslims on US soil remained tiny well into the mid-twentieth century. Contact between the United States and Muslim states frequently came in the context of either war or trade and, therefore, the perception of Islam that was developed in official circles up to the twentieth century was based on only scraps of encounter.

NOTES

1. Kambiz GhaneaBassiri, *A History of Islam in America*. Cambridge, New York: CUP, 2010, p. 9.
2. Michael Gomez, *Black Crescent: The Experience and Legacy of African Muslims in the America*. Cambridge, New York: CUP, 2005, p. 166; Allan Austin, *African Muslims in Antebellum America: Transatlantic Stories and Spiritual Struggles*. New York: Routledge, 1997, p. 22.
3. GhaneaBassiri, *Islam in America*, p. 16.
4. John Azumah, *The Legacy of Arab-Islam in Africa: A Quest for Inter-Religious Dialogue*. New York: Oneworld Publications, 2001. Chapter 4.
5. Michael Suleiman, "Early Arab Americans: The Search for Identity," in Eric Hoogland (ed), *Crossing the Waters: Arabic-Speaking Immigrants to the United States before 1940*. Washington DC: Smithsonian Institution Press, 1987, p. 45.
6. Ibid.
7. Jane Smith, *Islam in America*. New York: Columbia University Press, 1999, pp. 50–53.
8. Edward Curtis IV (ed), *The Columbia Sourcebook of Muslims in the United States*. New York: Columbia University Press, 2008, p. 438.
9. See Kemal Karpat (1985) "Ottoman Emigration to America," *International Journal of Middle Eastern Studies* Vol. 17, Iss. 2, pp. 175–209.
10. Approx. 23,000, although it is said that 86 percent of these returned to Turkey when the Republic was established in 1923. Talat Halman, "Turks," in Stephen Thernstrom (ed), *Harvard Encyclopedia of American Ethnic Groups*. Cambridge (MA): Harvard University Press, 1980, p. 993.
11. Detroit still represents the principle Muslim Arab-American population in the United States today.
12. Karen Leonard, *South Asian Americans*. Philadelphia (CT): Temple University Press, 1992, p. 153.
13. Muhammad Sadiq (1921) "My Advice to the Muhammadans in America," *Muslim Sunrise* Vol. 1, Iss. 2, p. 29.
14. See GhaneaBassiri, *Islam in America*, p. 31.
15. Data is very hard to come by. Alixa Naff has done a study on Californian Muslims and found that on 378 marriages took place between South Asian men and local women. Of these, approx. 80 percent were married to Hispanic women. See GhaneaBassiri, *Islam in America*, p. 190.
16. GhaneaBassiri, *Islam in America*, p. 48.
17. Abdo Elkholy, *The Arab Moslems in the United States*. New Haven (CT): College and University Press, 1966, pp. 44–46.
18. Sally Howell, "Federation," in Jocelyne Cesari (ed), *Encyclopedia of Islam in the United States*. Vol. 1. Westport (CT): Greenwood Press, 2007, p. 243.

19. Ibid.
20. Aminah McCloud, *African American Islam*. New York: Routledge, 1995, p. 69.
21. Ibid., p. 53.
22. Dizzy Gillespie and al Frazer, *To Be or Not . . . to Bop*. New York: Doubleday, 1974, p. 293.
23. See Roe Ahmed-Ullah and L. Cohen, "American Muslims Divided," *Chicago Tribune*, September 20, 2004. According to figures from the US Government Printing Office, there were 134,615 Muslim immigrants to the United States in 1960; by 1990, the number had risen to 871,582 for the year.
24. The organization's headquarters was originally at the al-Amin Mosque in Gary, Indiana; however, it moved to Plainfields a few years later. See Yvonne Haddad, "Arab Muslims," in Samer Abraham and Nabeel Abraham (eds), *Arabs in the New World: Studies on Arab American Communities*. Detroit (MI): Wayne State Press, 1983, p. 70. Even the NoI was seen as a gateway to Islam for bringing Islam to the United States: in 1957, the cleric al-Sharwabi proclaimed, "We need you here to bring the great truths of our faith to this country." Louis Decaro, *On the Side of My People: A Religious Life of Malcolm X*. New York: New York University Press, 1996, p. 168.
25. Larry Poston, *Islamic Da'wah in the West: Muslim Missionary Activity and the Dynamics of Conversion to Islam*. Oxford, New York: OUP, 1992, p. 102.
26. Robert Davis, *Christian Slaves, Muslim Masters: White Slavery in the Mediterranean, the Barbary Coast and Italy, 1500–1800*. London: Palgrave MacMillan, 2003. See also Giles Milton, *White Gold*. London: John Murray, 2005, and Adrian Tinniswood, *Pirates of Barbary: Corsairs, Conquests and Captivity in the 17th Century*. London: Vintage, 2011; Patrick Teye, *Barbary Pirates: Thomas Jefferson, William Eaton, and the Evolution of U.S. Diplomacy in the Mediterranean*. Unpublished Master's Thesis, East Tennessee State University, 2013, p. 6.
27. James Arnold, *The Moro War: How America Battled a Muslim Insurgency in the Philippine Jungle 1902–13*. New York: Bloomsbury, 2011.
28. See, for example, Christopher Gerrard and Alejandra Gutierrez (eds), "Part X, A Wider Context: Trade and Exchange, Europe and Beyond," in *The Oxford Handbook of Later Medieval Archaeology in Britain*. Oxford, New York: OUP, 2018, pp. 878–905.
29. According to Jack Goody's *Islam in Europe*. London: Wiley, 2013 (no page number) which references Metlitzki, 1977 English scholars "flocked to the Muslim West in search of Arab learning."
30. Nabil Matar, *Islam in Britain 1558–1685*. Cambridge: CUP, 1998, pp. 45–49.
31. Liane Saunders's PhD thesis discusses English-Ottoman diplomatic relations in this embryonic period, including the work of Sir Thomas Roe. See *The Motives Pattern and Form of Anglo-Ottoman Diplomatic Relations c1580–1661*. Unpublished PhD thesis, University of Oxford, 1993.
32. Many of these interactions are recorded and discussed in Gerald McClean (ed), *Britain and the Muslim World: Historical Perspectives*. Newcastle upon Tyne: Cambridge Scholars Publishing, 2011.

33. Humayan Ansari, *The Infidel Within: Muslims in Britain since 1800*. London: Hurst and Company, 2008, p. 25.

34. See Kathryn Hurlock, *Britain, Ireland and the Crusades, c.1000–1300*. Basingstoke: Palgrave Macmillan, 2013.

35. Denis Wright, *The Persians amongst the English*. London: I.B. Tauris, 1985, p. 1.

36. Gerald MacLean and Nabil Matar, *Britain and the Islamic World, 1558–1713*. Oxford, New York: OUP, 2016, pp. 42–58.

37. Ibid., p. 44.

38. Catherine Styler, *Barbary Pirates, British Slaves and the Early Modern Atlantic World, 1570–1800*. PhD Thesis, University of Pennsylvania, 2011, p. 52.

39. William Dalrymple, *The Last Mughal: The Fall of Delhi, 1857*. London: Blooomsbury, 2006.

40. Syed Ahmed Khan Bahadurk, *The Causes of the Indian Revolt*. Benares: Medical Hall Press, 1873.

41. Denis Judd, *Empire: The British Imperial Experience from 1765 to the Present*. London: Fontana Press, 1997, p. 418.

42. Eric Hobsbawm, *The Age of Empire: 1875–1914*. London: Abacus, 1989.

43. Judd, *Empire*, p. 183.

44. Andrew Porter, *Religion versus Empire? British Protestant Missionaries and Overseas Expansion, 1700–1914*. Manchester, New York: Manchester University Press, 2004, p. 65.

45. John Darwin, *Unfinished Empire: The Global Expansion of Britain*. London: Penguin, 2013, p. 191.

46. S. Pearce Carey, *William Carey*. New York: Wakeman Trust, 2008.

47. Nicholas Dirks, *The Scandal of Empire: India and the Creation of Imperial Britain*. London, Cambridge (MA): Belknap Press, 2006, pp. 298–300.

48. Darwin, *Unfinished Empire*, p. 245.

49. Dirks, *Scandal of Empire*, pp. 301–302.

50. Judd, *Empire*, p. 70.

51. Darwin, *Unfinished Empire*, p. 247.

Chapter 2

Views from the Top

In any government, the views of its leader on any given issue are of vital importance in determining the direction of travel on any policy field. For an autocratic or totalitarian regime the views of the leader will be key in determining policy, but in a democratic system those views will be important but not necessarily the determining factor on any given policy question. Nevertheless, the views of the leader, especially in the American presidential system, will be of vital importance.

For that reason, it is useful to explore the views of prime ministers and presidents on Islam as it shaped government approaches to, and understandings of, that faith. This chapter will therefore explore those views as expressed in diaries, memos, and meetings both within the overall context of the book's exploration of the US and British government understandings of Islam and in order to find out whether the governments over which they presided reflected those views or not.

However, rather than wading through the views of all presidents and prime ministers (although many did not make any record of their views), this chapter will focus upon the perspectives of British and American leaders whose premierships were seminal in their nation's history. Wherever possible, it is private reflections which will be examined; however, given the importance of 9/11 in the scheme of US-British-Muslim engagement, and the recent nature of those events, public statements for US-British leaders will have to be the source material as their private thoughts will not likely be publicly available for at least thirty to fifty years. This is, of course, unsatisfactory because public statements will rarely reflect private views, but even given these limitations, there are still some useful insights which can be gleaned from them.

Chapter 2

PRESIDENTS

As noted in the previous chapter, America had come to independence at the height of the influence of the Barbary Corsairs who operated in the Mediterranean basin and beyond. The public consciousness of this piracy and its accompanying outrage were apparent to the new political elites from the president to Congress who understood the political importance of being seen to be able to protect their citizens but also shared the fundamental horror at the plight of Christian slaves who, apart from being in that unhappy predicament, were also

> in a hostile foreign world. [Where] they would remain until they died, adopted Islam. . . . . Or were ransomed by their family, friends or government . . . those very factors made white slavery in the Muslim world seem cynical and galling to the Christian world.[1]

With this frustration at the plight of their captured citizens, and their duty toward them, American presidents set about trying to solve the problem, first with tribute and then with military action. Such was their desire to understand the problem properly that Thomas Jefferson and John Adams made a trip to see Ambassador Sidi Haji Abdrahman in London in 1786. Jefferson reported to John Jay (then secretary of state) that during the course of the conversation, Abdrahman had been asked why the North African rulers (via the Corsairs) felt it was alright to behave as they did. In response, Abdrahman had said (according to Jefferson) that

> [the right] was founded on the Laws of the Prophet, that it was written in their Koran, that all nations who should not have answered their authority were sinners, that it was their right and duty to make war upon them wherever they could be found, and to make slaves of all they could take as prisoners, and that every Mussulman who should be slain in battle was sure to go to Paradise.[2]

Abdrahaman had been justifying the actions of the North African corsairs with an appeal to the doctrines of Islam. Burkett and Leiner record that Barbary Corsairs often quoted Surah 47 of the Qur'an to justify their actions.[3] The *ayah* they likely refer to is Q47.4 which talks about the taking of non-Muslim slaves following successful military campaigns; however, this book is not concerned about interpreting the Qur'an, or other elements of the Islamic canon as it would be a volume in its own right. And, while the roots of the justification for the activities of the Barbary Corsairs as articulated in Ambassador Abdrahaman's discussion with Jefferson and Adams is interesting, it is only notable in this context from the perspective of what understanding of Islam this created in the minds of two future presidents of the United States.

For Jefferson, whatever his personal feelings about Islam, he did not make any further reference to the faith either in his public writings, or in his personal papers. He was clearly interested in Islam, but whether this was because he was attracted to it or was simply researching the motivations of one of his principal overseas adversaries cannot conclusively be assessed. But his noted skepticism for revelation generally suggests that the latter, rather than former, was the more likely explanation.[4]

However, his companion on the trip to London, John Adams, was far less circumspect in his opinions on Islam. For in his *Essay on the Turks*, published after his time in the presidency, he was scathing about the faith of Islam, especially what he understood to be their perception of non-Muslims:

> The natural hatred of the Mussulmen towards the infidels is in just accordance with the precepts of the Koran. . . . The fundamental doctrine of the Christian religion is the extirpation of hatred from the human heart. It forbids the exercise of it, even towards enemies. . . . In the 7th century of the Christian era, a wandering Arab . . . spread desolation and delusion over an extensive portion of the earth. . . . He declared undistinguishing and exterminating war as a part of his religion. . . . The essence of his doctrine was violence and lust, to exalt the brutal over the spiritual part of human nature.[5]

This angry assessment appears to have been largely formed upon the explanation which had been offered to him some forty years before by Sidi Haji Abdrahaman. Certainly the central accusation he flings at Muslims has strong echoes of Abdrahaman's explanation of the Corsairs' actions.

Adams' final salvo of accusation could be read as a warning to his presidential successors:

> The faithful follower of the prophet may submit to the imperious necessities of defeat: but the command to propagate the Moslem creed by the sword is always obligatory, when it can be made effective. The commands of the prophet may be performed alike, by fraud, or by force.[6]

This warning was written after America had defeated the Corsairs (1815), during the period of the Greek uprising against Ottoman rule and, in that context, it is clear that the former president was keen to make sure that neither America nor the Europeans who were also engaging with the implications of the Greek uprising (and Russian intervention) were lulled into what Adams saw as a false sense of security regarding both the Ottomans and the Corsairs. In this he also drew on the widely reported (in Europe and America) Ottoman massacres during the Greek War of Independence 1821–1825.[7]

It was similar events to those of the Greek War some 100 years later that prompted Theodore Roosevelt, a devout Christian, to write:

Armenians . . . for some centuries have sedulously avoided militarism and war . . . are so suffering precisely and exactly because they have been pacifists whereas their neighbors, the Turks, have not been pacifists but militarists.[8]

Before going on to add:

Christianity is not the creed of Asia and Africa at this moment solely because the seventh century Christians of Asia and Africa had trained themselves not to fight, whereas the Moslems were trained to fight. Christianity was saved in Europe solely because the peoples of Europe fought. If the peoples of Europe in the 7th and 8th centuries, and on up to and including the 17th century, had not possessed a military equality with, and gradually a growing superiority over the Mohammedans who invaded Europe, Europe would at this moment be Mohammedan and the Christian religion would be exterminated.[9]

His historical context was the Great War, the recent news of the Armenian Massacre, and the US engagement with the piracy in Moro noted in the previous chapter. The news of the Armenian massacre had broken throughout Europe and America and, although the United States had not entered the War by the time Roosevelt had written those words, he was aware of the events in Europe and was both a leader in the Progressive Movement and a Christian, attending the Reformed Church of America throughout his life.[10] For those reasons his perceptions of Islam were colored by the news he heard and the personal conviction he carried of the link between Western civilization and progress.

Forty years later, America had changed and so had the nature of the connections with Muslim majority states. Those connections now included substantial oil interests, a developing Cold War, with its need to ensure that Muslims would be allied with the United States rather than the Soviets, and, at home, a burgeoning Muslim diaspora. Furthermore, there had been an important shift in public life from the civilizational certainty of the righteousness of the West, and its Judeo-Christian values, toward a conception of civil society which focused upon more universal collective values. This was partly due to the horrors that had been perpetrated by the apparently civilized Western country of Germany upon the Jews (and others): actions which undermined belief in the Euro-American culture and the pervasive cosmopolitanism which was characteristic of developing international society.[11] The collective outworking of these substantial economic, cultural, and strategic shifts was seen publicly in Dwight Eisenhower's speech at the opening of the Washington DC Islamic Center in 1957, where, instead of assuming the ignorance and backward nature of Islam as his predecessors had done, he instead confidently stated that civilization owes to the Islamic world some of its most important tools and achievements . . . the Muslim genius has added much to the culture of all peoples.[12]

This public sense of welcoming and valuing the contribution that Islam had made to global society was perhaps sincerely meant, but it is also notable that in Eisenhower's private diary he expressed less enthusiasm for one particular Muslim ideology, as shall be seen in the following chapter.

With the conflict of the Cold War the focus of the presidency remained firmly upon the confrontation with the Soviet Union, although, as shall be seen in the next chapter, the Iranian Revolution did prompt research into the nature of Shi'a Islam specifically. This, however, led to little by way of either public or private remark at the presidential level and so, it was really with the ending of the Cold War, and the developing New World Order that presidential (and public) attention turned toward Islam for its own sake (rather than in relation to the geostrategic aims of the Cold War) once again. So it was not until 1991 that George H. W. Bush, the forty-first president, made public remarks about Islam once again, this time in relation to America's relationship with the Middle East and the Iraqi Invasion of Kuwait.

I'm not a student of religion, but I don't find anything in the principal teachings of Islam that put us in contradiction at all. In fact, the principles are the same as what—we have a diverse religious culture. But it's kindness, it's be good to your neighbor, it's love, and it's take care of children. It's all these things, so there's no anti-Islam.[13]

These remarks, made in the mists of the First Gulf War, show a significant shift in tone from the Eisenhower era, for it is clear that Bush (Sr.) was now having to address a narrative which had become embedded in the Middle East: that America was anti-Muslim.[14] This perception was a far cry from Eisenhower's triumphant tour of the Middle East in the 1950s where he was cheered at every port of call. Instead, this was an American president who was all too aware of the resentment against America that was bubbling in the region. And so it was that during his presidency Bill Clinton sought to foster a new relationship by acknowledging what he saw as the natural harmony between the traditional values of Islam and that of American society in a speech made the year after the publication of the controversial Samuel Huntington article which prophesied an ideological, identity-driven struggle between forces promoting globalization within a liberal democratic framework and that of other forms of identity, particularly Islam.[15] It was also the year after the attempted attack upon the World Trade Center in New York.[16]

> [Americans know] the traditional values of Islam, devotion to faith and good works, to family and society, are in harmony with the best of American ideals.[17]

Clinton's speech had been specifically directed toward refuting Huntington's thesis and it is therefore not necessarily representative of his true opinions. However, in light of the apparently strong links between the Clinton Foundation and a number of Gulf states, it seems reasonable to suggest that, at the very least, if the Clintons had a significant personal problem with Islam, it is unlikely that they would have taken money from such states.[18]

A similar theme to that articulated by Bill Clinton in Jordan seven years before was alluded to in what could arguably have been seen as the most important statement made by an American president in the modern era: that by George W. Bush in the wake of 9/11.

> Both Americans and Muslim friends and citizens, tax-paying citizens, and Muslims in nations were just appalled and could not believe what we saw on our TV screens.
>
> These acts of violence against innocents violate the fundamental tenets of the Islamic faith. And it's important for my fellow Americans to understand that. / The English translation is not as eloquent as the original Arabic, but let me quote from the Koran, itself: In the long run, evil in the extreme will be the end of those who do evil. For that they rejected the signs of Allah and held them up to ridicule. / The face of terror is not the true faith of Islam. That's not what Islam is all about. Islam is peace. These terrorists don't represent peace. They represent evil and war. / When we think of Islam we think of a faith that brings comfort to a billion people around the world. Billions of people find comfort and solace and peace. And that's made brothers and sisters out of every race—out of every race.[19]

The shift in emphasis from commonality, which was at the core of the Clinton remarks, to the language of peace in the Bush Jr. statement is entirely understandable in the circumstances and, rather than simply being for public consumption, it appears that Bush Jr.'s remarks were sincerely held opinions. His understanding of the true faith of Islam was revealed in an interview for the American television network ABC recorded during his presidency during which he was asked whether he believed that Muslims and Christians worshiped the same God, to which he replied in the affirmative.[20]

The commonalities between Islam and America, along with the peaceful nature of true Islam, were themes also articulated during the Obama presidency and his refusal to use the term "Radical Islam," especially following the Orlando nightclub attack in 2016, were the source of much criticism of his stance.[21] However, the then-president stood by his lack of reference to Radical Islam citing security concerns for Muslims within the United States.[22]

Whatever his personal opinions (he has described himself as a Christian), President Obama therefore carried on the public stance of his predecessor, albeit amended to signal a shift in focus away from the War on Terror of President George W. Bush.

Public rhetoric on Islam shifted once again under the presidency of Donald Trump. The current (at time of writing) president had maintained a similar position on the inherently peaceful nature of most Muslims but stopped short of making the kind of generalized statements concerning the perceived inherently peaceful nature of Islam as a faith that his predecessors had done since 9/11. Indeed, he made clear his belief in the connection between the faith and the actions of terrorists in interviews both during the presidential campaign and upon coming into office. For example, in an interview before he became president, the MSNBC host asked then-presidential candidate Donald Trump whether he thought that Islam was an inherently peaceful religion, he replied,

> Well, all I can say . . . there's something going on. You know, there's something definitely going on. I don't know that that question can be answered. . . . We are not loved by many Muslims.[23]

It was this assertion which led to the most famous of his campaigns concerning comments relating to acts of terrorism which were propagated in the name of Islam: the calling for a total and complete ban on Muslims entering the United States until answers to terrorism problems could be found.[24] A statement which connected the religion of Islam to terrorist acts perpetrated by some Muslims in an unequivocal way. In so doing, it could be argued that his perspectives on Islam bore a closer resemblance to those expressed by John Adams and, as we shall see later, the confrontationalists of the late Cold War and early post-Cold War era White House administrations.

The views of the presidents showed significant shifts over a long period of time and it is interesting to note that these shifts were not entirely governed by the events, or cultural and strategic circumstances of the time, or the proximity of Muslim diaspora peoples around them. Personality and personal perspective also played a part.

PRIME MINISTERS

British prime ministers had had cause to engage with Muslim heads of state and Islamic peoples for a deeper and longer time than those of the American presidents.

Their experiences, whether from afar or close at hand, were both negative and positive and yet they did not necessarily impact on their perception of

Islam as a whole in the natural way that one might have expected. The issues they engaged with covered the entire gamut of human experience, especially as the British Empire increasingly orientated toward the East following the loss of the American colonies.

It was the decline of the Ottoman Empire, rather than the Barbary pirates, which were the cause of comment in relation to Islam among British prime ministers, especially the rebellions against Ottoman rule in Greece (1821–1832) and, later that century, Bulgaria (1875–1878).[25]

What was particularly interesting in relation to British perceptions of Islam at this time was that because the Concert of Europe understood the Ottoman Empire as a civilization, the news of the massacres which took place in the region became all the more shocking. For example, the sensational reporting of the massacres perpetrated against the Christian Bulgarians so angered William Gladstone, who had left politics in 1875, that he returned to politics the following year, and in the process, wrote a pamphlet entitled *The Bulgarian Horrors and the Question of the East*.[26] In the text of his pamphlet, Gladstone revealed his perceptions of Islam and the Ottoman Turks specifically.[27] For, Gladstone was at pains to point out what he understood as the nuanced differences between differing Muslim peoples.

> Let me endeavor to very briefly to sketch in the rudest outline what the Turkish race was and what it is. It is not a question of Mahometanism simply, but of Mahometanism compounded with the peculiar character of a race. They are not the mild Mohametans of India, nor the chivalrous Saladins of Syria, nor the cultured Moors of Spain. They were, upon the whole, from the black day when they first entered Europe, one of the great anti-human specimen of humanity.[28]

Gladstone continues in much the same vein, although acknowledging, somewhat grudgingly, a tolerance toward non-Muslims which had developed within the Ottoman Empire over centuries. In making this acknowledgment it is likely that he was seeking to balance his discourse in the midst of his angry invective. But, leaving aside the tone and direction of his statement for a moment, two things are worthwhile noting from Gladstone's opinions. First, he was aware enough of non-European cultures to acknowledge differences between different Muslim groups which he characterized as "races" but might more accurately be assessed as a combination of creedal, cultural, and ethnic differences. Second, as we saw with Presidents Bush and Obama previously, he separated the faith from the actions of the peoples, though not as distinctively as they had done.[29]

His perceptions of Islam and Muslim peoples had not been based upon personal interaction (other than with the Ottoman ambassadors to London). Before being elected an MP in 1832 Gladstone had made the "Grand Tour" around Europe that many of his aristocratic peers also made. So his observations of Islam were made by a man who had made little contact with Muslim peoples. His views of Islam were filtered through the lens of his concern for the plight of the Christian minorities under Ottoman rule and it was this that drove his opposition to the British government's long-term policy of helping to maintain the Ottoman Empire, both for the purpose of protecting the trade routes to India, and also to prevent Russian influence spreading to the Mediterranean.

In contrast to Gladstone, one of Britain's other great prime ministers, Winston Churchill, had considerable exposure to Islam and Muslim peoples (at least compared to Gladstone) through his time in the Sudan and in the North-West Frontier of India. His views on Islam are worth noting not just because he was a highly influential public figure who left a long legacy but also because he was the prime minister who approved the grant which was made to British Muslims in 1940, which enabled the first two state-funded mosques to be built in the UK: Regents Park Mosque in West London and the East London Mosque on Mile End Road. That will be discussed in chapter 5.

Churchill wrote two books about his experiences in Africa. These books, in addition to describing his observations on the Sudanese rebellion, and the Boer War, which was the main focus of the narrative, also recorded his observations about Islam. And, as Gladstone had done in his pamphlet about the Bulgarian uprising, Churchill was keen to draw a distinction between the faith of Islam and the violence that he had seen in the Mahdi's revolt in the 1880s.

> What the horn is to the rhinoceros, what the sting is to the wasp, the Mohammedan faith was to the Arabs of the Soudan [sic]—a faculty of offence or defense. It was all this and no more. It was not the reason of the revolt. It strengthened, it characterized, but it did not cause.[30]

He therefore posits Islam as a magnifier, rather than a formative cause for violence. However, while he drew that distinction, he was not enthusiastic about what he saw as the role of Islam in preventing, rather than releasing, human flourishing.

> How dreadful are the curses which Mohammedanism lays on its votaries! Besides the fanatical frenzy, which is as dangerous in a man as hydrophobia in a dog, there is this fearful fatalistic apathy. The effects are apparent in many countries. Improvident habits, slovenly systems of agriculture, sluggish methods of commerce, and insecurity of property exist wherever the followers of the Prophet rule or live.[31]

It is a theme that he returned to in his book about his experiences in the North West Frontier Province.

> It is evident that Christianity, however degraded and distorted by cruelty and intolerance, must always exert a modifying influence on men's passions, and protect them from the more violent forms of fanatical fever, as we are protected from smallpox by vaccination. But the Mahommedan religion increases, instead of lessening, the fury of intolerance. It was originally propagated by the sword, and ever since its votaries have been subject, above the people of all other creeds, to this form of madness.[32]

In the light of this stinging assessment it would therefore be reasonable to ask why, some forty years later, he approved (along with the Cabinet) the grant for the building of a mosque. This will be discussed in chapter 5, but it is important to note that the context in which he had been writing were violent confrontations with Muslim peoples and that, furthermore, over forty years people's opinions on many subjects are likely to change with experience and understanding. Whether this lay behind Churchill's later actions will be seen shortly.

Moving on to more recent times, the views of Margaret Thatcher, the British prime minister during the furor over the Salman Rushdie book *The Satanic Verses*, became public in 2002 when the former prime minister wrote an article, published in *The Guardian* newspaper, entitled "Islamism is the new Bolshevism."[33] At the time of the Rushdie crisis the recently released documents show that both the prime minister and her Cabinet were primarily concerned about the disorder, rioting, and protest the book was causing, as well as the offense being caused to Muslims by the book's publication.[34] These pragmatic considerations were not foremost in her mind when, some twenty years later, in the wake of the evolving War on Terror she wrote her *Guardian* article.

> "In many respects the challenge of Islamic terror is unique" she argued ". . . The enemy is not a religion—most Muslims deplore what has occurred. Nor is it a single state . . . perhaps the best parallel is with early communism. Islamic extremism today, like bolshevism in the past, is an armed doctrine. It is an aggressive ideology promoted by fanatical, well-armed devotees . . . [that] requires a long-term strategy to defeat it."[35]

Her primary focus was on strategies to defeat Islamic extremism, but it is clear from her remarks that she did not see a connection between the faith of Islam and the actions of the terrorists. As a former, rather than current, politician, she had no constituency to appeal to, and it is likely therefore that her remarks came from personal belief. But it is also worth noting that she was clear that there were Western values to be defended from the threat of Islamic terrorism. This is a small but quite important step from the multiculturalist stance taken later in the decade when questions about what the West should stand for were being asked in earnest.

Moreover, this lack of linkage between the faith of Islam and the actions of the terrorists was particularly interesting in connection to the fact that she was the prime minister through the Rushdie Affair. Her view about the distinction between Islam as a faith and the actions of fanatics, even if they had been perpetrated in the name of that faith, suggests a strongly held conviction what Islam was, and was not.

The separation of Islam from the acts of terrorists was a perspective that appeared to have been shared by the prime minister at the time of the 7/7 attacks: Tony Blair. Although it seems that his views did not remain settled on the matter. For, while he was prime minister, Tony Blair had been keen to separate any linkage between the religion of Islam and the actions of terrorists either in connection with the 9/11 attacks or the domestic attacks of July 7 and 21, 2005.[36] Yet, after he left office, the former prime minister made a bolder assertion about the links between the actions of ISIS and the level of support among different diaspora Muslim communities. For, at a speech at the 9/11 Memorial Museum in New York, he argued that

> while the numbers who engage in violence through groups like Islamic State are relatively small, many of their views are widely shared./ The conspiracy theories which illuminate much of the jihadi writings have significant support even amongst parts of the mainstream population of some Muslim countries. There are millions of schoolchildren every day in countries round the world—not just in the Middle East—who are taught a view of the world and of their religion which is narrow-minded, prejudicial and therefore, in the context of a globalized world, dangerous.[37]

This was a subtle shift. The former prime minister was therefore careful not to make any connection with the doctrines or tenets of the faith of Islam and the actions of ISIS. That being said, he did take a step away from the position he adopted during his premiership, and that of Margaret Thatcher, by putting the blame for ISIS's perceived popularity on the deep-rooted belief in the inherent antagonism of the West toward Islam.

It was a finely judged distinction, because it made a general point about the perceived mind-set, or perspective of an entire religious group, while not attacking any of the theological or ideological positions adopted by denominations or sects within the House of Islam. In making this point it seems likely that Blair was drawing on polling data from a study done back in 2007 by START at the University of Maryland which had found that

Muslim respondents to the statement "the United States seeks to weaken and divide the Muslim world" generally agreed with it by large majorities.[38] For example, in Egypt, 92 percent agreed with the statement, while in Pakistan, 73 percent agreed with it.

Former prime minister Tony Blair's comments found a resonance in the words of David Cameron, who, in the same year as Tony Blair made his remarks in New York, articulated similar sentiments but with a far more categorical assessment of the ideological (rather than doctrinal) link between what he might have termed the seed-bed which bred the actions of extremists. Cameron was determined to confront the ideology and laid out what he saw as the battlefield in an important speech at a National Security Council meeting in 2015:

> For too long, we have been a passively tolerant society, saying to our citizens: as long as you obey the law, we will leave you alone. It's often meant we have stood neutral between different values. And that's helped foster a narrative of extremism and grievance. The government will conclusively turn the page on this failed approach. As the party of one nation, we will govern as one nation, and bring our country together. That means actively promoting certain values. Freedom of speech. Freedom of worship. Democracy. The rule of law. Equal rights regardless of race, gender or sexuality. We must say to our citizens: this is what defines us as a society. To belong here is to believe in these things. And it means confronting head-on the poisonous Islamist extremist ideology. Whether they are violent in their means or not, we must make it impossible for the extremists to succeed.[39]

The speech therefore recognized tacitly that the British values that he was espousing were not ones that were shared by those groups who were perpetrating the violence itself and the separatism which was a distinct but not unrelated stream of ideological thinking among some Muslims. In drawing this link he was clearer than Blair had been in his specific concerns with the ideology present among some Muslim groups. A theme he returned to later the same year when he again spoke about the proposed *Extremism Bill*.

> I know what a profound contribution Muslims from all backgrounds and denominations are making in every sphere of our society, proud to be both British and Muslim, without conflict or contradiction. . . . What we are fighting, in Islamist extremism, is an ideology. It is an extreme doctrine./ And like any extreme doctrine, it is subversive. At its furthest end it seeks to destroy nation-states to invent its own barbaric realm. And it often backs violence to achieve this aim—mostly violence against fellow Muslims—who don't subscribe to its sick worldview./ But you don't have to support violence to subscribe to certain intolerant ideas which create a climate in which extremists can flourish./ Ideas which are hostile to basic liberal values such as democracy, freedom and sexual

equality./ Ideas which actively promote discrimination, sectarianism and segregation./ Ideas—like those of the despicable far right—which privilege one identity to the detriment of the rights and freedoms of others./ And ideas also based on conspiracy: that Jews exercise malevolent power; or that Western powers, in concert with Israel, are deliberately humiliating Muslims, because they aim to destroy Islam. In this warped worldview, such conclusions are reached—that 9/11 was actually inspired by Mossad to provoke the invasion of Afghanistan; that British security services knew about 7/7, but didn't do anything about it because they wanted to provoke an anti-Muslim backlash . . . we must be clear. The root cause of the threat we face is the extremist ideology itself.[40]

Much of the speech's emphasis on engagement with ideology had been driven by the acknowledgment that, despite a decade of CONTEST by that point, the problem of homegrown extremism had become more acute. This was demonstrated not only in the beheading of drummer Lee Rigby on a South London street in 2013 but in the number of foreign fighters who were traveling to fight for ISIS and other terror groups such as al-Shabab and al-Qa'ida, which, at the time of Cameron's speech, was estimated to be approximately 600.[41] Indeed, away from violent extremism, revelations about the development of sharia zones, the grooming gangs that were first reported in 2016, along with what became known as the Trojan Horse Affair (where a number of school in Birmingham were found to be secretly adopting extremist ideologies, employ only religiously compatible staff, and to use practices, such as separating boys and girls, which are out of step with secular education) highlighted that extremist ideology was not simply a funnel for potential violence, but that it had the potential to create alternative, separate societies outside of British legislative control within the UK's own borders.[42]

His speech is interesting for a number of reasons, but perhaps most importantly, he was very specific in his criticisms. Perhaps because he knew that his remarks would be interpreted in any number of ways, or simply because, after a decade of PREVENT and CONTEST work there was a more nuanced understanding of what officials believed were the key specific issues for radicalization. Cameron's speech displayed a willingness to discuss what he understood to be the root causes of radicalization issues than his predecessors were either able to, or willing to, do.

This discussion of the views of British prime ministers has shown that there has been a conscious desire to separate the religion from the actions of Muslims all through the past two centuries. That is not to say that this separation has been consistently definitive throughout the period, but that there have been consistent attempts to nuance the frequently highly critical observations of actions of particular Muslim groups, by ensuring that not all Muslims are treated as having the same motivations or beliefs. This is an important distinction which appears to have been, in large part, motivated by policy considerations, even as those considerations have shifted over time.

CONCLUSION

It seems clear therefore that, for the most part, the views of British prime ministers have followed a similar pathway to those of US presidents insofar as the circumstances of the time have had some effect on the views that have been expressed by the leader. Personality and personal belief also have had an impact.

The underlying narrative in both the views of the presidents and those of the prime ministers is clearly a shift from the perceived superiority of their own government, and an explicit rejection of the culture of Islamic government, followed by a reorientation in which commonalities are expressed and any claim to superiority is rejected. Of course, historical circumstances are important in this, but, as the discussion in the introduction concerning the shifting political theory during the period showed, this narrative has been driven from within, rather than without. In that context, the proximity of Muslim peoples and states to the leaders, while playing some part in these changing opinions, was probably not the decisive factor. It appears that internal, rather than external, political and cultural factors have had a bigger part to play. At the same time, it needs to be acknowledged that this cultural shift in political thinking has also been connected to geostrategic needs. It is hoped that the discussion through the rest of the book will help to evidence that claim, while nuancing the multiple, sometimes competing, threads of opinion on Islam found within the governments of both countries over the period in question.

This will be important to bear in mind as we analyze the experiences of American and British officials, for, by default, we will also gain insight into the level of impact that the personal views of the leader of either government had on each administration's understanding of Islam.

NOTES

1. John Burkett and Frederick Leiner, *The End of Barbary Terror: America's 1815 War against the Pirates of North Africa*. Oxford, New York: OUP, 2006, p. 35.

2. "American Commissioners to John Jay, March 28, 1786," *Founders Online*, National Archives, last modified on June 13, 2018, http://founders.archives.gov/documents/Jefferson/01-09-02-0315. Original source: Julian Boyd (ed), *The Papers of Thomas Jefferson, vol. 9, 1 November 1785–22 June 1786*. Princeton: Princeton University Press, 1954, pp. 357–359.

3. Burkett and Leiner, *End of Barbary Terror*, pp. 2–3.

4. The question of Jefferson's personal faith is given more in-depth treatment in Mark Beliles and Jerry Newcombe, *Doubting Thomas? The Religious Life and Legacy of Thomas Jefferson*. New York: Morgan James Publishing, 2015.

5. Lynn Parsons, *John Quincy Adams—A Bibliography*. Lanham: Rowman and Littlefield, 1999, p. 41.

6. Ibid., p. 29.

7. This will be returned to in the British Prime Ministers section of this chapter in relation to the Bulgarian Massacre. See also, Alex Heraclides and Ada Dialla, "Intervention in the Greek War of Independence, 1821–32," in *Humanitarian Intervention in the Long Nineteenth Century*. Manchester: Manchester University Press, 2015.

8. Theodore Roosevelt *Fear God and Take Your Own Part* (Originally Published 1916). New York: Forgotten Book, 2017, pp. 61, 64.

9. Ibid.

10. Christian Reisner, *Roosevelt's Religion*. Oxford: Clarendon Press, 1922, pp. 304–306.

11. For a more in-depth discussion of these shifting dynamics, see Adam Watson, *The Evolution of International Society: A Comparative Historical Analysis*. London: Routledge, 1992; Timothy Dunne and Christian Reus-Smit, *The Globalization of International Society*. Oxford, New York: OUP, 2017; Alan Dawley, *Changing the World: American Progressives in War and Revolution*. Princeton: Princeton University Press, 2003.

12. Full text of President Eisenhower's speech on June 28, 1957 can be found at https://www.whitehousehistory.org/ press-room/press-fact-sheets/u-s-presidential-visits-to-domestic-mosques.

13. His remarks about Islam were made in the context of a Question and Answer session with Arab journalists on March 8, 1991. The session followed a speech the President had just made concerning the end of the Gulf War. See the transcript at https://www.presidency.ucsb.edu/documents/interview-with-middle-eastern-journalists.

14. The rise of anti-American feeling in the MENA region is analyzed in Amaney Jamal, *Of Empires and Citizens: Pro-American Democracy or No Democracy At All?* Princeton: Princeton University Press, 2012.

15. The article became the foundation for his book *The Clash of Civilizations and the Remaking of the World Order* (Originally published 1997). London, New York: Simon and Schuster, 2002.

16. See Charles Shields, *The 1993 World Trade Center Bombing*. New York: Chelsea House Publishers, 2002.

17. "Remarks to the Jordanian Parliament" Amman, Jordan. Transcript. October 26, 1994, https://www.presidency.ucs b.edu/ws/index.php?pid=49373 &st=islam&st1.

18. A balanced report of the connections between the Foundation and various Gulf regimes can be found in Amy Chozik and Steve Eder, "Foundation Ties Bedevil Hillary Clinton's Presidential Campaign," *The New York Times*, August 20, 2016.

19. George W. Bush, "Remarks," Islamic Center, Washington, DC, September 17, 2001, https://www.presidency.ucsb.edu/documents/remarks-the-islamic-center-washington.

20. George W. Bush, "Interview," Good Morning America, December 14, 2003, https://www.youtube.com/watch?v=UGu0-kTi3Eg.

21. The approaches to Islamic issues of George W. Bush and Barack Obama are compared in Corinna Mullin (2011) "The US Discourse on Political Islam: Is Obama's a Truly Post-'War On Terror' Administration?" *Critical Studies on Terrorism* Vol. 4, Iss. 2, pp. 263–281.

22. See Ken Dilanian, "Why Won't Obama Say Radical Islam?" www.nbcnews.com, June 13, 2016.

23. Jenna Johnson, "Donald Trump Would 'Strongly Consider' Closing Some Mosques," *The Washington Post*, March 20, 2017.

24. Donald Trump, Campaign Rally Press Conference, Mount Pleasant, South Carolina, December 7, 2015, https://www.youtube.com/watch?v=hLgTF8FrYlU.

25. These events are discussed in the context of the post-1815 context of the "Concert of Europe" system developed by Count Metternick in Carsten Holbraad, *The Concert of Europe: A Study in German and British International Theory*. London: Prentice Hall Press, 1970.

26. The public outcry and political effect of the Bulgarian Massacres are analyzed in H.C. Matthew, *Gladstone, 1809–1898*. Oxford: OUP, 1997, pp. 271–282.

27. William Gladstone, *The Bulgarian Horrors and the Question of the East*. London: John Murray, 1876.

28. Ibid., p. 9.

29. Gladstone's engagement with the Ottoman Empire is analyzed in detail in Fahriye Yildizeli, *W.E. Gladstone and British Policy towards the Ottoman Empire*. Unpublished PhD thesis, University of Exeter, 2016.

30. Winston Churchill, *The River War: An Account of the Reconquest of the Sudan* (First published 1899). Mineola (NY): Dover Publications Inc, 2012, p. 52.

31. Ibid., p. 53.

32. Winston Churchill, *The Story of the Malakand Field Force* (First published 1898). London: Bloomsbury Academic, 2015, p. 29.

33. Margaret Thatcher, "Islamism Is the New Bolshevism," *The Guardian*, February 12, 2002.

34. CAB/128/94/3, F5. *Cabinet Meeting Minutes*, June 29, 1989. The course of what became known as "the Rushdie Affair" is recounted and analyzed in Kenan Malik, *From Fatwa to Jihad: The Rushdie Affair and Its Legacy*. London, New York: Atlantic Books, 2009.

35. Thatcher, "Islamism."

36. Milan Rai, *7/7: The London Bombings, Islam and the Iraq War*. London: Pluto Press, 2006, pp. 28–31.

37. As reported in Anon, "Tony Blair: Islamic Extremists' Ideology Enjoys Support of Many Muslims," *The Guardian*, October 6, 2015.

38. Michelle Nichols, "Muslims Believe US Goal to Weaken Muslims," www.reuters.com, April 24, 2007.

39. Office of the Prime Minister, Press Release: *Counter-Extremism Bill—National Security Council Meeting*. May 13, 2015, https://www.gov.uk/government/news/counter-extremism-bill-national-security-council-meeting.

40. David Cameron, "Extremism," Transcript. Ninestiles School, Birmingham, July 20, 2015, https://www.gov.uk/government/speeches/extremism-pm-speech.

41. F. Cocco, "How Many Foreign Fighters Have Joined Islamic State," www.theweek.co.uk, June 24, 2015.

42. J. Fergusson, *Al-Britannia, My Country.* Milton Keynes: Bantam Press, 2017, pp. 98–101.

Chapter 3

Foreign Affairs

Three key areas will be looked at in this chapter in relation to analyzing British and US perceptions of Islam in the area of foreign policy: first, the negotiations which resulted in the Treaties of Sevres and Lausanne, second, the Anglo-American attempts to encourage anticommunist Muslim unity in the early Cold War, and third, the US-led War on Terror in the post-9/11 era.

The reason why these three incidents have been chosen is because they speak to broader shifts in attitude of US and British administrations toward issues that involved religion, whether it be in the civilizational spheres of the First World War period, the ideological nationalisms of the Cold War period, or the evolving New World Order multiculturalism and multipolar era of the Age of Identity.

THE TREATIES OF SEVRES AND LAUSANNE

As the British prime minister David Lloyd-George set off for the peace conferences in 1919, he was in a confident mood. The Germans, Austro-Hungarians, and Ottomans had been defeated and both he and the French premier Clemenceau looked forward to shaping the peace. None of the defeated foe had strong negotiating hands, it appeared, and there were a number of strategic acquisitions which Lloyd-George felt would greatly assist the security of the British Empire, which he felt there was every expectation of being able to acquire. Negotiations with the Ottomans, he blithely asserted, would take a matter of weeks.[1] Yet, the treaty that was finally concluded at Lausanne four years later was not at all favorable to Britain and, indeed, has been hailed in Turkey ever since as one of Turkey's greatest diplomatic triumphs.[2] What, then, undermined the Allied position?

The first mistake came very early on in 1919. Both Lloyd-George and President Wilson thought that, in its exhausted state, the Ottomans would not be able to resist the creation of an independent Kurdistan and the division of Anatolia among its Greek and Italian minority populations. The Greeks, seizing the opportunity they felt they had, landed a force in Smyrna in order to encourage Turkish acquiescence to any peace treaty which the allies sought to impose on them.

But the allies had misscalculated. Despite the presence of British warships in the Dardanelles and a considerable (though rapidly reducing) British army across Turkey, the Turks were determined not to be cowed into an unacceptable peace. Weakened though they undoubtedly were, the specter of a permanent Greek presence in Turkey was so appalling that Turkish troops in the process of being demobbed ran to the arms depots where their weapons had been handed in, and promptly took them up once again. In the growing chaos, General Mustapha Kemal declared that the Sultan Mehmed VI's government was effectively a puppet of the allies and declared independence at Amasya, quickly forging alliances with the Young Turks which, even in its fractured state, still had functioning networks. Their modernizing, religious nationalism was a useful ideological tool for Kemal as he sought to oppose the imposition of an abhorrent peace, aided as it was by a Sultan-Caliph who was more interested in holding onto his crown than he was concerned about the prestige of his empire.[3] As Peter Fromkin argues,

> Despite Kemal's strong secular bias, Moslem [sic] holy men proved to be his strongest adherents.[4]

Kemal continued to struggle for independence right through the period of negotiations which led to the Treaty of Sevres, and then, following that treaty's rapid collapse, the later Treaty of Lausanne. Even though Sultan Mehmed VI signed Sevres, with its effective breakup of both the Ottoman Empire and Turkey itself, it could not be imposed. Indeed, events within Turkey and the pressure being brought to bear on the allies by their infighting and external Muslim lobbying, effectively rendered the Treaty of Sevres dead on arrival.[5] The agreement which was reached at Lausanne four years later was a shadow of what Lloyd-George and Clemenceau had envisaged and, while the factors given earlier were significant, the lack of enthusiasm for the plans for the Middle East displayed by President Wilson was a decisive factor. For, despite his complicity in this action, President Wilson was a reluctant coconspirator.

Wilson's views on Islam as a faith he kept to himself, but from a policy perspective American trade with the Ottomans at the time of the First World War was negligible. One might have assumed that he would have been happy to declare war against Turkey without many reasons to pause. But he refused to declare war on the Ottomans, even when he declared war against German and Austria-Hungary in 1917. The Senate Foreign Relations Committee asked the then-secretary of state Robert Lansing for an explanation, especially as Point 12 of President Wilson's famous Fourteen Points had been about the Ottoman Empire.[6] Lansing's reply was lengthy, identifying just two reasons in its discourse: first, that the Ottomans had not declared war on the United States and, therefore, there was not good reason to antagonize them by declaring war, especially as Wilson feared reprisals against Christian and Jewish minorities in Turkey. Second, he pointed out that two Christian colleges, which were supported by one of President Wilson's close friends and financial backers, Cleveland Dodge, would likely be harmed by the declaration. The institutions had received over 2 million dollars of investment, so Lansing argued that such a significant sum needed protecting.[7]

Yet neither of these points appears to have been the overriding factor in Wilson's thinking. For, under further pressure from the Senate and Congress, Wilson refused to buckle, and it seems that his real underlying concern was not those which Lansing had expressed in his letter but instead, he appears to have been more interested in the impact that the declaration of war would have on the money flowing to American missionaries in the Ottoman Empire who were looking after Syrian and Armenian refugees.[8] However, while this philanthropic instinct prevented direct military action, that did not stop Wilson from imposing a travel ban in 1915 on all subjects of the Ottoman Empire in theory but which, due to the caveats in the Executive Order (2932), effectively targeted Muslims alone.[9]

But in spite of this punitive measure against those who were not enemy citizens, Wilson's interest in the Ottomans owed more, not just to his concern about Ottoman religious minorities, but more pertinently, to his opposition to the secret Sykes-Picot agreement which, upon specific request, had been sent to him by Lord Balfour in 1917. Wilson believed it was a recipe for future disaster and had said as much to Balfour upon his reading of it. These twin concerns were probably the bait which drew Wilson into the postwar peace process with Turkey.

With no territorial ambitions of his own in Turkey, Wilsons's foreign policy in relation to the Ottoman Empire as an Islamic state seems to have owed little to any personal feelings toward Islam as a faith one way or another but instead to more strategic considerations around the long-term stability of the Middle East and the status of religious minorities. Lloyd-George also does not appear to have had any openly expressed opinions on Islam or Muslims as such, but his motivations in his relations with Turkey/the Ottomans were instead governed by the tantalizing prospect of further strategic territorial gains in the Middle East and North Africa (MENA) region and his concern about the prospect of trouble with Muslim diasporas in India especially, who quickly became very active and vocal in their advocacy on behalf of the Ottoman Sultan-Caliph.[10]

The evidence of these events therefore suggests that, for both President Wilson and for Prime Minister Lloyd-George, Islam and Muslims were something that represented a particular set of issues which were, in many ways, divorced from one another. On the one hand, the considerations of the Muslim citizens of the British Empire presented Lloyd-George with a limiting framework when seeking to advance the British Empire's territorial and security ambitions. For President Wilson, however, Islam was remote and therefore removed from his foreign policy considerations. Indeed, it appears only to have come into his consideration in two areas: first, the plight of religious minorities in Ottoman lands and second, in relation to the machinations of his European allies whose ambitions Wilson was both suspicious of and alarmed by.

THE COLD WAR

The early period of the Cold War was a key period in which the new order of the world was established in the form it would take for the next forty years. In this evolving confrontational context, the potential for making Islam and Muslims an ally was once again explored, as it had been in differing geostrategic contexts.

The traditional Islamic heartlands, as well as the newly independent South Asian states, represented key potential areas for Soviet expansionism in the Cold War era.[11] Britain was bankrupt after the Second World War but wanted to assist the United States in the developing confrontation.[12] The United States was conscious of the fact that its support for the newly created state of Israel had the potential to drive the surrounding Muslim states into the hands of the Soviets.[13] Their concern was well founded. The growing ideology of Arab Nationalism had its ideological roots in a hybrid of socialist aspiration and perceived Muslim oppression.[14] This combination gave the Soviets a natural platform for the propagation of their message and influence in the Middle East and North African (MENA) region.

The connection between Muslims and communists went right back to the very earliest days of the Russian Revolution. Leon Trotsky noted in 1923 that in some colonies as many as 15 percent of Communist Party members were believers in Islam.[15] A communiqué sent out on December 6, 1917, less than three weeks after the Revolution began, articulated the common cause the Bolsheviks had with Muslims and clearly sought to capitalize on what the Bolsheviks felt to be a natural alignment between the aims of the Muslim

Leagues across the British Empire, and their own fight against inequality and autocracy:

> The waking people of Russia are animated by the desire to secure an honest peace and to help all oppressed people in the world to find their freedom. In this holy undertaking Russia is not alone. The great call of freedom given by the Russian revolution is voiced by all working men of west and east. . . . Muslims of the east, all those persons and property, freedom and fatherland, have been exploited during centuries by greedy European despoilers . . . do not lose time but cast from your shoulders the yoke of the despoilers of your countries.[16]

The fledgling Bolshevik state saw in the growing Muslim consciousness an opportunity to undermine European control of many of the lands that the Russians themselves were seeking to influence. For the ideology of pan-Islamism, which had been fostered by the Ottomans in the decades leading up to the First World War and then spread through the teachings of Jamal-ad Din al-Afghani, represented an alternative to the emergent Christian-infused, liberal progressivism of the first Globalist Age.[17]

The Middle East was particularly fertile ground for communist insurgency even before the creation of Israel for a number of reasons, including the breakup of the Ottoman Empire, but it was the Anglo-Russian Entente of 1907 which initially galvanized anti-European feeling to the extent that British intelligence officials talked of a "conscious wave of resentment running through the Moslem world."[18] At the Baku Congress of the Peoples of the East in September 1920, Russian Bolshevik leaders issued a call for a "holy war" against Western imperialism. Two years later the Fourth Congress of the Communist International endorsed alliances with pan-Islamism against imperialism.[19]

This did not remain the case indefinitely of course. Emil Aydin notes in his chapter "The Question of Orientalism in Pan-Islamic thought: The Origins, Content and Legacy of Transnational Muslim Identities" that, even though they had initially supported the pan-Islamic movements,

> the Bolsheviks could not accept the idea of an alternative Eastern civilization entrenched within Pan-Islamic discourses.[20]

He began to

> fear that, instead of using them they [Communists] could become instruments of this other rival internationalism.[21]

A fear that became reality with the Iranian Revolution of 1979. Nevertheless, the commonality of the discourse of oppression brought revivalist Islam and socialism into a sympathetic alignment which continues to this day.

This perception of natural alignment between socialism and Islamic revivalism was a view that British officials were desperate to oppose in the post–Second World War period for two very pragmatic reasons: first, many Muslims lived within their imperial borders, both within Britain itself and in its territories. Second (and connected to it), there was much economic investment in these Persian, Levantine, and Arabian regions, so a loss of favor and/or territory would not simply have meant a loss of face but involve very real economic consequences.

The British had experienced the potential for their enemies to exploit Islamist or pan-Islamic groups during their imperial days in India and Sudan, and more recently had seen how the Nazis were able to use the activities of the Muslim Brotherhood for their own end during the Second World War. Intelligence files, covering October 1942, reveal that the British had investigated the activities of Hasan al-Banna following accusations that the Ikhwan had been indulging in anti-British activities, a claim furiously denied by al-Banna who had submitted a memorandum to the Egyptian prime minister on September 7, 1942, stating that the Ikhwan's activities were purely religious, not political.[22] Nevertheless, the British investigation revealed that leading members of the Ikhwan, including al-Banna himself, had been writing and printing pro-Nazi leaflets at the Al-Nasr printing press in Alexandria, although the process was highly secretive.[23] This link is discussed in Rubin and Schwanitz's 2014 book in the context of examining the roots of cooperation between Muslim political activists and the Nazis in seeking Jewish destruction.[24] The focus of Rubin and Schwanitz's work is the anti-Semitic cooperation between them, but, in the context of this book, their research is invaluable in highlighting that the protection of Jews was not a British priority, for even though this cooperation was known about by British intelligence officials, there was still a desire to have the Brotherhood onside, rather than in opposition. In other words, the knowledge that the British officials had of the pro-Nazi cooperation of the Brotherhood, and the known anti-Semitism of both groups, was not considered a barrier to potential cooperation. Here, the important issue was not the protection of the rights of religious minorities (as has been seen already) but instead the focus was on the potential strategic value in having the Brotherhood either neutral or on the side of the British. Evidence of this lack of interest in protecting minorities will be seen again shortly, but the same file which discusses Nazi links also reveals that the British had, earlier the same year, already decided to use government money to support the Ikhwan, perhaps hoping to buy their loyalty.[25]

Evidence from this intelligence shows that this had not worked, but this did not prevent the British seeing, in the Ikhwan, an organization which could potentially have some benefit for them.[26]

These centuries-old imperial concerns about whether revivalist Islamic ideologies could be harnessed or should be seen as a threat (or both) entered a new phase as the Cold War began and drew America into labyrinth of ideological issues and security threats which had part of the British imperial experience for more than a century.

Clearly, Britain had exhausted her capacity to take part in the Cold War militarily, but her commonwealth connections and knowledge of some of the key areas of engagement, including the Middle East, were very useful to the Americans. The issue for both Cold War allies was therefore how to keep Muslims onside while trying to ensure Islamist ideology was not used against them. If it could be used for them, that was something useful.[27] It was in this connection that the idea of a Muslim Bloc was raised in 1949 and the American State department sought to facilitate a process which would ensure that an ideology of Islam that was sympathetic to their cause was developed.[28] Matthew Jacobs has argued that this policy arose from the prominent perception in successive American administrations that Islam was a force for stability due to its perceived lack of interest in change and generally conservative outlook and so would be amenable to encouragements an anti-Soviet bloc on the grounds of preventing potentially destabilizing ideologies from taking root in the region.[29] Jacobs's observation is confirmed by the work of Andrew Rotter and Salim Yakub who both point out that, through to the late 1960s, US officials sought to use Islam, through the medium of King Faisal of Saudi Arabia's influence, into an ideological force which would combat nascent Arab Nationalism.[30]

The US government had known that its support of Israel would likely drive Arab states into the arms of the Soviets. In a memorandum for the National Security Council dated July 6, 1954, James Lay Jr., executive secretary to the Office of the President, stated that if America was to have any chance of creating the kind of Middle Eastern anti-Soviet bloc which the British had tried to encourage (which the United States restyled Middle East Defense Organization [MEDO]), then it would need to "seek to engage the participation of intellectuals [Muslim leaders] in Western-orientated activities."[31] The policy was openly stated here but had clearly been in operation since the very early 1950s. It was a policy which was also being used extensively in Persia from 1951 onward.

On January 13, 1953, an internal State Department memo from the office of the secretary, Alan Dulles, spoke of the encouragement (and financial assistance) that the State Department had given toward a colloquium entitled the "Colloquium on Islamic Culture" to be held at Princeton University which was also sponsored by the Library of Congress. It was to be a "meeting in September 1953 between leading intellectuals of the Islamic world and the United States."[32] Its purpose as stated was to make an important contribution, at this time to both short term and long-term United States political objectives in the Moslem area.³³

The statement of goals went on to express the hope that

> the discussions between intellectual leaders of the Islamic world and the United States will stimulate interest in and research on the Islamic world within American educational circles.

However, it was not the education of Americans that primarily interested the colloquium. Of the seven principal topics discussed over the three days at Princeton, the longest discussion centered around ways of propagating a form of Islam that would be attractive to young people, drawing them into Islam, rather than Socialism.³⁴

Many of the Muslim delegates were given funding for an additional three months' stay in order for them to research and lecture on Islam at US universities. The colloquium was not just to be held at Princeton. The second part of the colloquium was held in Washington and included a visit to President Eisenhower in the Oval Office.

One of those who was paid for was Saeed Ramadan, an acknowledged senior member of the Muslim Brotherhood who later moved to Switzerland to set up the Brotherhood organizations in Europe.³⁵ Eisenhower recorded in his private papers that he found Ramadan's views repugnant, indeed, close to fascist.³⁶

The record of the colloquium was published and it reveals that the discussions had given Ramadan in particular an extensive opportunity to articulate his vision for the Muslim Brotherhood, expressing among other things its desire to be an all-encompassing ideology which would include provision for welfare, education, and healthcare as part of an Islamic structure for a new age. It was a vision welcomed by Kopper and several other officials at the colloquium.

It is important to acknowledge that even while these literalist forms of Wahhabi and Brotherhood Islam were being cautiously explored as foreign policy tools, there were also conscious attempts to spike the influence of those Muslim schools whose dogma was seen as too dangerous for the West. This is not dangerous in the sense of an ideology which stood opposed to Western values; this was dangerous in the sense that the institution had the capability of drawing people away from the narrative that the allies desired Muslims to hear.

However, concerns about the spread of "Islamic Radicalism" were not felt until the Iranian Revolution of 1979 and the correspondence from that period concerning the US government's views on Shi'a Islam are highly illuminating.

The United States had been highly, even intimately, involved in Iran since before the Second World War, but it was in the early Cold War that the United States replaced Britain as the primary foreign influence in the country.[37] By the late 1950s US-Iranian relations included American military and intelligence cooperation with the Shah. Indeed, Dilip Hiro argues that

> the US Embassy in Tehran became as important a center of power as the Shah's court.[38]

America was therefore locked into every facet of Iranian life, other than that of religion. Whether this was because of the traditional US culture of separation of church and state or this absence was due to concerns over cultural sensitivities is not apparent.

The British had also been reluctant to engage in religious matters, whether during the period of the Empire or the post–Second World War context, although, as will be seen, the line was sometimes rather blurred, but there were moments in which British authorities had decided to deliberately step into faith issues such as in relation to the 1858 Proclamation already discussed, and in relation to the securing of a proclamation from the North Indian "Ulema" declaring the British rule in India dar al-Islam.[39] Furthermore, certain religious practices such as sati had been specifically banned. But the British did not have the same church-state relationship that the United States did, and so it is interesting, given the differing cultural norms of each, that both had such similar approaches in this context.

During the period of the US-Shah dominance in Tehran, Iran became the principal supplier of oil to Israel. But the United States did not back Tehran unconditionally; under the presidency of John F. Kennedy, for example, further military assistance to the Shah was made dependent upon reforms, including dealing with the endemic corruption in the regime.[40] Nevertheless, the cooperation between America and the court of the Shah was such that, in the early 1970s, the Shah was being given a two-hour briefing by the CIA head of Station every Saturday morning.[41] The eventual revolution therefore was not simply an issue of regional destabilization in the context of the Cold War for the United States; it was a matter of important national security concern at all levels. As such, it jolted the United States not only in the context of their own strategic aims but also in realizing that the understanding of Islam as a stabilizing force in the region might not be either the whole truth or true at all.

The Iranian Revolution occurred during the administration of President Carter and, with the recent release of files from the period there has been opportunity for scholars to research the correspondence which pertained to those events. Of the attitudes to Islam these files reveal, the most important headline must be the perception that Shi'i Islam, rather than Sunni Islam, was the more revolutionary-minded.[42] This perception was understandable given the circumstances which they were observing and dealing with, but it is perhaps a signal of how perceptions have changed over the course of the past forty years, and the events around al-Qa'ida and ISIS, that greater concerns have been raised about Sunni Islam than Shi-ism.[43]

In the early phases of the growing opposition to the leadership of the Shah, Shi'a Islam was dismissed as both a religious force for resistance and a general force in the country. However, a report by the State Department's Bureau of Intelligence in 1977 did note that the form of the developing resistance to the Shah did have within it the "hallmarks of the Shi'a doctrine of dissimilation in the face of a superior force."[44]

At the very least, the US experiences in Iran therefore taught them that, while they had those within the administration who were expert enough with the ideologies they were engaging with. That knowledge, and the assumptions of the relative weakness of religious feeling versus secularization which also infused the correspondence, was enough for the Carter administration, from the president down, to underestimate the potency of religious feeling in the region. For that reason, it was realized that a more rigorous and thorough understanding of the religion of Islam itself, rather than the sociocultural briefings which were the mainstay of State Department briefing, was necessary.

Consequently, on June 24, July 15, and September 30, 1985, the Subcommittee on Europe and the Middle East of the Committee on Foreign Affairs for the House of Representatives (99th Session) held hearings on Islamic Fundamentalism and Islamic Radicalism.[45] The hearings were geared toward helping American policymakers to understand how religious and sociocultural movements in the Islamic world would impact on the advancing of US interests in those regions. In order for the committee to engage with the issue, they commissioned two experts to give reports: Dr. Hermann Eilts, of Boston University, and Dr. John Esposito, then of Holy Cross College.[46]

Covering the detail of the subcommittee would take too long, as the hearings minutes are 452 pages long. However, there are one or two particularly significant elements of discussion that are useful to draw out because they speak into the formation of US government attitudes to Islamic radicalism as a phenomenon.

Esposito was the first of the experts to give testimony and he pointed out that

> Moslems see Westerners as perpetuators of a Crusader mentality toward Islam, which they believe informs a policy of American neocolonialism, both by government and by multinationals. Thus, they see a danger that America will

seek to dominate political, economic and even social life in ways not unlike European imperialism.[47]

before moving on to summarize the beliefs which, he believed, characterized all Muslim organizations.[48] He ended by delineating what he felt to be the key differences between what we would now describe as Islamic Fundamentalists and Salafis, against those of other interpretations of the faith.[49]

> For radical movements, the following assumptions or beliefs are incorporated in addition to the foregoing. One, a crusader mentality, neocolonialist ambitions, and the power of Zionism have resulted in a Western Judeo-Christian conspiracy which pits the West against the East, or the Moslem world, in this case. Two, since the legitimacy of Moslem governments is based on Islamic law—sharia—governments, such as Anwar Sadat's in Egypt, which do not follow Islamic law are illegitimate. Those responsible for such an atheistic state are guilty of unbelief and, as such, are lawful objects of holy war (Jihad), and thus that government must be overthrown. Moslems are obliged both to overthrow such un-Islamic governments and to fight other Moslems who do not share their own total commitment. Militants regard such persons as no longer Moslems, but rather unbelievers. Three, jihad against unbelievers is a religious duty. Four, Christians and Jews are often considered unbelievers rather than, as has been traditional in Islam, as tolerated people of the Book. Five, opposition to illegitimate Moslem governments often extends to the official Ulama or clergy—the Shi'ites of Iran and Lebanon are exceptions—and to state-supported mosques, since they are considered to be co-opted and controlled by the government.[50]

The overwhelmingly negative view of the US Esposito outlined made it clear to US government officials and politicians that negative Muslim perspectives of America had already been germinating for some time. So when Esposito went on to propose that the United States should adopt a new stance in the Arab Muslim world, it flowed from a place of blame: blame of the United States for interfering in the Middle East. Esposito's recipe for changing that negative perception was centered around his central thesis that "it is usually U.S. presence and policy in a given country or region, not a generic hatred of America, that motivates actions against the American Government and business interests."[51] A perception that led to the suggestion that the United States should support regional nonstate actors since the United States was seen as supporting un-Islamic leaderships. He also advised that the United States should do all in its power to avoid being seen as a neocolonial power.

As has been seen already, Esposito's testimony and opinions very much fitted in with the prevailing view of the time in the US government on the value of Islam as a regional stabilizer and that, in this context, the events in Iran in 1979 could be considered an anomaly, rather than part of an ongoing normative pattern arising out of doctrines within the faith itself. Indeed, as Krysta Wise asserts, the United States believed that the Iranian Revolution was an anomaly and that, once the initial fire of revolutionary fervor had died down, moderates would assume control.[52]

For both the US and British governments, therefore, the Cold War was a period of seeking to bring as many Muslim states into the Western sphere of influence. It was a period of learning about the faith and most especially, revising previously held views on the potency of religious feeling in the Middle East.

THE WAR ON TERROR

No single event in the modern era has had the instant impact that the attacks of 9/11 had. By the time the dust had settled from the collapse of the Twin Towers and the cleanup operation had begun, President George W. Bush had declared a "War on Terror" which has helped to shape international events ever since. As Cofer Black of the CIA said to the Joint House and Senate Select Intelligence Committee,

> all you need to know is that there was a before 9/11 and after 9/11. After 9/11 the gloves came off.[53]

This section will focus almost entirely on the US engagement with the War on Terror. Not only because they were the lead protagonist but also because the British engagement in a foreign affairs context was primarily in relation to US aims and desires. However, it is important to note that the British were not simply involved in the War on Terror to support an ally: sixty-seven British nationals were among those killed on September 11, 2001. So Britain had reason to be involved on its own terms. Indeed, the events of 9/11 stimulated the British prime minister Tony Blair into what Oliver Daddow described as hyperactivity in which Blair saw a new world order being made using British leverage and American power.[54] Daddow argues that the Blair foreign policy was a blip which was quickly changed under his successor's back "towards its ethically informed, but cautiously realist roots."[55] As was discussed in chapter 2, the British government had had a long-standing relationship with the Middle East which stretched back, for better or worse, to the Crusades and before. A Foreign Office submission to a Parliamentary enquiry in 2013 concerning the relationship between Britain and Saudi Arabia (and Bahrain) characterized the relations between the two countries as "amongst our most enduring in the world."[56] It was this long-standing relationship that was subsumed into the response to the 9/11 attacks.

9/11 was not the first jihadi attack of the global terrorist era, nor was it the last: al-Qa'ida had already attacked the USS *Cole* off the coast of East Africa three years before, and back in 1993 a plan to blow up the World Trade Centre had almost succeeded. The bombings in Madrid (2004) and London (July 7 and 21, 2005) as well as subsequent smaller and less sophisticated attacks in France (notably Paris, 2015, and Nice, 2016), Germany (including Berlin and Ansbach, 2016), and further attacks in the UK, America, and France. In addition to these attacks the specter of homegrown foreign fighters had also heightened concern about the influence of jihadi propaganda from Islamic State of Iraq and Levant (ISIL, also known as ISIS Daesh and IS) among Muslim diaspora communities in the West.

Huge numbers of publications, both books and articles, have sought to pars and interpret the religious, cultural, and political implications of these events. Indeed, later in this book (chapter 8) the issue of radicalization and homegrown jihadism will be explored, but this chapter will focus only upon the perception of Islam and Muslim states which have been understood by Britain and America through the overseas elements of The War on Terror.

In his article "The War on Terror in American Grand Strategy," Michael Boyle highlighted that the US declaration of war following the 9/11 attacks

> constituted the single most ambitious reordering of America's foreign policy objectives since the Second World War.[57]

Before citing the new delineation in world affairs as defined by President George W. Bush,

> every nation, in every region, now has a decision to make. Either you are with us, or you are with the terrorists.[58]

For Muslim states the choice was not an easy one for, on the one hand, America was an important ally, particularly for Saudi Arabia and Pakistan. On the other hand, the US support for Israel and the broader conflation of US-Crusader narratives which had permeated through the MENA region and South Asia made the open support of the United States and her allies publicly difficult to manage for regimes.[59]

The popular notion that the post-Cold War world was to be defined in terms of adherence to, or competition with, the Pax Americana had become embodied in the belief in The Cultural Confrontation, or The Clash of Civilizations as famously proposed by Harvard professor Samuel Huntington. It was a belief that was deeply embedded in the psyche of the Muslims of the Middle East, South and Southeast Asia, and had superseded the previous narrative that had dominated the late Cold War and early post-Cold War period that the issues underlying inequality had been framed in terms of the material—social, economic and military—inequalities that separated north from post-colonial south. This new theory however, involved the belief that relations between the Middle East and the west had become those of civilizational confrontation, based on a western hostility to "Islam."[60]

Fred Halliday argues that this myth was perpetuated from 1991 onward by those in both the United States and Middle East. For both Iran and the Arabs the concept was embodied as cultural aggression.[61] Mehran Kamrava cites the drivers of a "highly ideological" US foreign policy as Condolezza Rice (national security advisor), Donald Rumsfeld (secretary of defense), and Dick Cheney (vice president).[62] Fawaz Gerges contextualizes these "confronationalists" with an exploration of the political and intellectual impact of scholars such as Bernard Lewis and Samuel Huntington in a book which was published before the events of 9/11.[63] Gerges quotes Mortimer Zuckerman, Charles Krauthammer, and Daniel Pipes who all posited Islam as the new threat, taking over from the communist USSR, in a series of opinions which were, at that stage, heavily influenced by the shock of the Iranian Revolution and the impact of the World Trade Center bombing.[64] Indeed, such was the level of fear about Islamic activism that Walter McDougall, former aide to President Nixon, proposed an alliance with Russia to protect Christendom against the Muslim world.[65]

It would therefore be reasonable to assert that, when the 9/11 attacks occurred, there was already fertile soil within the upper echelons of US administrations, fertilized over more than twenty years, that felt that the 9/11 attacks were simply the continuation of a civilizational war that had been going for centuries. The administration of Bill Clinton had, for a time, bucked that trend, replacing the civilizational confrontation ideology with the language of partnership and common concern with the Muslim peoples to see responsible government and human rights. His administration was at pains to separate Islamic extremism from Islam. Two speeches given in 1994 sought to identify a distinction between the faith and the work of Islamists.[66] In each Islamic extremism was posited as a tool for the acquisition of power.

Halliday makes a distinction between US relations with Muslim states over the post-Cold War period and those of transnational Muslim organizations such as al-Qa'ida. The former, he argues, remained on essentially the same terms throughout the period; it was relations with the later which shifted dramatically from the US support of the Mujahidin in the 1980s to the confrontation with the Mujahidin's successors, the Taliban and jihadi groups, more broadly from the 1990s onward.

The observation is, on the surface, accurate, yet it misses the clear souring of relationships with the United States' key strategic partners in the War on Terror (Pakistan and Saudi Arabia) in the post-9/11 period.

The George W. Bush administration required assistance if it was going to perpetrate the War on Terror outside the United States. For that reason, the dominant clash narrative required tapering and, what's more, partnership with states in the Middle East and South Asia which represented the epitome of all that the US officials rejected—Saudi Arabia, the home of most of the 9/11 attackers, and Pakistan, whose state intelligence service had a close working relationship with the Taliban and al-Qa'ida.

For Pakistan, President Bush's stark delineation offered the prospect of a renewal of relations with a state which had become increasingly distant from it. Indeed, as Christine Fair pointed out in her article, the events of 9/11

> afforded then President Musharraf the opportunity to cast off . . . sanctions and rehabilitate Pakistan's standing in the community of nations.[67]

In such circumstances, therefore, Musharraf had little choice but to agree to allow the United States to use naval, army, and air force bases. But in the decade which followed, relations became more, rather than less, strained. The sharing of intelligence, which was intended to be the bedrock of the coalition, did not produce the results that the United States was searching for. Indeed, when Osama Bin Laden was discovered hiding in a large house in Abbottabad (a city which is home to Pakistan's largest officer training academy), the Americans chose to insert a special forces team, kill Bin Laden, and extract from the country before the Pakistanis were even informed of the operation. Nor was that the only occasion that the United States acted unilaterally.[68]

For the Saudi royal family, the shock of learning that fifteen of the nineteen 9/11 hijackers were Saudi nationals concentrated the mind, especially given that the World Trade Centre bombing had also been the work of Saudi nationals. In such circumstances, cooperation was the route toward repairing a relationship which had already been under strain from internal Saudi and US voices.[69] Condolezza Rice, then-secretary of state, summed up the frustration on the American side in a speech in 2005:

> For sixty years, my country, the United States, pursued peace and stability at the expense of democracy in this region here in the Middle East—and we have achieved neither.[70]

Yet, while Saudi-US relationship was going through this most turbulent period another Muslim organization was actually improving its relationship with the United States over the same period as both the Saudi and Pakistani relations were souring.

President Bush appointed a special envoy to the Organization of the Islamic Conference (OIC) in 2008 with the remit of increasing cooperation with the OIC on Conflict Resolution, Counterterrorism, Human Rights, Humanitarian Assistance, Global Women's Issues and Health.[71] The range of these issues indicates that the United States was pivoting toward engagement with transnational organizations to try to engage with the deep problems of the MENA region and wider Human Rights concerns, rather than maintaining its state-focused agenda.

This spirit of civilizational cooperation has continued in recent years. For example, America has lent its cautious support to the Istanbul Process, which arose from the Human Rights Council's Resolution 16/18. The resolution committed the HRC to

> combatting intolerance, negative stereotyping and stigmatization of, and discrimination, incitement to violence, and violence against persons based on religion or belief.[72]

In this it has been joined by the UK whose work in this area is being headed by the Foreign and Commonwealth Office. The British ambassador to the United Nations Geneva, Mark Matthews, addressed the British government's interest in, and engagement with, Resolution 16/18 in a speech hosted by the Universal Rights Group in Geneva in 2017.[73] In it, Matthews highlighted the work being done by both the British government itself, as well as the other members, in seeking to reduce hate crimes internationally. The tone and substance of Matthews' speech showed that, while the War on Terror remains, at least theoretically, the operational doctrine of the United States and its allies, it is clear that the strident, stark delineation laid out by President Bush in the wake of the 9/11 attacks has been replaced with the language of cooperation. This, argue Michelle Bentley and Jack Holland, was the object of President Obama's foreign policy.[74] Yet it is worthwhile noting that this change in tone has come about while the terrorist threat itself has not diminished at all and it is strongly indicative of a recognition of the self-defeating nature of the binary oppositions which had been set up in the early post-9/11 era. However, it looks as if the tone and policies of President Trump's administration have returned the United States to a more confrontationalist stance. That being said, he made a trip to the Gulf region early in his tenure and the thrust of his remarks was strongly suggestive of a desire to cooperate with, and engage in, regional issues, although the sense of his remarks strongly suggested that his primary concern had switched from winning the War on Terror itself, to wanting to limit or roll back growing Iranian influence in the region.[75] For that reason, it can be argued that his policy of containment is likely to offer new opportunities for US-Saudi relations to deepen in the near future.

In the context of the focus of this book, therefore, it seems that the War on Terror era did little to impact underlying perceptions of Islam and Muslims as such. Indeed, the intelligence required and the military resources to be deployed have, if anything, deepened US-Saudi relations, even as their mineral needs have altered their economic relationships. However, as shall be seen later, concerns over the impact of homegrown terrorism have added a new dimension both of US understanding of some streams of Islamic ideology and raising further concerns over the impact of Wahhabi and other literalist interpretations of Islam in US mosques.

CONCLUSION

The three episodes under discussion in this chapter have revealed a number of important dynamics and patterns.

The first pattern is a clear and consistent concern about wider Muslim opinion concerning the particular event under discussion. That opinion was noted and, while it did not necessarily change the action, it did prompt serious consideration of messaging strategies which could mitigate the negative perception that the actions might draw.

The second pattern or theme in the correspondence was that Islam could be both an ally and a potential enemy depending on the circumstance and it was interesting that the perception, even leading up to the Iranian Revolution, was that Shi'a Islam was more of an inherently socially destabilizing ideology than Sunni Islam was.

The third observation which could be made about the correspondence was that it shows that there were good levels of expertise available to policymakers in all these contexts, but that other political considerations sometimes meant that their advice was not implemented.

In terms of the overarching theme of the book, however, the key observation which could be made is that policymakers on both sides of the Atlantic understood that any relationship between America and Britain on the one hand, and Muslim majority states on the other was fragile and prone to crack at any point. The perception of Islam and of Muslims which they therefore understood in this context was that close relations, while being a pragmatic necessity, were neither desired nor expected with the United States and Britain.

NOTES

1. Jukka Nevakivi, *Britain, France and the Arab Middle East 1914–1920*. London: Athlone Press, 1969, p. 104.

2. Kathleen Burk, *Lion and the Eagle: The Interaction of the British and American Empires 1783—1972*. London, New York: Bloomsbury Press, 2018, p. 157.

3. Markus Dressler (2015) "Rereading Ziya Gokalp: Secularism and Reform of the Islamic State in the Late Young Turk Period," *International Journal of Middle East Studies* Vol. 47, Iss. 3, pp. 511–531.

4. David Fromkin, *The Peace to End All Peace: The Fall of the Ottoman Empire and the Creation of the Modern Middle East*. London: Phoenix Press, 2000, p. 407.

5. This is detailed in Bernard Lewis, *The Emergence of Modern Turkey*, 3rd edn. Oxford, New York: OUP, 2002, pp. 247–250; Fromkin, *Peace to End all Peace*, pp. 405–407. Sean Oliver-Dee, *The Caliphate Question: British Government and Islamic Governance*. Lanham (MD): Rowman and Littlefield, 2009, pp. 109—119.

6. The point referenced the Ottomans in the context of the wider principle of "Self-Determination": "The Turkish portions of the present Ottoman Empire should be assured a secure sovereignty, but the other nationalities which are now under Turkish rule should be assured and undoubted security of life and an absolutely unmolested opportunity of autonomous development." This wording represented a softening of Wilson's stance as an earlier version had proposed the complete destruction of not just the Ottoman Empire but of Turkey itself. See Charles Seymour, *The Intimate Papers of Colonel House*. Boston: Houghton Mifflin, 1928, p. 51, in Fromkin, *Peace to end all Peace*, p. 259.

7. Laurence Evans, *United States Policy and the Partition of Turkey: 1914–1924*. Baltimore: Johns Hopkins University Press, 1965, p. 39.

8. Ibid.

9. Karpat, "The Ottoman Emigration to America, 1860–1914." Nancy Gentile Ford, *Americans All! Foreign-Born Soldiers in World War I*. College Station (TX): Texas A&M University Press, 2001, pp. 60–61; Mustafa Aksakal (2011) "Holy War Made in Germany? Ottoman Origins of the 1914 Jihad," *War in History* Vol. 18, Iss. 2, pp. 184–199.

10. See M. Naeen Qureshi, *Pan-Islam in British-Indian Politics: A Study of the Khilafat Movement. 1918–1924*. Leiden: Brill, 1999.

11. David Sanders, *Losing and Empire, Finding a Role: British Foreign Policy since 1945*. Basingstoke: MacMillan, 1990, pp. 65–81.

12. Michael Kirby, *The Decline of British Power since 1870*. London and New York: Routledge, 2014, p. 83.

13. Steven Hurst, *Cold War US Foreign Policy: Key Perspectives*. Edinburgh: Edinburgh University Press, 2005.

14. Adeed Dawisha, *Arab Nationalism in the Twentieth Century: From Triumph to Despair*. Princeton (NJ): Princeton University Press, 2016.

15. Joseph Massad, *Islam in Liberalism*. Chicago, New York: University of Chicago Press, 1994, p. 94.

16. Translation found in Intelligence Bureau Memorandum, Section F "The Russian Moslems and the Bolsheviks." no date. FO 141/587. F93-94.

17. For discussion a discussion of Al-Afghani and Pan-Islamism, see Qureishi, *Pan -Islamism* and Sean Oliver-Dee, *Muslim Minorities and Citizenship: Authority, Communities and Islamic Law*. London, New York: I.B. Tauris, 2012, pp. 108–112.

18. Analysis piece. "The Islamic Consciousness," FO141/587. no date. F113.

19. Jon Jacobson, *When the Soviet Union Entered World Politics*. Berkley: University of California, 1994, pp. 55–56.

20. Emil Aydin, "The Question of Orientalism in Pan-Islamic Thought: The Origins, Content and Legacy of Transnational Muslim Identities," in Sucheta Mazumdar, Vasant Kaiwar and Theirry Labica (eds), *From Orientalism to Post-Colonialism: Asia, Europe and the Lineages of Difference*. Abingdon: Routledge, 2010, p. 211.

21. Ibid.

22. DS(E) 140/1, General HQ, Middle East, Cairo. October 10, 1942.

23. W.A. Smart, *Memorandum*, November 11, 1942.

24. Barry Rubin and Wolfgang Schwanitz, *Nazis, Islamists, and the Making of the Modern Middle East*. New Haven (CT): Yale University Press, 2014. See also Klaus Michael Mallmann and Martin Cuppers, *Nazi Palestine: The Plans for the Extermination of the Jews in Palestine*. New York: Enigma Books, 2010; Matthias Kuntzel, *Jihad and Jew Hatred: Islamism, Nazism and the roots of 9/11* (trans. Colin Meade). New York: Telos Press, 2007.

25. DS (E)/200/42. Minutes of Meeting with Amin Osman Pacha at British Embassy May 18, 1942.

26. Ibid. Appendix A to the Minutes.

27. Ernest Woodward, *British Foreign Policy in the Second World War*. London: HM Stationary Office, 1962, pp. 148–149.

28. It was reported that the Soviets had in fact accused Britain of engaging in this policy, but that, by the time they had done so, the policy had been abandoned for reasons that will be explored shortly. FO371/75047 File No. 1019, *Third Quarterly Report on Islamic World*, Eastern Section, October 1949.

29. Matthew Jacobs, *Imagining the Middle East: The Building of an American Foreign Policy, 1918–1967*. Chapel Hill (NC): University of North Carolina Press, 2011, p. 118.

30. See Andrew Rotter, *Comrades at Odds: The United States and India, 1947–1964*. New York: Ithaca Press, 2000; and Salim Yakub, *Containing Arab Nationalism: The Eisenhower Doctrine and the Middle East*. Chapel Hill (NC): University of North Carolina Press, 2002.

31. NEA:NE:FHAwalt:bbh 3/11/52.

32. Ibid.

33. Dr. Wilson Compton to Mr. Bruce, January 13, 1953. IIA:IPO:GHDamon:bv.

34. Ibid.

35. Foreign Service Dispatch, 237. 511.80/7-2753. July 1, 1953.

36. See Eric Walberg, *Postmodern Imperialism: Geopolitics and the Great Games*. Atlanta: Clarity Press, 2014.

37. Dilip Hiro, *Cold War in the Islamic World*. New York, Oxford: OUP, 2018, p. 61.

38. Ibid., p. 62.

39. See Oliver-Dee, *Muslim Minorities and Citizenship*, p. 35.

40. April Summitt (2004) "For a White Revolution: John F Kennedy and the Shah of Iran," *Middle East Journal* Vol. 58, Iss. 4, pp. 560–575.

41. Dilip Hiro, *Iran under the Ayatollahs*. New York, London: Routledge, 2013, pp. 166–167.

42. Mattin Biglari (2016) "Captive to the Demonology of the Iranian Mobs: US Foreign Policy and Perceptions of Shi'a Islam during the Iranian Revolution, 1978–79," *Diplomatic History* Vol. 40, Iss. 4, pp. 579–605.

43. This will be seen in the following chapter and chapter 8, which engage with post-9/11 correspondence.

44. Franklin Huddle, *The Future of Iran: Implications for the US*, INR, Iran Documents 01144, DSNA January 13, 1977.

45. Subcommittee on Europe and the Middle East of the Committee on Foreign Affairs for the House of Representatives (99th Session) *Islamic Fundamentalism and Islamic Radicalism*. Washington DC: US Government Printing Office, 1985.

46. Eilts was one of the State Department Arabists for many years before retiring and setting up the center for International Relations at Boston University. He held posts in Saudi Arabia, Libya, and Egypt before his retirement. He died in 2006. Professor John Esposito has become one of the most sought-after and respected authorities on Islam in the West. He is currently director of the Prince Al Walid Centre for Muslim-Christian Understanding at Georgetown University in Washington, DC.

47. Esposito, *Hearings, Islamic Radicalization*, p. 2.

48. Ibid., p. 3.

49. Terminologies to describe such groups are often controversial and contested. The terms given earlier are those based upon the definitions given in the annually published *Muslim 500*, which includes in every publication a set of definitions of all the differing theological and ideological streams within Islam. See S. E. Scheifer (chief editor). 2017. *The Muslim 500 (2018): The World's 500 Most Influential Muslims*. Amman: The Royal Islamic Strategic Studies Centre.

50. Esposito, *Hearings, Islamic Radicalization*, p. 5.

51. Esposito, *Hearings, Islamic Radicalization*, p. 6. See also Samer Shehata, *Islamist Politics in the Middle East: Movements and Change*. New York, London: Routledge, 2012.

52. Krysta Wise (2011) "Islamic Revolution of 1979: The Downfall of American-Iranian Relations," *Legacy* Vol. 11, Iss. 1, pp. 1–16.

53. Testimony to joint SSCI/HPSCI hearing, September 26, 2002, in Thomas Ayers (2005) "Six Floors of Detainee Operations in the Post-9/11 World," *Parameters* Vol. 35, p. 33.

54. Oliver Daddow (2013) "The Use of force in British Foreign Policy: From New Labour to the Coalition," *The Political Quarterly* Vol. 84, Iss. 1, pp. 110–119.

55. Ibid., p. 110.

56. House of Commons Foreign Affairs Committee *The UK's Relations with Saudi Arabia and Bahrain* Fifth Report of Session 2013–14. Vol. 1, November 12, 2013, p. 18.

57. Michael Boyle (2008) "The War on Terror in American Grand Strategy," *Journal of International Affairs* Vol. 84, Iss. 2, pp. 191–209.

58. George W. Bush, "Address to a Joint Session of Congress and the American People," September 20, 2001, http://www.whitehouse.gov/news/releases/2001/09/20 010920-8.html.

59. This narrative and its effects are analyzed in Nathan Funk and Abdul Aziz Said (2004) "Islam and the West: Narratives of Conflict and Transformation," *International Journal of Peace Studies* Vol. 9, Iss. 1, pp. 1–28.

60. Fred Halliday, *The Middle East in International Relations: Power, Politics and Ideology*. Cambridge, New York: CUP, 2005, p. 155.

61. Ibid.

62. Mehran Kamran, *The Middle East: A Political History since the First World War*. Berkley, Los Angeles: UCLA Press, 2005, p. 207.

63. Fawaz Gerges, *America and Political Islam: Clash of Cultures of Clash of Interests?* Cambridge: CUP, 1999.

64. Ibid., p. 23.

65. Ibid.

66. See Anthony Lake (1994) "Building a New Middle East, Challenges for US Policy," Address to the Soref Symposium of the Washington Institute of Near Eastern Policy, May 17, 1994, US Department of State; Robert Pelletreau (1994) "Symposium: Resurgent Islam," *Middle East Policy* Vol. 3, Iss. 2, pp. 1–21.

67. C. Christine Fair (2012) "The US–Pakistan Relations after a Decade of the War on Terror," *Contemporary South Asia* Vol. 20, Iss. 2, pp. 243–253.

68. Daniel Markey, *No Exit from Pakistan: America's Tortured Relationship with Islamabad*. Cambridge, New York: CUP, 2013, pp. 72–169.

69. Rachael Bronson's *Thicker than Oil: America's Uneasy Partnership with Saudi Arabia*. New York, Oxford: OUP, 2008 assesses the voices of dissent in both states that, from the earliest years of their relationship, were calling for an end to it on both the US and Saudi sides.

70. Condoleezza Rice, "Remarks at the American University in Cairo," https://2001-2009.state.gov/secretary/rm/2005/48328.htm, June 20, 2005.

71. See State Department Statement, https://www.state.gov/s/rga/oic/268129.htm, January 20, 2008.

72. The text of HRC Resolution 16/18 can be found at https://www2.ohchr.org/english/bodies/hrcouncil /docs/16session/a.hrc.res.16.18_en.pdf, April 12, 2011.

73. Mark Matthews, "UK Statement at the Implementation of Council Resolution 16/18 on Combating Religious Intolerance," February 14, 2017, https://www.gov.uk/government/news/uk-statement-at-the-implementation-of-council-resolution-1618-event-on-combating-religious-intolerance-hosted-by-universal-rights-group.

74. Michelle Bentley and Jack Holland, *Obama's Foreign Policy: Ending the War on Terror*. New York, London: Routledge, 2014.

75. The full transcript of President Trump's "Speech to the Muslim World," delivered in Saudi Arabia on May 21, 2017 can be found at https://www.haaretz.com/middle-east-news/read-in-full-transcript-of-trump-s-speech-to-the-muslim-world-1.5474977.

Chapter 4

Economics

In many ways, as with many of these issues, the subject matter crosses a number of other subject areas and elements of this chapter could easily have been located within a number of the other chapters. However, although separating economics as a distinct strand is, in one sense, a false distinction, it has been done in this way in order that differing elements of economic engagement, which are such an important part of the Anglo-US engagement with Muslims, is given space for analysis on its own terms.

The discovery and exploitation of oil in the Middle East, along with the development of sharia finance instruments, have become important elements of both the US and British relationship with Muslim majority states and diaspora peoples. Oil has been a more indirect element of Britain's relationship with Islam and this chapter will analyze the nature of that relationship through an investigation of the correspondence surrounding the granting of exploration concessions to the US and British companies in Arabia in the 1930s and 1950s. It will also explore sharia finance initiatives through the British engagement with the Muslim World Bank in 1954, the opening of the largest US sharia bank Lariba in 1987, and the correspondence around the possible collaboration between the UK and the Islamic Development Bank in 1978.

This chapter will therefore seek to show that there have been sound economic considerations which have bought both Britain and the United States into *Courting Islam*. At the same time, it will examine the events and the correspondence surrounding them in order to help us to understand what perceptions of the faith and Muslim leaders were formed by US and British officials through those interactions.

Chapter 4

OIL EXPLOITATION

The British and American need for oil to power both the growing domestic car markets and their increasingly mechanized militaries became more urgent as the nineteenth century gave way to the twentieth. But as far back as 1814, oil had been produced (about one barrel per day) in Marietta, Ohio, although the mechanization process which would create the demand had not yet begun, so it meant that little use was found for it. The first commercial oil well had been founded in America back in 1859 (near Titusville, Pennsylvania), and its founding coincided with the first significant commercial requirement for oil: the kerosene lamp, whose clean burn immediately found favor with consumers, creating the first commercial need for oil which could be refined for kerosene. It was in response to this growing demand that J. D. Rockefeller founded Standard Oil (SO) in 1870: the first large-scale commercial production in the United States.

Britain first began to use coal-gas for street lighting in 1807, but just a few years later, in 1815, oil-gas began to be used. As the use of street lighting increased, the demand for oil-gas also began to increase.[1] In 1861, the first recorded import of oil came from the United States to Britain aboard the ship *Elizabeth Watts* and that process continued with Britain continuing to import from the United States and from Dutch Sumatra when oil was discovered there in 1885. That increase in oil import began with the discovery of oil in Persia by William Reynolds in 1908, but it was Winston Churchill's decision as First Sea Lord to switch the British Navy from coal-fired to oil-fired engines shortly before the outbreak of the First World War which brought oil into significant usage in Britain.[2] The British government became the major shareholder in the Anglo-Persian Oil Company (APOC) setting the seal on British interests in the Persian region. As Adelson observes, that decision turned the Persian Gulf into a "British lake."[3]

Even before that momentous decision had been taken, though, the discovery of oil in Persia had prompted APOC to expand its horizons. For that reason they had already made enquiries of the political resident as to whether an oil concession was available from the Ruler of Kuwait, Mubarak al-Sabah II (1911). Indeed, they had even managed to secure an agreement with Mubarak II through the political resident which said that no Kuwait oil concession would be given except to a person nominated and recommended by the British government (1913).[4] Yet this attempt to rapidly secure all the oil interests in the region fell short. The First World War stalled progress on the development of the agreements with the rulers of Kuwait to the extent that negotiations did not resume until 1923. Captain William Henry Shakespear, an officer in the Indian Political Service, acted as the political agent initiating APOC's negotiations for oil concession agreement with Ahmad al-Jaber al-Sabah, who had come to the throne following the death of his brother Salim in 1921. Captain Shakespear had developed a personal relationship with Abdul Aziz Ibn Saud during his time in Arabia before the outbreak of war and it was hoped that this personal relationship would assist the British government as a whole when it came to acquiring oil rights.[5] Major Holmes of Eastern and General Syndicate sent a telegram to Sheikh Ahmad informing him of his acquisition of the Hasa field from Ibn Saud and advising him not to grant any oil concession before first considering his own company's terms. Sheikh Ahmad rejected APOC's terms as unacceptable. The following year APOC's negotiating rights for Kuwait oil fields agreement lapsed and they were quickly acquired by the American firm Gulf Oil Corporation (GOC) Holmes, on behalf of the EGS and the GOC, negotiated unsuccessfully with Sheikh Ahmad for concession. The United States requested the right of equal freedom in negotiations with the Kuwaiti ruler. Seeing their negotiating power weakening, Britain agreed to an American request for an open door policy for American oil in Kuwait. Sheikh Ahmad, seeking to play the British and Americans off against one another in order to secure the best deal, requested a comprehensive concession proposal from both APOC and the GOC. In the end, both APOC and GOC merged to mine the oil field jointly and in the process created the Kuwait Oil Company in 1934, when the Kuwait Oil Concession Agreement was signed by Shaikh Ahmad of Kuwait.[6]

The pathway to the agreement of the Kuwait Oil Concession Agreement signed on December 23, 1934, was therefore long and complex and in one sense the history given earlier is not vital to the central discussion of the book. However, its sheer length and complexity are a sign of the value placed on the securing of the concession by the British government. This is relevant to the overall ark of the book insofar as it was clear that the British were prepared to go a long way to ensure that they had access to the resources. This context is important because it seems to have opened the negotiators to permitting a form of terminology in the agreements which did not fit within the context of the cultural milieu within which the British sat. For, most strikingly, the agreement was made "In the name of God the Merciful" (as was the 1948 agreement—translated as "Allah" in the Arabic version of the agreement) and that second, both the 1934 and 1948 agreements contained a clause which committed the KOC to build schools and hospitals.[7]

It is interesting that God should be invoked in this agreement, especially for what is a purely commercial venture: there is no religious commitment in the agreement at all. Not even a commitment to honor the religious freedom of employees, or the religious customs of the country in which KOC is operating. It maybe however that the language had been the personal desire of Sheikh Ahmad himself as Chisholm records in his book about the negotiations over the KOC that when Sheikh Ahmad had ascended to the throne, he had made a specific commitment with his people to rule under sharia.[8] Chisholm makes no record of this language being resisted, or even commented on and it is entirely possible that the British believed that there was no sense that having such language carried any implications at all. Yet the use of phrase carries the connotation that the agreement is being made under the sovereignty of Allah, rather than the liberal context of the people. Of course, in the English text, the term "God" is used instead, but the fact that the Arabic version of the agreement uses Allah, instead of Ilah which could be used as a generic term for God in Arabic, is worthwhile noting as well.

In terms of education, this commitment to build schools was, in many respects, unremarkable to Western eyes, but to revivalist and reformist Muslims, the idea of having Western-styled educational and welfare establishments created in a Gulf state was an anathema.[9]

The course of this protracted negotiation had shown vividly at least two things: first, that American power internationally was on the rise and British power was on the wane; second, that both countries understood very clearly the importance of oil to their increasingly mechanized societies and militaries. Indeed, the British had specifically ended their defense of the Kuwaiti oil concession because they knew that without America as an ally they were going to be in trouble,[10] especially with the rise of the fascist powers becoming a reality and the threat of war that they brought.

In the context of the lack of understanding of the American and British of the agreement being made under the sovereignty of Allah rather than as a secular international contract, it showed the British officials as ignorant of the potential implications of the wording of the contract in relation to whether, for example, the contract was to be honored under international law terms, or under sharia terms. The question about the implications of that did not seem to be even peripherally understood by the negotiators. For them, the Kuwaiti agreement was simply an economic or trade deal. Yet it committed the United States and Britain to a long-term engagement to the region which included not simply the development of education and welfare support in Kuwait but also wider duties of care. Perhaps the British negotiators had simply assumed that the education they had committed themselves to would be of a liberal or secular nature, yet no specification had been made.[11] The agreement therefore, at least in theory, carried the potential of funding of madrassa education.

Indeed, up to 1961 Britain controlled the foreign affairs and defense of Kuwait and in the same period all Western foreigners fell under the jurisdiction of the British political agent, not the Shaikh. The United States did not even establish a consulate in Kuwait until 1951. Furthermore, until 1971 the British retained ultimate responsibility for the Persian Gulf. Only after withdrawal east of Suez finally took place in that year did the United States become directly involved in the Gulf, an involvement that led to the Carter

Doctrine of 1980. But the fact that Britain was willing to pour money and resources into Kuwait demonstrated the strategic importance of the relationship both to Britain itself and to the West in general.

ISLAMIC FINANCE

The growth and development of Islamic finance in both countries is a recent phenomenon although such products had been used informally for several decades. British prime ministers and chancellors have, over more than a decade, openly expressed a desire to see London become the Islamic finance capital for the globe. As such there has been a drive within the City of London and on Wall Street to see increasing investment. Sharia-compliant finance represents a significant new revenue stream at a time when many of the world's OECD countries, including the UK and United States are running significant structural deficits.

British merchant banks and the Bank of England had Islamic finance units going back into the 1970s and in the 1990s the Saudi Baraka bank offered sharia-compliant mortgages to the public.[12] The first institutional engagement with Islamic finance in the UK came in 2003 when the Bank of England changed the rules on Stamp Duty to make *sukuk* mortgages more competitive.[13] In practice this meant that, rather than having to pay Stamp Duty twice, as would have happened under the pre-2003 system if an *sukuk* mortgage product was desired, the changed law ensured that it would only have to be paid once. This ensured the *sukuk* mortgage's viability as an alternative financial product. Two years later officials in the Treasury stated that there would be no objection to having Islamic financial products in UK markets and in the same year the Labor government passed legislation which brought sharia-compliant mortgages under the umbrella of other financial instruments.[14]

However, it was in London's bond markets that sharia-compliant products were eagerly awaited. The Financial Services Authority (since defunct) explored the possibility of a regulatory framework to encompass the emerging sharia bond market. The then chief secretary to the Treasury, Stephen Timms, stated publicly that

> Britain wants to support increasingly sophisticated Islamic finance and increased trade with Muslim countries.[15]

He made no secret of the fact that he was working to try and remove any legal or tax barriers which might inhibit sharia financial capital flow and went on to express the desire for London to become the global base for sharia financial products. Timms was supported by the then-chancellor Gordon Brown who declared at the Islamic Finance and Trade Conference (held in London, 2006) that he wanted London to become the "gateway for shari'a finance."[16]

This drive for Islamic finance was one element of an investment strategy to tap new markets and Britain's Muslim population was seen as a significant new source of finance. Lloyds TSB announced in 2006 that all of their branches would offer sharia-compliant branches and the following year the FSA founded the Bank of London and the Middle East as the first entirely sharia-compliant financial house in the UK. It was quickly followed by the Islamic Bank of Britain in 2008.[17]

Yet in this rush for investment, the British government had overlooked the fact that a study published in 2004 showed that three-quarters of Muslims in the UK were not interested in using Islamic finance and 83 percent questioned the necessity of sharia-compliant products. Indeed, only 9 percent of Muslims showed an interest in using such products. So the demand has not been there, even though the belief in the demand was absolute. But rather than back away from using the products any further, government buildings have now had sharia financial products secured on their use. Part of the agreement for the £200million bond the British government issued in 2016 was that the government agreed that the buildings would abide by certain aspects of sharia rules, so Muslim investors did not feel they were making money out of something they regard as forbidden in Islam.[18] Indeed the *The Independent* reported that the buildings were "now governed by sharia law."[19] Andrew Bridgen, the Conservative MP for North West Leicestershire, told the website:

> I do find it unbelievable government buildings are governed by sharia law. I don't see the bars as being an essential part of Parliament but it's the principle that matters. Most of our constituents will be absolutely amazed that the principle could ever have been authorized.[20]

It is unclear which aspects of sharia are being adhered to by the managers of the buildings concerned, but according to a government for the article in the *Independent* it had been agreed that serving pork in Richmond House would not affect the sharia compliance of the *sukuk*. Furthermore, the Treasury were adamant that

> the sukuk is issued under, and governed by, English law which applies at all times.[21]

Concerns have been raised about the commercial banking sector's use of sharia finance as well. In 2014, in response to enquiries, the Liberal-Conservative coalition government cited a number of organizations, including the Executive Sharia Committee of HSBC Saudi Arabia, as saying the bonds were sharia compliant but suggested potential investors should seek opinions from their chosen experts.[22]

But whatever the concerns being raised about the use of such financial instruments for government buildings it is clear that sharia finance remains an important element of the British government's investment strategy. Concerns about the potential impact of such instruments, both in terms of the legal ramifications and the use of Islamic finance to advance a separatist agenda, have either been ignored or have been dismissed. Whether the concerns about the use of such products come to be realized in the future is of course impossible to say, but, from the point of view of this book, the importance of sharia finance lies in its promotion, rather than opposition, by successive British governments. In that context therefore, it appears that, on the surface at least, British governments have no concerns about sharia finance and indeed and in favor of its increased use. Of course, this is likely to be a pragmatic decision in relation to financial needs, but it also perhaps suggests that the British government sees such products as ethical investments and therefore have no qualms about using such instruments.

The earliest use of sharia finance products in the United States can be traced to the work of LARIBA who, in 1987, began to offer sharia finance home financing products in Pasadena, California. A significant step came in 1997 when the United Bank of Kuwait, operating as a federal branch in the United States, applied for a license to sell ijara products (lease to purchase) for homes in a program they called al-Manzil. Over the next two years it expanded its operations over a further eleven states. What brought IF much more into the mainstream though was Freddie Mac's decision to buy Islamic mortgages from LARIBA in 2001. Fannie Mae followed in 2003. The investment of these banks into the sharia finance market enabled the large-scale financing of multiple IF products in the housing sector.[23]

Successive US administrations have sought to encourage the use of Islamic Finance (IF) by US banks and brokerages. Back in April 2002 the Treasury Department and Harvard University convened a seminar for business leaders, banks, and financial institutions to explain the principles and benefits (as they saw them) of sharia finance. The stimulus for the meeting had come from a presentation on the benefits of IF that had been made at the G-7 finance ministers' meeting that had been held in Ottawa earlier that month. In the Ottawa meeting, the governor of the Central Bank of Malaysia made a presentation on sharia finance in order for the finance ministers to understand sharia finance better. There is no record of the meeting, but the very fact that the Treasury-Harvard meeting happened so soon afterward suggests that the then-treasury secretary felt was something worth pursuing.

The subject appears to have gone quiet for about six years (while IF assets began to grow in the United States) until, in the midst of the "Downturn" in

November 2008, the US Treasury Department sponsored a seminar called "Islamic Finance 101" which again used state sponsorship to encourage the use of sharia finance.[24] The course actively promoted it through sponsorship of a teaching program run through Harvard University's Islamic Finance Project.

These encouragements appear to have borne fruit. According the materials available to the Global Islamic Finance Forum conference in Malaysia in September 2012 North America has fifteen financial institutions in the United States offering sharia-compliant banking products which include home financing, personal financing, mutual funds, business financing, and investment services.[25] In addition, there are also a number of corporations in the United States that have issued *sukuk* bonds including the International Finance Corporation, a member of the World Bank group and GE Capital, which is the finance arm of General Electric. Furthermore, the United States is now the fourth largest market in the world for sharia-compliant asset fund management with over $3.8 billion in assets under management across seven funds. Their growth has been fueled by the inauguration of the Dow Jones Islamic Market Index in 1999 and the introduction of Standard & Poor's Shariah Indices in 2006. It was further enhanced with Freddie Mac's use of sharia-compliant products in relation to mortgages from the early noughties.[26] The Islamic Society of North America has spotted the potential for further development of Islamic financing within the Muslim communities in the United States and outside them as well. To that end it hosted an Imam training even in Southern California in 2011 to train Imams in giving advice on sharia-compliant products. The event was sponsored by the Guidance Financial Group, a property and investment company that has investment portfolios in both the United States and Saudi Arabia.[27]

At present major companies such as AIG, Bank of America, Citicorp, Goldman Sachs, J.P. Morgan Chase, Merrill Lynch, Morgan Stanley Capital, and Wacho- via/Wells Fargo all engage in IF. Two dedicated IF companies, LARIBA and Guidance Financial Group, along with three banks Devon, University Bank, and HSBC Amanah, offer sharia finance only products. In 2005, University Bank announced that it had formed a new totally sharia-compliant subsidiary, University Islamic which would offer mortgages to Muslims only.[28] In the financial markets, The Dow Jones Islamic Market Index has been in operation since 1999, before the US government began to explicitly encourage the use of sharia finance products. Standard and Poor has also been operating a sharia finance index since 2006.

One recent example of the sharia finance deals being done in the United States has been the $219 million property deal completed in June 2016 for property developer Sharif el-Gamal in New York, two blocks away from the site of the World Trade Centre. The site had been purchased for $4.5 million in 2009 but had run into controversy because of the developer's desire to build a mosque and Islamic center at the site. However, the development of offices has been agreed with the developers securing sharia finance terms from Maybank (based in Malaysia) and Warba Bank (based in Kuwait), Intesa Sanpaolo (Italian), and MASIC, which is the investment wing of the al-Suveaei family of Saudi Arabia.[29]

So sharia finance has expanded at the encouragement of successive governments in the United States over twenty years, yet there are in-built regulations at state and national level which are nonspecific against IF, that have acted as a brake to faster IF growth in the United States. For example, a mosque in Tennessee lost its property tax exemption after it took out a sharia finance mortgage. As the bank and not the mosque itself now became the technical owner of the property the property tax exemption for a religious institution no longer applied, and the bank became liable for the property tax.

However, one of the primary causes of the low level of investment in sharia finance are the costs and relative lack of clarity in determining which financial products are permissible and which are not in Islam. Indeed, there is a fundamental dispute between different Muslim scholars concerning whether all interest, or only excessive interest, is considered wrong in the faith.[30]

The other major brake on investment into the sharia finance market is fears over Islamic terrorism financing. Back in 2005 a Senate enquiry was launched into the possible link between terror finance and sharia finance. The enquiry concluded that there was no evidence that it was more likely to financing terrorism than its mainstream counterpart yet there can be little doubt that there remains enough concern about the financing of terror from within sharia finance that US investors are nervous about getting involved in the market. And with good reason. For while the Senate hearings remained inconclusive, a paper for the *Global Security Studies Journal* by Steve Barber, published in 2011, was able to make a direct link between sharia finance and terror funding. Barber demonstrated that the key mechanism for terror funding (though not the only one) is the Mudaraba account which is obliged to be opened by any user of it. The Mudaraba account is the account from which zakat (charitable donation) is taken. Under some investments, the Mudaraba account's money is dispersed at the discretion of the investor themselves. However, in other Mudaraba accounts, the investment is under the control of the sharia committee which oversees the sharia compatibility of the sharia finance product within the financial institution. The scholars are therefore free to disperse the funds to whatever causes they desire and there is little or no transparency for either the investor or the authorities over where that money goes.[31]

Sharia finance has therefore seen expansion in the United States but also a growing wariness to become involved on the part of US financial institutions. Some of this wariness has been due to the relatively chaos and low rates of return that are seen in the sector, yet continuing worries about the financing of terror are also impacting investor enthusiasm. Some Muslim commentators have characterized this as evidence of Islamophobia; however, such labels ignore the real concerns associated with a financial system which is not accountable and is religiously unnecessary.

However, despite this cooling of interest in the commercial sector, the US government appears to have remained consistently enthusiastic about the investment potential associated with sharia finance. Indeed, this has remained the case despite the 2016 change of president to one who has been generally characterized as antagonistic toward Islam and Muslims.

Summary

Both the US and British governments appear to have taken a positive view of sharia finance as a source of income and have shown, despite changes in government and growing concerns about Islamic separatism among some Islamic diaspora communities, a continued desire to see its expansion. As such, their approach to sharia finance can be seen as a continuation of the dynamics set up through the development of the oil concessions over the previous century, in which any concerns over cultural impact (from either Muslim or Western perspectives) are overridden by the desire to create capital. For that reason, it could be argued that the US and British government approaches to sharia finance are an encapsulation of the shifting culture within both states where any sense of cultural protectionism as expressed in the nineteenth and twentieth centuries are eroded by the cosmopolitanism of the political elites in Washington DC and Westminster.

HALAL

On January 21, 2013, the *Huffington Post* reported that McDonald's had settled out of court a case in which their Dearborn branch had advertised burgers as halal, which in fact were not.[32] The case was interesting on several levels, but the key underlying interest from the perspective of this book was not that the chain had deliberately misled customers, but that it underlined the wider penetration of halal products into the North American food markets.

This penetration has been quietly taking place over quite some time.

Back in 2008 Niraj Warikoo of the *Detroit Free Press* had posted an article which attempted to show in microcosm how the US cultural landscape was shifting. In it, Warikoo highlighted the fact that the local KFC in Dearborn was advertising itself as selling halal meat as a choice.[33] A decade later there is evidence to suggest that what began as a local choice in high Muslim population areas such as the Chicago region has now entered the North American mainstream food market to the extent that halal meat is being widely sold without notification that it is such. Indeed, recent scandals in the UK have revealed that unlabeled halal products have been sold there as well.[34]

Part of the reason for this drive toward halal food in America lies in a desire to capture the ethical trade market, which is presently dominated by kosher foods, for there are only 5.3 million Jews in the United States, but kosher food is a $12.5 billion market. These figures show that many outside the Jewish communities in the United States are buying these products and Muslim businessmen are seeing an opportunity to position halal as a viable alternative in order to capitalize on it. One example is Adnan Durrani, the founder of Saffron Road who is now the CEO of American Halal. He wants consumers to understand halal as being

> wholesome and pure. Sustainable, fair trade, and just practices in terms of the environment and animal welfare.[35]

Neither the British nor US governments appear to have expressed concern, or even commented about the development of halal products. In both cases this is probably due to the fact that kosher slaughter has been practiced on both sides of the Atlantic for many years and sanctioned by in the UK since 1928, when it was given legal status in the Slaughter of Animals Act (1928) in Scotland and in the Slaughter of Animals Act (1933) in England and Wales. These domestic laws later adopted the Welfare of Animals (Slaughter or Killing Regulation) (1995) under Schedule 12 of EU regulation SI 731.[36]

A Food Standards Agency (UK) survey carried out in 2011 found that 194 establishments in the UK carried out the slaughter of 43,772 cattle of which 3 percent were killed by Jewish ritual and 4 percent were slaughtered by Muslim ritual. It is a signal of the growth of the industry and the consequential interest in the commercial possibilities which would be of natural interest to governments.[37]

The public statements coming from government or legislative sources in the UK about any issues relating to halal products have not engaged with any potential theological or sovereignty issues arising from the principle of allowing halal (or kosher) slaughter in a liberal democratic state but instead have focused on the lack of disclosure around the halal slaughter on the labeling of products. It was to that end that the Conservative MP for Shipley, Philip Davis, brought a private members Bill to Parliament in 2012.[38] The Bill was defeated, but it is interesting to note that Masood Khawaja, president of the Halal Food Authority, had agreed with the principle of labeling halal products.[39]

In the United States the Humane Slaughter Act, 1958 permitted ritual slaughter as one of two methods of animal slaughter.[40] Halal slaughter, like kosher, is therefore legal throughout the country; however, individual states have passed legislation in relation to labeling. For example, in Illinois regulations have been passed which specify that if a restaurant sells both halal and non-halal food, then each has to be clearly labeled. Furthermore, in Illinois, Maryland, Michigan, and Minnesota, it is illegal to label a product as halal, when it is not.[41] It seems therefore that the laws are consistently being created with a view to protecting those Muslims who wish to buy halal products, rather than seeking to ensure that all customers, whether Muslim or non-Muslim, are able to make a choice about the ethical origins of their purchase.

This issue, parallel to that of the labeling issues in the UK three years before, appears to be gaining public consciousness and concern in the United States. A report by National Public Radio in April 2018 drew national attention to the lack of labeling and suggested that the reasoning behind the move was a deliberate attempt to avoid potentially Islamophobic attitudes.[42] Given the parallel lack of labeling of halal products in the UK, it could very well be that the concerns in the UK mirrored those of US suppliers of halal. However, jumping to conclusions (or accusations) of Islamophobia could be precipitous and would require further research to be evidenced against, for example, a choice to avoid any form of animal ritual slaughter product, Jewish or Muslim.

For the purposes of this book, however, the question of labeling or non-labeling of food is interesting only in the context of government perspective and it is important therefore to observe that there has not been any government comment, positive or negative, about either halal products in general or the labeling issue. On both sides of the Atlantic this could be taken as a tacit approval of the growth of halal and the tax revenue the commercial growth will help to raise. However, in the United States it is likely also that the question of government interference in religious questions will have had a bearing on decisions relating to discussion of ethical, or religious, food.

CONCLUSION

As has been seen in all the sections on economic engagement, it is clear that the need for investment and the requirement to secure resources for their citizens have brought both the British and American governments to a place where the need for ongoing relations with Muslim states and diaspora peoples are a key component of their economic viability. For that reason, maintaining good relations with Muslim powers has remained a vital part not only of foreign policy, as we have seen, but also of economic policy. Both Britain and the United States have been exploring alternative energy sources over the past decade and even though the United States is finding alternative homegrown energy sources, there is still substantial investment by British and American companies in the oil fields of the Middle East which is unlikely to discontinue in the short to medium term.[43]

The exponential growth of sharia-compliant products and the much-needed investment they bring into economies which are running substantial structural deficits have added a new financial dimension to the ongoing trade and commercial relationships which exist between the Anglo-American powers and the Gulf region. Even with the growth of the BRIC economies and the new markets and revenue streams they offer, it is likely that continued financial relationships with Muslim powers and investors will continue for the decades to come.

But, in the context of the overarching theme of this book, and leaving aside from the commercial, economic, and resource needs being fulfilled in the relationships, it is clear that neither the British nor American administrations have any concerns about the growth of religiously related products and services within their states. For that reason, it would be reasonable to propose that the officials and leaders engaging with Islam in the sphere of economics have separated any feelings, positive or negative, toward the faith of Islam from the economic and commercial needs they are fulfilling. In that context, therefore, one could say that the officials' perceptions are a product of a culture in which public-private faith is the norm, and religious is separated from public (in this case commercial or economic) life. Moreover, it would be important to note that economic interactions have perhaps encapsulated the pragmatism which has characterized Muslim interactions with the US and British governments more perfectly than the other thematic areas this book explores. At the same time, although not related to the pragmatism of the policies, the sweep of time over which this economic discussion has passed also captures the shifting political culture of the political elites insofar as the economic engagement between Muslims and the Anglo-American sphere has helped bring Islam from its traditional heartlands to the United States and Britain and, in the process, has helped shape the emerging political norms of both.

NOTES

1. See Sonia Shah, *Crude: The Story of Oil*. New York, London: Seven Stories Press, 2011. Chapter 1.
2. Ibid.

3. Roger Adelson, *London and the Invention of the Middle East: Money, Power and War, 1902–1922*. New Haven (CT): Yale University Press, 1995, p. 7.

4. Efraim Karsh and Inari Karsh, *Empires of the Sand: The Struggle for Mastery of the Middle East (1789–1923)*. Cambridge (MA), London: Harvard University Press, 2001, p. 178.

5. Michael and Elanor Brock (eds), *Herbert Asquith Letters to Venetia Stanley*. Oxford and New York: OUP, 1982, p. 168.

6. Record of the negotiations over these years were published by Archibald Chisholm *The First Kuwait Oil Concession: A Record of Negotiation, 1911–1934*. London: Frank Cass, 1975.

7. Ibid., p. 89.

8. Ibid., p. 90.

9. For a contextual discussion of education in Islamic doctrine, see Sebastian Gunther, "Education," in Gerhard Bowering (Editor in Chief), *The Princeton Encyclopedia of Islamic Political Thought*. Princeton, Oxford: Princeton University Press, 2013, pp. 145–146.

10. Note by Sir A. Chamberlain, "Belligerent Rights at Sea and the Relations between the United States and Great Britain," October 26, 1927, C.P. 258(27), CAB 24/189; Foreign Office memorandum by G. Thompson, November 17, 1927, A6768/133/45, F.O. 371/12041; and file 36/45 of 1928, F.O. 371/12809 & 12810. See also minutes of the meeting May 1928 on A3195/A3438/36/45, F.O. 371/12810. For a general account of Anglo-American relations in this period, see B.J.C. McKercher, *The Second Baldwin Government and the United States, 1924–29*. Cambridge: CUP, 1984. For informal intervention, see correspondence in the State Department, Papers relating to the Foreign Relations of the United States. 1932, Volume II, pp. 3–6; and for formal representations, US Chargé, London to Secretary of State for Foreign Affairs, March 29, 1932, E1549/121/91, F.O. 371/16001.

11. In his 1955 article on the effect of Oil production on the Gulf states, Sir Rupert Hay does not specify what form this education took. Rupert Hay (1955) "The Impact of the Oil Industry on the Persian Gulf Shaykhdoms," *Middle East Journal* Vol. 9, pp. 361–392.

12. Elaine Housby, *Islamic Financial Services in the United Kingdom*. Edinburgh: Edinburgh University Press, 2011, pp. 23–45.

13. Nicola Woolock, "No Interest-but a Surefire, Best Selling Hit," *Daily Telegraph*, November 15, 2003.

14. Anon, "Islamic Finance in the UK," *Islamic Finance Home*, December 19, 2003. See also Valentino Cattelan, *Islamic Finance in Europe: Towards a Plural Financial System*. London: Edward Elgar Publishing, 2013.

15. "Speech by the Chief Secretary to the Treasury," Islamic Trade and Conference, HM Treasury. June 13, 2006.

16. Anon, "UK's Brown backs Islamic Finance," *BBC News*, June 13, 2006. See also Harris Irfan, *Heaven's Bankers: Inside the hidden world of Islamic Finance*. London: Hachette, 2014.

17. Anon, "Bank of London and the Middle East Launches as London based Islamic Bank," *AME Info*, July 9, 2008.

18. See Charlie Watson and Ian Cooper, "Five Whitehall Buildings Held by Wealthy Businessmen Now Operating Under Sharia Rules," *The Independent*, March 3, 2016.

19. Matthew Dathan, "Revealed: The Buildings Across Westminster Governed by Sharia Law—Including Admiralty House, Once Home to Members of the Royal Family and Sea Lords," *The Independent*, March 3, 2016.

20. Ibid.

21. Watson and Cooper, "Whitehall Buildings."

22. See Elaine Housby, *Islamic and Ethical Finance in the United Kingdom*. Edinburgh: Edinburgh University Press, 2013.

23. Victoria Lynn Zyp, *Islamic Finance in the United States: Product Development and Regulatory Adoption*. Master's Thesis, Georgetown University, 2009, p. 10.

24. The program is available at http://www.saneworks.us/uploads/news/applications/7.pdf.

25. Kabir Hassan and Michael Mahlknecht, *Islamic Capital Markets: Products and Strategies*. Oxford: Wiley, 2014.

26. As reported in Blake Gould (No Date), *Islamic Finance in North America 2009*. Yassar Media. https://umgroup.ca/2019/06/yasaar-media-islamic-finance-in-north-american-2009/.

27. The company's website is: http://www.guidancefinancial.com.

28. Kimberly Tracy (2006) "Islamic Finance: A Growing Industry in the United States," *North Carolina Banking Institute*, Iss. 355, pp. 29–31.

29. Anon, "Manhattan Tower Secures $219million in Shari'a Compliant Financing," *The Financial Times*, June 21, 2016.

30. Anon, "Islamic Finance's Global Surge Remains a Missed Opportunity for Banks in the US and Canada," www.theconversation.com, March 6, 2015.

31. Steve Barber (2011) "The "New Economy of Terror": The Financing of Islamist Terrorism," *Global Security Studies* Vol. 2, Iss. 1, pp. 38–51.

32. Jeff Karoub, "McDonalds to Pay $700,000 To Settle Allegations that the Franchise Falsely Claimed Food Complied with Halal," *The Huffington Post*, January 21, 2013.

33. Niraj Warikoo, "Halal Food at KFC," *Detroit Free Press*, March 30, 2008.

34. The reaction of non-Muslim British citizens to halal products is discussed in Rana Ayyub (2015) "Exploring Perceptions of Non-Muslims towards Halal Foods in the UK," *British Food Journal* Vol. 117, Iss. 9, pp. 2328–2343.

35. Adam Bluestein, "Bringing a Muslim Culinary Tradition Mainstream," www.inc.com May 3, 2012.

36. See Christopher Barclay, *Religious Slaughter* House of Commons Library SN/SC/1314 June 11, 2011, p. 2.

37. Ibid., pp. 2–3. The report also contains figures for the slaughter of sheep and poultry not cited here.

38. See House of Commons Debate, April 24, 2012, *Hansard*, pp. 823–825.

39. Barclay, *Ritual Slaughter*, p. 6.

40. 7 USC 1901–1907. *Humane Slaughter Act*. Text can be found at https://www.animallaw.info/statute/us-food-animal-humane-methods-livestock-slaughter.

41. See https://halaltransactions.wordpress.com/2014/12/29/halal-laws-in-the-usa/.

42. Esther Hoing, "You Might be Eating Halal Meant and Not Even Know It," *National Public Radio*, April 5, 2018.

43. See George Abed, "Middle Eastern Oil Producers Still Have Strong Hand," *The Financial Times*, April 5, 2017.

Chapter 5

Public Activism
Cartoons and Mosque-Building

Central to the discussion are government attempts to come to grips with the international Muslim consciousness which was a cause of concern right through the imperial period and into the present day for differing, though related, reasons. In order to do that we will explore reaction, both historically and currently, to the publication of materials deemed insulting, even blasphemous to Muslims by way of helping us to understand the manifestations of Muslim activism. We will examine both Muslim activism and the reaction of the government to it as a window into understanding US-British government reactions to Muslim concerns and what they say about US-British governmental perceptions of Islam and Muslims.

On September 30, 2005, a series of cartoons were published in the Danish newspaper *Jyllands-Posten*.[1] The cartoons' publication came two months after bombs had ripped through London in what was, up to then, the most devastating terrorist attack on a European capital city. Even though there had been a bombing in Madrid in 2002, the London bombs seemed to galvanize public opinion in the UK and in the rest of Europe in a way that the attacks in New York and Madrid had not. This was perhaps due to the fact that the terrorists responsible were homegrown radicals. From a policy perspective, it prompted the then-Labor government in the UK to bring into force CONTEST (counterterrorism strategy), which included among its proposals the development of the Prevent strategy. Prevent's (Preventing Violent Extremism) task was to stop Muslims who were deemed susceptible of sliding into radicalization from heading down that route.

But at a public level the response to the bombings was one of anger and questioning of the loyalties of Muslim citizens. Numerous polls (usually with very small samples) were published in a series of papers which painted

Muslim communities as heavily radicalized.[2] Others began to question more openly the contention by many Muslims that terrorist acts such as 9/11 and 7/7 had nothing to do with Islam as a religion.[3] It was in that context that the *Jellands-Posten* cartoon was published. At first its publication went largely unnoticed and it was not until January 2006, when the Norwegian newspaper *Magazinet* republished the cartoons that rumblings of protest began and spread across the Middle East. The first violent response occurred on January 30, when gunmen attacked the EU offices in Gaza and demanded an apology from the officials on behalf of the cartoon's publishers. The Danish newspaper apologized the following day and yet, on the day after that, newspapers across Europe (baring the UK) reprinted the cartoon again. Protest and violence increased as the Norwegian and Danish embassies across the Middle East were attacked in response to the cartoons. In response to which the French magazine *Charlie Hebdo* reprinted the cartoons in an edition which had as its front cover a picture of Muhammad saying, "It's hard to be loved by imbeciles."[4] The cycle of violent protest and reprinting of the cartoon continued for some time. It reached a high-profile peak in January 2015 when the offices of *Charlie Hebdo* were attacked by jihadis Said and Cherif Kouachi who both claimed to be from al-Qa'ida in Yemen.[5] Yet, since that attack, the drawing of provocative cartoons and the violent responses to them have continued. Notably in Texas, where two gunmen were killed while trying to enter a building to attack a competition going on to draw cartoons of Muhammad.[6]

In many ways, therefore, the publication of the cartoons and the debate that has taken place around them (along with the violence) have become axiomatic of the difficulties that both Muslims and non-Muslims have had in adjusting to the perceptions and expectations of the other. Managing those tensions has been one of the key issues for Western governments whose ultimate goal is social cohesion. Understanding the concerns of Muslims, while not being seen to be limiting free expression has become an important element of the US-British government work in this field. This chapter will therefore explore not only historical examples of the same issue to understand what the issues were but also what the US and British officials came to understand about Islam through their engagement with these issues.

CARTOONS

Looking back, Muslim anger created by cartoons is not at all a new problem. File L/PJ/6/1911 deals with correspondence relating to the publication of a cartoon which was seen to be insulting Mohammed in 1925. A. R. Dard, Imam of the Ahmadiyya mosque, wrote to the secretary for home affairs on

August 26, 1925, to express his outrage at a cartoon published on August 18, 1925, in *The Star* newspaper.[7] The reason for the Imam's outrage was a cartoon in which the famous cricketer Jack Hobbs was pictured as a huge figure towering over a number of historical figures including the Roman emperor Julius Caesar and French emperor Napoleon. One of the historical figures included was Muhammad.

What made Imam Dard angry was firstly the representation of Muhammad at all but also the fact that Muhammad, along with the other historical figures, was dwarfed by the size of Jack Hobbes. The cartoon was therefore deemed religiously insulting from the point of view of representing the image of Muhammad and belittling that any other human being should be represented in the same space and frame as that of Muhammad.

The question of the representation of Muhammad in any pictorial form is a sensitive one. For, while the Qur'an does not prohibit the depiction of Muhammad, there are a number of Hadith that do.[8] The paper's reaction was swift: they printed an apology on September 25, 1925. The reason was not very difficult to find for Muslims in India (a very significant market for the paper at that time) were making strong calls for the paper to be boycotted.

Interestingly, the British government was clearly aware of the religious sensitivities that the cartoon raised for correspondence shows that officials felt that the paper ought to have known better than to have allowed the cartoon's publication.[9]

This is an interesting response from several perspectives. First, because rather than seeking to defend free speech (as much of the debate around the Danish Cartoon mentioned earlier focused upon), the secretary of state for India Frederick Edwin Smith, first earl of Birkenhead, remarked that newspapers should be more aware of this kind of sentiment but, since the paper had already apologized, there was no need to take it further.[10] Smith clearly therefore had no interest in seeking to defend the rights of the newspaper to include any public figure they wished in their cartoon and instead expected that the paper would be aware enough to self-censor. Second, there was enough awareness of Muslim views on depictions of Muhammad that the secretary of state was able to opine on the matter in a manner which suggested that not only were Muslim attitudes to Muhammad depictions common knowledge in government circles but that they were more widely understood as well.

The secretary of state believed that the matter had quickly been resolved and in many ways it had. However, in a move reminiscent of the recent Muhammad cartoon controversy (although there is no clear evidence to suggest that this was deliberate in the same way the recent cartoon incident was) the *Weekly Dispatch* published a cartoon in which Muhammad was depicted as a coal seller with the caption:

If the mountain doesn't go to Mahommed [*sic*], Mahommed will have to come to the mountain.[11]

If the *Weekly Dispatch* did know about *The Star* cartoon controversy, then the publication could have been seen as an act of free speech defiance but that is unlikely. What was more likely is that they simply did not think through the implications of the depiction of the cartoon.

Following the *Weekly Dispatch* cartoon publication one letter of protest was received by the British government. That of Khalistan Sheldrake who was the editor at the office of *The Minaret*. Sheldrake was careful to point out that he was not a lone protester but that other protests about the cartoon had been made in France as well.

The panic was immediate and Sir Arthur Hirtzel suggested that the editors of the weekly dispatch should be alerted to print an apology.

Hirtzel's response is instructive because there is no sense from his note that he sought to reason with the *The Minaret* in relation to suggesting that this was a one-off mistake by the paper and that it would not happen again.[12] Or that, in a free society, the newspaper should be allowed to print what it wished. Instead, Hirtzel's focus related entirely to pacifying injured Muslim opinion and encouraging the paper to immediately apologize for the offense caused. His panicked response tells a different story to that offered in Johan Mathew's article on Pan-Islam in which Mathew quotes Hirtzel's 1919 memorandum in which he characterizes the pan-Islamic movement as something which will only become dangerous if it is given the oxygen of attention.[13] Six years later, he had obviously realized that there was danger in it and Hirtzel's response was likely guided by concerns over keeping the peace as there had been riots between Muslims and Parsees in Bombay in 1851 over the publication of a depiction (not satirical) of Muhammad in the newspaper *Chtra Dynan Darpan* and in 1874 over the discussion of the life of Muhammad in the book *Famous Prophets and Communities* by Rustomji Jalbhoy.[14] Furthermore, in 1891, 1896, and 1897, Calcutta (Kolkotta) had also been subject to Hindu-Muslim riots.[15]

It was in that context that Moulvi Mohamed Hirodin wrote to Lord Hamilton, then-secretary of state for India on February 17, 1896, concerning the possible benefits of engaging with the Anjuman i-Islam which had offices in both India and London.[16] Moulvi Hirodin suggested that seeking some official representation of Muslim interests both in India and in the UK might be a way to pacify Muslim concerns over both their own personal safety in a Hindu majority country but also seeking ways in which the concerns of Muslims in relation to "insults to their faith" might be heard. The Moulvi forwarded to Lord Hamilton the Anjuman i-Islam London's rules and regulations which Lord Hamilton had clearly expressed a desire to see.

A Mr. Khan, who was the home secretary for the Anjuman i-Islam, then sent a compliment's slip to Lord Hamilton offering a meeting. On the compliment's slip Khan briefly highlighted that the Anjuman i-Islam had been established in 1886. Its purpose was to promote commonality among Muslims living in the UK, and to act as hosts to Muslims visiting the UK. It had a political interest and one of its functions was to watch the press and to, when appropriate, enlighten the British public. In essence, therefore, it was like a forerunner of organizations such as the Muslim Council of Britain in the UK and the Council on American-Islamic Relations in the United States.[17] Lord Hamilton's particular interest clearly focused upon whether this group represented any one sect or denomination. His concern was that, if they did, then the Anjuman i-Islam should not be seen by him as it could be seen as negotiating with selected persons to the exclusion of others.

Yet, something needed to be done to prevent further outbreaks of violence between Muslims and other groups. In 1898 more riots occurred following the publication of a pamphlet in which a convert from Hinduism to Christianity had accused Muhammad of lechery and outright lies when dealing with God.[18] As a result Muslims in India and London petitioned Queen Victoria and the government in order to have the pamphlet removed from circulation.[19] The Viceroy's office declined to take action on the matter because it was not something for the executive government to engage with the matter; if libel was proved, the advice was that the matter should be taken up by the courts.

In each of the cases outlined in the chapter, therefore, the perception of Islam and the response to the issue by the British government were virtually identical: that officials were aware of Muslim sensitivities around both criticisms and the publication of images of Muhammad. This knowledge rather than seeking to encourage Muslim citizens of the period to allow freedom of expression resulted in a desire to placate Muslim views. There is no record of government officials in the UK questioning the validity of Muslim sensitivities in this area, instead, they appeared to take a pragmatic approach to freedom of expression which placed a far higher importance on social cohesion than any other concern. As such the British attitude very much reflected the rubric of "religious freedom" which was laid out in the 1858 Proclamation by Queen Victoria in which religious freedom was defined in terms of preventing unrest and promoting social cohesion. In that context, for example, Christian mission to both Hindus and Muslims was discouraged due to the potential for causing social upheaval that evangelism and conversion would bring. This will be discussed further in chapter 6.

For the United States, the publication of insulting cartoons has been a far more recent issue. The shootings in Texas have already been mentioned and there was little comment on the cartoons published in *Charlie Hebdo* and the shootings which followed from President Obama's administration other than the president's questioning of *Charlie Hebdo*'s judgment.[20] Other than that, the government seemed keen to steer clear of any engagement with the issue at all. There was no defense of free speech and it was noticeable that the US government did not send representatives to the memorial held in France following the *Charlie Hebdo* attacks.

In the light of that response, it seems reasonable to suggest that when US administrations have been faced with this problem of insulting cartoons being published, they appear to have followed the British framework for responding to the crisis. Whether their response, or lack of it, was a direct result of researching British precedent is not known, but there can be no doubt that the two responses were very similar.

MOSQUE-BUILDING AND MESSAGING

Chapter 3 highlighted the awareness of both US and British officials to the need for direct and coordinated messaging to Muslim majority states and diaspora peoples. This section will analyze their messaging for its underlying narratives but also for what it revealed about what officials thought would appeal to Muslims. In so doing it will analyze what implicit understandings of Muslims were at work within the administrations.

IOR L/PS/11/85 P4715, F7 is a record of the discussions on December 30–31, 1914, at the French ministry for foreign affairs between M. Déclassé (French foreign minister), Mssr Gout (his secretary), and Sir Henry McMahon concerning joint concerns about Turkey's entry into the war and possible effects on imperial Muslim populations.

The minutes of the meeting specify that the French were able to report that both Algerian and Moroccan troops were fighting loyally on the Allied side but that there had been some issues with the Tunisians who had some sense of sympathy with the movements among the Young Turks. McMahon was similarly able to report that Indian and Arab troops also had been loyal, helped by the positive statements on Britain's behalf made by the Aga Khan and other Muslim notables. In this climate of positive feeling of Muslims toward the Allies, the British were keen to ensure that there would be no hint of any interference in Muslim internal affairs, such as the question of the Caliphate, if that positive state of affairs was to continue. Déclassé agreed.[21] They then discussed pushing the publication of various positive publications by Muslims for the wider audience, which the French also concurred with.

This concern for, and discussion around, the possibility of Muslim revolt on behalf of the Caliph against Franco-British rule signaled that both were aware of the importance of the potency of the pan-Islamic ideology which had been spread around imperially controlled North Africa, the Levant, and South Asia.[22]

One signal of this was that there appeared to be an awareness of the significance of the Khutbas in the meeting, for McMahon asked Déclassé if the Sultan's name was being mentioned in the Khutbas in Algeria, Tunisia, and Morocco. Déclassé thought they were but in his capacity as Caliph, not as Sultan. This question and its reply were significant because the mentioning of the Caliph's name in the Friday Prayers in the Mosque were a signal of the sense of loyalty that Muslims felt toward those who were in authority over them.[23] This was understood by the British and French leadership and investigations into the number of mosques saying the name of the Caliph in their *Khutbah* became an indicator of where the sympathies of Muslims within the Empire lay.[24]

After the First World War, a letter from Sir Horace Rumpole (high commissioner in Constantinople) to Lord Curzon in London raised similar concerns in the post-conflict world.[25] Rumpole attached an appeal for a Muslim congress that had been circulating and which had encapsulated these concerns. The appeal had been published in *Hakimiet-i-Millie* (Turkish journal) and the high commissioner was clearly concerned about the effects of the appeal. For it was arguing that the "Christian" countries of Europe were enemies of Islam and that Muslims need to be unified against it. Rumpole observed that the appeal was part of the Kemalist regime's desire to keep the Muslim world onside following Kemal's insurrection against from the Caliph. Nevertheless, Rumpole was convinced that the charge held weight with a good many people and that its reception showed the underlying resentment against non-Muslim rule that existed in the Muslim majority parts of the British Empire.[26]

An article in the French newspaper *Temps* on September 12, 1914, lent credence to the Muslim concerns about anti-Muslim bias when it suggested that the War against the Turks was a Crusade.[27] Unsurprisingly both governments sought at once to counter the concept of anti-Muslim bias by showing that they were both countries in which Muslims were able to live freely and to worship freely as well and it was in this connection that the building of a mosque in both London and Paris was discussed for its propaganda value.

Yet it was not until well after the end of the First World War that activity in connection to mosque-building began in earnest. In IOR/L/PS/276, there is a letter from Ameer Ali, dated March 14, 1927, on behalf of the London Mosque Fund to Sir Arthur Hirtzel asking permission to write to prominent Muslim rulers such as the Amir of Afghanistan, to secure the necessary funds for the mosque. Ali stated that the mosque was to serve the many Muslims who have come to London, but despite this, they had been unable to raise the funds from among Muslims themselves and so sought to enlist the help of the British government.[28] The trustees of the mosque fund were listed as Lord

Ampthill, Lord Lamington (a lifelong orientalist and friend of Lord Curzon), Sir Mohammed Rafique, and Ameer Ali himself: a list which showed that the push for a British Mosque was not simply coming from Muslims but also from British establishment figures.

The letter revealed that the London mosque project had been a developing concern since before the First World War. According to the letter, the project began in 1910 when letters were sent to promenade persons such as the Nizam of Hyderabad, Ahmed Shah, ex-Shah of Persia, and the former Sultan-Caliph of Turkey (then in exile in Cyprus), but none of these had produced the funds required for the project. Coming to the British government was a natural next step for Ali, especially as he must have sensed that the British government was keen on ensuring good relations with the Islamic world for he concluded his letter with a plea that played to the propaganda value of Crown assistance with mosque-building:

We know your majesty has, at heart, the promotion of Islamic culture.[29]

It was a plea which ignored until 1940 when, during a cabinet meeting at the height of the Blitz, Prime Minister Winston Churchill and his colleagues authorized £100,000 for the express purpose of buying land in London to build a mosque.[30]

Clearly much had been happening from the late 1920s onward in what became the Stock Market Crash of 1929, and the subsequent rise of Nazism. Indeed, the Quit India Movement which had also developed through the 1930s had also been an important field of policy discussion through the period and, it may have been that the British government did not feel in a position to grant funds for a mosque in a situation where it was needing to be seen as impartial between Muslims and Hindus through the Round Table Discussions and the gathering pace of the calls for Pakistan. Yet, these "distractions" in relation to the granting of the mosque funding request could not have fallen on ears that had been more ably primed to receive it for, as Bimla Prasad argues, Syed Ahmed Khan's policy of friendly engagement with the British authorities laid the groundwork for British acceptance of Muslim views and opinions.[31] It was a policy that continued through the university (Aligarh) that Khan founded, long after his death.

Khan had been a staunch supporter of British rule in India, much to the chagrin of other Muslim leaders such as Muhammad Ali. Yet, Khan was not a man who accepted British rule as an ongoing inevitability: he was a Muslim who strongly desired to Islam resurgent once again and saw that the best way of achieving that was by courting the British rulers, rather than working against them.[32] Furthermore, he was theologically grounded in the Qur'an and Hadith whose message, Khan believed, required loyalty to non-Muslim rulers. This did not mean that Khan did not desire to advance Muslim presence and power, but he was content to do so within the context of a long-term strategy of friendship diplomacy rather than uncompromising demand.[33]

Whether, as Prasad argues, this work was decisive in orientating the British toward Muslim agendas over Hindu ones in the run toward Independence, during which the decision-making about the mosque some forty years after Khan's death was made, is a case which is hard to make. But it would not be unreasonable to propose that Khan's diplomacy laid the groundwork for Muslim agendas to be considered. Certainly, Mohammed Mujeeb, principal of Aligarh, was in no doubt of Khan's importance in creating the conditions for Muslim agendas to be advanced.[34] His analysis does not engage with wider political considerations of the time: particularly the British desire to use Muslim grievances and concerns to help weaken the bargaining position of the Hindu-dominated Congress Party.[35]

But whether Sayyid Ahmed Khan and the Aligarh University were decisively important in the case of the mosque in London itself or not, Khan's work with the British establishment had borne fruit as the peers willing to attach themselves to the committee for the London Mosque testified.

By mid-1942 it seems that there were sufficient funds available for the mosque to go ahead.[36] A number of British diplomats to the Middle East were asked for their opinion on the matter. Out of the eight asked, five were in favor, two expressed misgivings, and one expressed doubt (Sir Miles Lampton) on the basis that he felt that the whole scheme was the pet of the Egyptian Ambassador and that, in giving this money, it left open the possibility that the mosque would fall into undesirable hands and/or the hands of other sects.[37] Sir John Maffey expressed the opinion that the propaganda value would be limited and that the mosque might "involve them [the government] in some future responsibilities or embarrassments"[38] But all agreed that overall, it was felt the propaganda value was such that the proposal should go forward, especially in the light of the fact that London had a bigger Muslim population than Paris, Rome, and Berlin, all of which had mosques.

This awareness of the importance of propaganda in relation to British-Muslim relations was seen once again in file IOR L/I /1/877 entitled "Muslim Influence in World Affairs." A request from the India Office for a program about Muslim opinion on the war (the Second World War) to be broadcasted by the BBC. The India Office had approached Sir Hassan Suhrawardy for a script, but his offering was rejected on the grounds of having too many Qur'anic quotes and it was too long. Also, there was a feeling that it might lead to other religions wanting the same opportunity. So on March 20, 1941, a Mr. Coatman at the BBC was asked to produce a new draft, which was subsequently broadcast.[39] It is useful to see what messages the British government were seeking to convey to the British public about the importance of Muslims as a group.

The script itself was three pages long and it begins with an overview of why Muslim opinion concerning the war was important. It cited the numbers of Muslims in different regions, especially the sensitive Middle East as well as the importance of the oil in Muslim countries such as Iraq and Iran. The script stated that the most important reason for Muslim relations was that over half were in the British Empire as well as that the British had "renewal of the ancient friendship with Turkey."[40] The film sought to convey the message that both Germany and Italy had behaved very badly toward their Muslim subjects in Africa and went on to show how Nazi ideals were opposed to the ideas of Islam. It moved on to characterize Islam as having a similar outlook to that of Puritanism, or Old Testament conduct, further citing the importance of Jesus in Islam and that therefore the "Christian" powers of Europe (Britain and France) were therefore not very different to those of Muslim countries.

The film does contain a number of minor errors, for example, Muslims include themselves among the citation of Christians and Jews as "Ahl al Kitab."[41]

The final part of the script gave a personal illustration of the common Greek heritage by relating an incident between two Muslim soldiers on the Northwest Frontier who were arguing and one said to the other, "who do you think you, are, Plato?"[42] The illustration was clearly there to show that Greek culture was so endemic to Muslim culture that it was part of common parlance.

It is clear therefore that in the period of the wars, through the building of mosques and the development of propaganda materials such as that which we have discussed, that the British government has not just sought to keep Muslims onside for various pragmatic reasons but had sought to encourage the British public also to think of Muslims as citizens with common principles and outlooks who could and should be free to be Muslims within the context of the British Empire (then Commonwealth). This dynamic continued after the war period and was most clearly seen in the development of the exhibition of Islamic culture which was planned for 1976.[43] Although Klas Grinel argues that

> the Festival's framing of the Muslim world did not really include contemporary British Muslims, and further that Islam was framed as a fundamental other to modernity, which implicitly excluded Muslims from a modern British identity.[44]

Grinel's contention is that the exhibition deliberately framed Islam as an "other," something alien to British culture. The argument is convincing, yet it is possible that, given that the correspondence reveals that there was a marked lack of interest from Muslim states to be involved with the exhibition (the Saudis had promised both money and items for the exhibition but neither materialized in the end and that it was only the UAE which provided funds), perhaps an alternative explanation for this characterization of the Islamic world was really due to the principally British organizing committee who, with the best will in the world, did not understand the narrative about Islam that the exhibition would frame.

It would be fair to say, therefore, in the context of this book's overarching theme, that British governments showed themselves very willing to encourage positive images of Islam and promote Muslim interests in relation to providing money for a place of worship. Of course, there were strategic interests prompting these actions and there is no suggestion in the correspondence of a culture of Islamophelia in Whitehall, but there was a recognition that Britain needed Muslims and Islamic states to be onside. In this sense, it was a pragmatic engagement which certainly showed none of the negativity about Islam expressed by Churchill and others as was detailed back in chapter 2. It therefore appears that British policies, at the very least, divorced any private concerns about Islam as a faith, from policy considerations, including Churchill himself.

Turning to the United States, it is noteworthy that there were some parallel in the tactics they used to encourage Muslim support but also significant differences with the British approach. For, although we see in Washington DC the building of a National Mosque, as there had been in the UK, there appears to have been a far wider effort to engage the US population at a more grassroots level in building bridges between the United States and Muslim-majority countries and their peoples.

It does not appear to have been until the early 1950s, with the advent of the Cold War, US support of the newly created state of Israel and the United States' engagement in oil exploration in the Middle East that significant account began to be taken of Muslim opinion of America. For example, the first Islamic center in Washington DC was built in the mid-1950s and inaugurated by President Eisenhower in 1957.[45] But back in 1952 there was the first documentary evidence that Muslim opinion was becoming more important to US policymakers in a Department of State memorandum reporting the meeting of the Working Group on Special Materials for Arab and other Moslem [sic] Countries on March 25, 1952.[46] The meeting was focused on the creation of propaganda materials which could be distributed in Arab-speaking countries and arose from an earlier meeting which had discussed the "causes, nature and extent of Arab mistrust of the United States."[47]

Huntingdon Damon (chairman) began the meeting by highlighting the need for effective propaganda tools to be developed in relation to the US presence in the Middle East. Damon had two main concerns: that "Arabs did not understand the true nature of the communist threat" and that US interests were being "miss-represented" as imperialist.[48] In reply Harold Glidden, one of the State Department's Arabists, argued that the program developed should

> fit the point of view of the Arabs and that it suited their outlook and susceptibility and not what we project upon them.[49]

Gliddens characterized Arabs as those who think of themselves in group, rather than individual terms, and as such the US propaganda needed to play to that, rather than stressing individuality. This point, while interesting, does not seem to have been followed up in the meeting and instead the chairman turned attention to one of the other suggestions that had been made: about doing an exhibition of US educational books in the Arab world as a means of showing Arabs what was being taught to American children about Arabs and their culture. Two of the books they discussed were *Allah, The God of Islam* which had been published in 1950 for the specific purpose of teaching ten-year-olds in the United States about what Arabs believe and *Strange Lands, Friendly People* by Justice Douglas, which had five pages of "sympathetic analysis" of Islam in it.[50] Glidden is very definite that they should stay away from religion all together, but Damon instead saw the propaganda value to be had in citing the mosques in the United States.

> Here is the "Washington Mosque." There are almost unlimited public relations you could build around the construction of the mosque.[51]

Clearly Damon was seeking to show that America was religiously free, and that Muslims already in the United States were able to live as Muslims in that land. This both sought to counter the narrative of the United States as an imperialist Christian country and highlighted the lack of religious freedom for any faith in the USSR. Javier Guerrero notes in his article on the Carter administration's attempts at countering Soviet messaging in Muslim states, that the theme of 'freedom' continued to be a vital seem of propaganda throughout the Cold War period.[52]

Following on in that vein, another State Department official suggested that use could be made of a Muslim scriptwriter who worked at the State Department called Dr. Zaki Abu Shadi, whose work focused on "trying to relate cultural goods in the US with those of Islam."[53] The idea was that Shadi would be commissioned to write a series of scripts which would fuse the one hundred greatest classics of the American and Muslim worlds. Gladden specifically cited Lincoln's Gettysburg Address, with its accent on United Nations, freedom, and ending slavery as something that Arabs "would swallow that hook, line and sinker."[54] Other suggestions included an essay competition in the United States entitled "The Impact of Islam on Christianity," with the winning essay to be published in Arabic in the region.

However, a significant portion of the meeting was given over to discussing several suggestions by a Turkish-American called Mr. Begg, whose department is not named but appears to have been focused on working on Arab-American relations through private enterprise, rather than formal government links. Begg makes a number of suggestions for developing ties between US and Arab links which include some of the events which would be familiar in modern cultural exchange, such as encouraging sporting tours and town twinning. One of the twinnings that took place was between Baton Rouge and Cairo.[55] According to Begg,

> They [people of Baton Rouge] got excited about it. They put on public exhibition of Egyptian art ... they started special classes at the university there about the Arabic world and particularly about Egypt. ... They have gotten in touch with students in Cairo and they wanted to have American baseball equipment and basketball because we sent someone over there to train them in American games, so the students in Baton Rouge are collecting such equipment to send to Cairo.[56]

It is not known how far this association went, but Begg continued with the outlining of a plan to bring the Salim Bey, the Egyptian minister of information to Baton Rouge to speak about his country. Baton Rouge is a substantial city, and one that might have the resources to look further afield for affiliations, yet it was not just cities that were encouraged to connect with the Middle East. Further on in his discussion, Begg highlights the work of Senator Gillette, who had been working to try and get some smaller towns in Iowa interested in affiliations with the Middle East.[57]

In their book *Searching for Cultural Diplomacy* Jessica Gienow-Hecht and Mark Donfred discuss the very limited impact that such efforts made in the long term and also highlight the tensions that existed between the US government and the private firms (such as TWA and Ford) who were rather dismissive of the obvious propaganda the US government was trying to push. Private enterprise was particularly scathing about the Voice of America broadcasts and print chapter which were sent throughout the Middle East.[58] Their particular concern was the fact that they believed that the US government's broadcasts and chapters would be quickly seen as the propaganda pieces they were and would quickly be dismissed by the populous at large.

So the fears of TWA and Ford were well founded, yet to dismiss the entire work as an expensive propaganda exercise misses the point in the context of this book that there was an openness to discovering Muslim culture that sat at odds with the increasing civil rights agitations which were also growing over the same period. After all, the same city, Baton Rouge, whose citizens came in large numbers to hear a talk on Egyptian culture, including Islam at the Town Hall, was the same city in which there was segregation between black and white. Of course there is the sense that Islam was (at that time) a remote and fascinating "Eastern," or "Oriental" culture and represented no immediate threat culturally in the way that African-American culture might be seen.[59]

The initiative also included the financing of private Middle Eastern citizens to come in groups to speak at town hall meetings in the United States. One such visit had already taken place when this strategic meeting happened. Begg reported that it had been a great success with large numbers of people in Milwaukee coming to hear citizens from Iran talking about their lives.[60]

As can be seen, the "Working Group on Special Materials for Arab and other Moslem [sic] Countries" meeting included multiple differing ideas and strategies to promote the idea of America as "Islam and Arab friendly." This was juxtaposed with the Soviets who were characterized as being against all religion even though, as we have already seen, one of the first acts of the Bolshevik revolutionary government was to make an appeal of brotherhood to Muslim Leagues throughout the European colonial territories. But the core fact was that the United States understood the importance of having Muslims onside not only in relation to their foreign policy aims but also in relation to encouraging the loyalty of their Muslim diaspora citizens in the United States.

CONCLUSION

A desire to appear Muslim-friendly pushed both the United States and United Kingdom to do more and more to provide evidence of their goodwill. As has been seen already, there were very specific economic and geopolitical motivations underlying this enthusiasm and it should not be read as being anything other than a diplomatic necessity, and not as a general goodwill toward that faith. But it is important to note the extent to which both the United Kingdom and United States were prepared to go in order to ensure that Muslims were made aware of the goodwill of both states toward Muslims and Islam as a whole. The funding of mosques was unique in relation to state sponsorship of places of worship and as such is one of the strongest indicators of the lengths the Anglo-American governments went to secure Muslim loyalty and goodwill toward them.

In relation to the overall understanding of Islam which is seen in these incidents, however, it is clear that both British and US officials were aware of the fact that there was a deep suspicion, even resentment, by Muslims toward both countries. It is that knowledge which lay behind the propaganda work which both engaged in and yet, other than specific worries about Crusading imagery, there is no sense in the files that there was an understanding of what prompted those resentments. Or at least, there was an assumption that the issues were short term, such as in relation to the Turkish propaganda in the First World War, rather than longer-term worries about the very presence of British domination (or later American) of areas which had been dominated by Muslim rulers. Nor even were there apparent understandings of the source of religious upset that arose from the portrayal of Muhammad in picture (no matter what the picture), even though both governments had been given such ample evidence of the feelings stirred up in this area.

For both British and US governments, therefore, the issues that officials were dealing with were understood in short-termist frameworks, rather than within the context of longer-term and theological issues which the cartoons prompted. Furthermore, the naive belief that the building of a mosque, or a cultural exchange, would make Muslims believe that either the British or Americans were friends of Islam shows how shallow the understanding of the roots of the resentments and suspicions Muslims had of them was. And, while short-termist perceptions are not necessarily, by definition, a problem, they can be when dealing with highly complex issues such as these. For in these cases it created unrealistic expectations of the effort needed to ensure the loyalty and cooperation of Muslim communities.

NOTES

1. This is discussed in more detail in Jytte Klausen, *The Cartoons that Shook the World*. New Haven, London: Yale University Press, 2009.

2. See for example Gramme Wilson, "Young British Muslims Getting More Radical," *The Daily Telegraph*, January 28, 2007.

3. Melanie Philips, "It's Pure Myth that Islam is a Religion of Peace," *The Times*, June 29, 2015.

4. There is an insightful discussion of these issues in Elizabeth Eide and Risto Kunelius, *Transnational Media Events: The Mohammad Cartoons and the Imagined Clash of Civilizations*. New York: Coronet, 2008.

5. Andrew Higgins and Maia De La Baume, "Two Brothers Suspected in Killings Were Known to French Intelligence Services," *The New York Times*, January 8, 2015.

6. Kevin Conlon and Kristine Sgueglia, "Two Shot Dead after They Open Fire at Mohammed Cartoon Event in Texas," www.cnn.com May 4, 2015.

7. L/PJ/6/1911. F1, August 26, 1925.

8. See al-Bukhari, *Sahih* Book 7, Hadiths 834, 840, 844 and 846 in Bukhari, Muhammad and Muhammad Khan, *The English Translation of Sahih Al-Bukhari with the Arabic Text*. Baltimore (MD): Al- Saadawi Publications, 1996.

9. L/PJ/6/1911, F5, October 8, 1925.

10. Ibid.

11. L/PJ/6/1911, F7, December 5, 1925.

12. L/PJ/6/1911, F21-28.

13. Johan Mathew (2017) "Spectres of Pan-Islam: Methodological Nationalism and British Imperial Policy after the First World War," *The Journal of Imperial and Commonwealth History* Vol. 45, Iss. 6, pp. 942–968. Mathew's argument fails to take into account the long-term concerns about the potential for disrupting the *Pax Britannia* that was imprinted on British government consciousness that has been described both in this book and in previous publications such as *The Caliphate Question: British Government and Islamic Governance*. Lanham (MD): Rowman and Littlefield, 2009, and *Muslim Minorities and Citizenship: Authority, Communities and Islamic Law*. London: I.B. Tauris, 2012.

14. See Mark Doyle, *Communal Violence in the British Empire: Disturbing the Pax*. London: Bloomsbury, 2017, pp. 108–110.

15. Ibid.

16. L/PJ/6547, F2, February 18, 1896.

17. L/PJ/6547, F3, p. 7.

18. Correspondence concerning a libeling of Muhammad by Muslims in both London and India in 1898. Meena Menon highlights that communal riots were a regular occurrence over the period 1890–1945 and took place for a wide variety of reasons. As such, the British were well aware of high ongoing inter-communal tensions and the risks they posed. See Meena Menon (2010) "Chronicle of Communal Riots in Bombay Presidency (1893—1945)," *Economic and Political Weekly* Vol. 45, Iss. 47, pp. 63–72.

19. It is interesting to note that the Muslim grounds for their petitions were not based upon an "insult to Muhammad," but rather on the grounds that it was against free thinking.

20. Eline Gordts, "Mohammed Cartoons: White House Questions 'Judgement' behind Charlie Hebdo cartoons," *The Huffington Post*, September 20, 2012.

21. IOR L/PS/11/85 P4715, F8-9.

22. See Jacob Landau, *Pan Islamism: History and Politics*. London, New York: Routledge, 2015.

23. Since the revival of pan-Islamism that had been developing across the Muslim world from the late 1850s onward, there had been an encouragement from Ottoman ambassadors across the lands under the control of the Europeans to say the Caliph's name as part of the prayers, as a way of signalling their loyalty to the most powerful Muslim leader in the world at that time. Ibid., pp. 43–51.

24. For a fuller discussion of the significance of the Caliph's naming in the *Khutba* see Naeem Qureishi, *Pan-Islamism in British Indian Politics*. Leiden: Brill, 2011, pp. 211–236.

25. IOR L/PS/.11/85 P4715, F8.

26. File FO 371/6470, May 18, 1921. Much of this was dealt with in *The Caliphate Question* so it will not be rehearsed again here.

27. IOR L/PS/.11/85 P4715, F1-6.

28. IOR l/PS/12/883, *Letter*, March 14, 1927.

29. Humayan Ansari offers a Muslim perspective on the development and advocacy for a London mosque in "'A Mosque in London Worthy of the Tradition of

Islam and Worthy of the Capital of the British Empire': The Struggle to Create Muslim Space 1910–1944," in Susheila Nasta (ed), *India in Britain: South Asian Networks and Connections, 1858–1950*. London, New York: Palgrave Macmillan, 2013, pp. 80–95.

30. CB/OS/323/12. *Cabinet Minutes*, August 14, 1940.

31. Bimla Prasad (1967) "The Emergence of the Demand for India's Partition," *International Studies* Vol. 9, Iss. 3, pp. 241–278.

32. Oliver-Dee, *The Caliphate Question*, p. 41.

33. Ibid., pp. 41–43.

34. Mohammed Mujeeb, *The Indian Muslims*. Aligarh: Aligarh University Press, 1967.

35. See, for example, Masood Ghaznavi (1974) "Recent Muslim Historiography in South Asia: The Problem of Perspective," *Indian Economic and Social History Review* Vol. 11, Iss. 2–3, pp. 183–215; Theodore Wright (1966) "Muslim Education in India at the Crossroads: The Case of Aligarh," *Public Affairs* Vol. 39, Iss. 1, pp. 50–61.

36. FO371/24548 letter from Sir Luke, Colonial Office to Sir Caccia dated August 22, 1942. Says that that the secretary of state for the colonies has decided that there are sufficient funds for a mosque to be built in central London. He goes on to say "Lord Lloyd considers that the good impression which the provision of a site by His Majesty's government would make upon Moslem opinion throughout the world would be well worth the sum involved."

37. FO 371/24548, F5-7.

38. Ibid.

39. IOR L/I/877, F7-9.

40. IOR L/I/877, F8.

41. For a doctrinal discussion of the nature of the 'ahl al-Kitab see Gudrun Krämer, Denis Matringe, John Nawas and Everett Rowson, *Encyclopaedia of Islam* (Three). Leiden: Brill, 2011, Volume 1, pp. 183–185.

42. IOR L/I/877, F9.

43. PC4/1 "World Heritage of Islam Festival in London."

44. Klas Grinel (2018) "Framing Islam at the World of Islam Festival, London, 1976," *Journal of Muslims in Europe* Vol. 7, Iss. 1, pp. 73–93.

45. As was discussed earlier.

46. DoS 511.80/4-252, CS/Y Office Memorandum dated April 2, 1952, from the Working Group Chairman G.H. Damon to Near East Policy Director, Richard Sanger.

47. Ibid., p. 1.

48. Ibid., pp. 2–3.

49. Ibid., p. 6. Gliddens was an interesting character who is described in Justin Hart's book on US engagement in the Middle East as the most famous of the State Department Arabists and the author of a controversial report published in the *American Journal of Psychology* on "Arab Emotions." Justin Hart, *The Empire of Ideas: The Origins of Public Diplomacy and the Transformation of U.S. Foreign Policy*. Oxford, New York: OUP, 2013, p. 236.

50. Ibid., p. 20.

51. Ibid., p. 21.

52. Javier Guerrero (2017) "Propaganda Broadcasts and Cold War Politics: The Carter Administration's Outreach to Islam," *Journal of Cold War Studies* Vol. 19, Iss. 1, pp. 4–37.

53. Ibid., p. 24.

54. Ibid., p. 25.

55. Ibid., p. 43.

56. Ibid.

57. Ibid., p. 44.

58. Jessica Dienow and Mark Donfred, *Searching for Cultural Diplomacy*. Oxford: Berghahn Books, 2010, p. 169.

59. In his article on the perception of Islam in the minds of American, Fawaz Gerges unpacks the evolution of US views of Islam and Muslims over the course of two centuries. See Fawaz Gerges (2003) "Islam and Muslims in the Mind of America," *Annals of the American Academy of Political and Social Science* Vol. 588, pp. 73–89.

60. These exchanges and the wider geostrategic context of them are discussed in Matthew Holland, *America and Egypt: From Roosevelt to Eisenhower*. Westport (CT): Praeger Publishers, 1996.

Chapter 6

Proselytizing and Conversion

There is no subject that a Western government likes discussing less than proselytizing or conversion. From a policy perspective, few events can disturb apparently peaceful and cohesive communities like conversion and the instability this brings can, potentially, become a catalyst for wider civil unrest.

This chapter will therefore discuss the expressed views of US and British governments in the case of three people and one incident, in order to understand the nature of those concerns, and how they are related to the US and British government perceptions which the book is analyzing. However, this chapter will principally be focused around British engagement with this area because the main context of the engagement took place within British imperial realms.

Back in the introduction to this book the history section highlighted how the so-called Pious Clause proposed by George Grant in relation to the East India Company charter renewal in 1813 helped to galvanize public opinion in favor of advancing not necessarily Christianity but the civilizing work of the *Pax Britannica*.

The underlying perception which the debates around the Pious Clause had prompted was that Hinduism and Islam were not religions to be engaged with and respected but instead tools of ignorance. As John Darwin puts it,

> They were equally nervous of offending local religious belief or lending open support to Christian missions despite their suspicion that Islam (for example) was intellectually bankrupt and Hinduism a medley of superstition and ignorance.[1]

This became the cultural context in which British officials wrestled with the issues thrown up by evangelism. Yet, as will be seen, the attitudes identified by John Darwin here were not the primary framework for the consideration of the issues described in the chapter.

EVANGELISM AND RELIGIOUS FREEDOM

In September 1879, the foreign secretary, Lord Salisbury, wrote to Sir Austen Layard, British Attaché to the Ottoman court, concerning the arrest of a German-born, Church Missionary Society (CMS) missionary and his Turkish religious scholar ('ulama) assistant Ahmed Tewfik Effendi, who had been helping the German translate St. John's Gospel and the Church of England's Book of Common Prayer (1662) into Turkish.[2] The German missionary, Rev. Dr. Koelle and Tewfik Effendi were imprisoned and, even though the British Attaché to the Ottomans was given assurances for their safety, the Turkish scholar was sentenced to death. Sir Austen, with the assistance of the French and German Ambassadors, made repeated, strong representations to the Sultan and other relevant religious authorities while reporting to London that public opinion was being enflamed against Effendi (and Dr. Koelle). The incident could hardly have occurred at a less advantageous moment from a British, or indeed Ottoman, perspective.

In general, the British had maintained a good relationship with the Ottomans. The Ottomans and British had been allies in the Crimean war against Russia and it was a fatwa by the Ottoman Caliph which undermined the legitimacy of the rebellion against British rule in India that was credited with being a decisive factor in the ending of the conflict.[3] That good British-Ottoman relationship was therefore an integral element of British security strategy for, quite apart from the important trade routes which went through their land to India (and elsewhere), the Ottoman Caliph-Sultan's status as the head of the Sunni Muslim world (a status which was taking on new significance at that time with the work of the revivalist preaching's of Jamal ad-Din Al-Afghani and the evolving doctrines of Pan Islamism) was of special significance to the British with their large imperial Muslim population.[4]

A balance therefore needed to be struck between the need to keep a vital ally onside, the commitment to religious freedom, and the protection of those under British rule on the other.

On the Ottoman side, the country was going through a period of significant constitutional change. The dominant Hanafi fiqh which had been the fundamental basis for the Ottoman legal structure had been completely reshaped in the *Tanzimat* reforms over a seven-year period between 1869 and 1876 during which the Citizenship Law (1869) had been introduced, granting equal status to Muslim and non-Muslim alike, and the *Mejella*, the constitutional document which fused elements of European (mostly French) civil legal norms, with elements of Hanafi sharia had been published in 1876, just three years before the incident in question.⁵

Those changes had been met with fierce opposition from conservative religious elements in Turkey and so the Koelle-Effendi case was one that was being watched closely from a number of differing perspectives. On the one hand the conservative Turkish religious authorities saw the incident as an opportunity to make wider claims about the insidious impact of Western thinking in Muslim societies: highlighting the fact that a member of the 'ulama had been "seduced" by this openness. On the other hand, the British and other European powers were interested in both the approach to religious freedom in the newly secularizing Ottoman state, as well as the fundamental principle of how non-Turks would be treated in that country. The issue of religious freedom therefore was bound into a number of other geopolitical and long-term cultural questions.

Internal correspondence between Lord Salisbury in Whitehall and Sir Austen Layard in Istanbul therefore concerned two interrelated issues. First, they sought to establish whether Dr. Koelle, a German by birth, was under British jurisdiction because he was working for a British organization (CMS). Clearly this was done in order to ascertain the nature of the engagement with the Ottoman authorities. In other words, should the cause of protest and representation to the Ottomans be on the basis of the arrest of a British subject and the extent to which that person should be subject to Ottoman law? Second, having established Koelle's status as a German subject under the aegis of a British agency, they sought to understand why his activities should warrant arrest.

However, before the matter escalated into an international standoff, Dr. Koelle was released. As was Ahmed Effendi. Layard's personal interactions with the Sultan appear to have been the decisive factor. But, even though the matter was concluded with relatively little incident, the issues it raised went deeper and the argument was reignited by the Sultan's foreign minister Sawas Pasha in a personal letter to Layard. In that strongly worded letter, Pasha made accusations against Koelle, even though Koelle was freed, which were vigorously refuted by Layard in a letter of January 13, 1880. There is not the time to discuss all the issues Sir Austen raises in his response, but it is important to note the heart of Layard's refutation to Pasha, for it demonstrates the impact of the attitudes articulated in the 1858 Proclamation:

> Everyone has a right to hold the opinions he may have formed upon religious and other matters so long as he does not publish such as are calculated to insult the religion of the country in which he resides, or to cause a public scandal or a disturbance of the peace.⁶

Sir Austen's words are effectively a paraphrase of the 1858 Proclamation and, as such, they demonstrate the wider application that the Proclamation's words had taken on. This was demonstrated in a similar but differing context some forty years after the Koelle case. When a travel application was made to William Batten, the British Agent in Jeddah, requesting a visa to travel into the Hijaz for the purposes of evangelization.

The Worldwide Evangelization Crusade (formerly known as "Heart of Africa Mission") expressed the desire to place a Mr. and Mrs. Millar as missionaries in the Hijaz in 1922.[7] The Worldwide Evangelization Crusade (WEC) had been formed a year before the First World War by C. T. Studd and Alfred Buxton who initially believed that God had called them to mission in Africa but quickly decided that it was instead a global mission that God was calling them to.

Their enthusiasm for missions to Arabia though could not, from a British government perspective have been worse timed.

The British and their allies, were in the midst of very delicate diplomatic activity which was seeking to limit the pan-Islamic appeal of the defeated Ottoman Caliph, while at the same time taking into consideration the feelings of the Muslims, particularly Indian Muslims, who were repeatedly petitioning the British government to allow the Caliph (Abdul Hamid II) to remain in post.[8] In the two years before the WEC application to evangelize the Hijaz, Prime Minister David Lloyd George had hosted two rather fractious meetings between himself and members of the Indian Khalifat Delegation at Downing Street. During the course of their meetings one of the delegation had quoted a hadith attributed to Ibn Abbas which said

> the "Island of Arabia" should remain inviolate and entirely in Moslem [sic] control. This is based on the dying injunction of the Prophet himself.[9]

The upper echelons of the British government were therefore highly aware of the religious significance of maintaining the "Islamic purity" of the Arabian Peninsula. What is more, the meetings had been taking place against a background of agitation in India against what was happening to the Caliph. Furthermore, there was a growing concern among Muslims in the British Empire about perceived British anti-Islamic bias which had grown as a result of the perception that the British were dealing more harshly with the Ottoman Empire, than they were with the other defeated powers.[10] As if that was not enough, the Arab tribesmen who had joined T. E. Lawrence against the Ottomans on the promise of independence were watching closely to see if the British kept their promises while, at the same time conflict was raging between Hussein, King of the Hijaz, and Ibn Saud, Lord of the Nejd.

The British government was therefore in an impossible situation, which was mostly of its own making, seeking to balance the representations of the

Khilafat Delegation on behalf of Indian Muslims, against the promises made to the Arabian tribes and the symbolic importance of Arabia to Islam.[11]

The internal government correspondence which was prompted by the WEC request between Jeddah and Whitehall clearly had the difficult international situation in mind. For, although the visit of the Khilafat Delegation to London was not specifically mentioned, frequent allusion was made to "the question of the settlement of the status of the Ottoman Sultan and the concerns being expressed by Indian Muslims."[12] Which William Batten was urged to bear in mind, along with the "sensitive situation in the Arabian Peninsula" at the time when making his decision on the Millar's entry visa.[13] It is clear that Whitehall was seeking to direct Batten without giving a direct order and Batten understood the implication of what was being said for, he did refuse permission to the Millars. However, what is interesting is that Batten did not allude to the political situation at all in his letter of refusal to the Millars but instead appears to have opted to use his religio-cultural knowledge to find grounds for the Millar's refusal. For, in his reply Batten stated that

> the Hidjaz is a country, every inch of which is holy ground to the Moslem [sic] world, and which is nominally closed to Christians. . . . It is a time of pilgrimage for Moslems and we see it as a duty to owe them some protection against incidents likely to wound them in their religious sentiments.[14]

Batten's reply is fascinating because religious sensitivity of the kind he was describing was not one of the reasons for refusal of the Millars that Whitehall had given him. It is unlikely that the Cabinet Office minutes of the Khalifat Delegation meetings would have been available to him, although they would have been circulated around senior civil servants in Whitehall, especially the India Office. But those who had access to the minutes to the meeting, such as Malcolm Harvey, the Whitehall civil servant responding to Batten's request for advice concerning the Millar's application, would have had access to that information. It is therefore interesting that Harvey did not mention Mohamed Ali's scriptural reference in this seemingly highly relevant situation, instead choosing to focus on political issues, whereas Batten, who did not have access to the minutes of the Khilafat Delegation but clearly had his own regional cultural and religious knowledge, chose to refuse the Millars on the grounds of certain religious principles rather than the political ones.[15]

Batten's refusal was entirely understandable in the political context, but it was also in line with the sentiment expressed in the 1858 Proclamation: the fundamental principle that religious freedom, in this case the freedom to evangelize, should be constrained within the bounds of maintaining peace and security.

There is no further correspondence from the Millars in the file and it prompts the question of whether they accepted the answer, or whether they sought to enter the region illegally. Nothing more is known about them, but the request they made, and the considerations they prompted, serve to throw into sharp relief the continued impact of the philosophy which underpinned the 1858 Proclamation's conception of religious freedom.

That being the case it is interesting to note Muslim missionaries coming to Britain from the late nineteenth century onward were not impeded. Muhammed Ally has shown that, among the wealthy merchants, students and professionals such as Lawyers who came to Britain in increasing numbers from the 1840s onward, included among them were

> learned Moulvies, the expositors of Mohammedan Law and faith were included among them.[16]

Few details of these missional activities are known, and in one sense they are not important in this context for it is likely that British authorities were either unaware of their existence, or not concerned about their work insofar as their numbers appear to have been so small. Certainly no correspondence exists in British government files discussing the existence of Muslim missionaries either in Britain or other parts of the Empire. Given the rubric of the 1858 Proclamation, it is likely that the government would only have been interested if the activities of the missionaries began to cause social tensions. In that context therefore, it could be argued that the lack of government action on Muslim missionaries showed consistency of application of the Proclamation.

CONVERSION TO ISLAM BY GOVERNMENT OFFICIALS

St. John Philby

But it was not just evangelism and conversion as potential cohesion breakers which worried officials. There were also concerns expressed about the potential implications of conversions to Islam by British officials. One such convert was St. John Philby, father of Kim Philby who was caught spying for the USSR in the Cold War.

Mr. Philby converted to Islam in 1930 while working as a businessman in the Middle East following his period as a diplomat in the region during the First World War. A letter from Hope Gill, the British Agent in Jeddah, to G. W. Rendell in India (who forwarded the letter to the India Office) mentioned Philby's conversion in the context of a concern that Philby might become a member of the Wahabbi Brotherhood.[17] Hope-Gill noted that Philby had been encouraged to write about his conversion by King Ibn Saud himself as the two knew each other. Ibn Saud presumably wanted Philby to write about his conversion as an encouragement to other Europeans to follow Philby into Islam. Indeed, there was substantial interest in Islam among the British aristocracy at the time both in relation to a broad interest in "the Orient," but in relation to exploring Islam as a religion specifically.[18]

Hope-Gill's concern was not with Philby's conversion per se but rather, he was worried that Philby might be used as a pawn by Ibn Saud. In that connection, Hope-Gill mentioned that Philby might become a member of the Brothers and hinted at a degree of desperation and naivety about Philby's conversion for he reported that Philby's conversion was most likely prompted by his business going badly and being out of money. His conversion almost certainly meant that he would get work. Apparently the locals had christened Philby "slave of tuppence" rather than the name 'Abdullah that he had actually taken.[19] Gill was convinced that Philby had no religious conviction at all.

In the end, Hope-Gill was clearly intrigued enough to invite Philby for a personal chat. A further letter (dated August 30, 1930) from Hope-Gill highlighted that Philby had said himself that his conversion was not at all spiritual, rather, it was a rejection of HMG policy in the Middle East. Philby decided to convert to express his commonality with the Arabs and all things Arabian.[20] This letter was passed to the Foreign Office in London who in turn made it known to Khan Bahadur Tasaddaq Husain of the Home Intelligence department in India who had learnt from a chapter in *The Pioneer* (dated September 26, 1930) of Philby's conversion. The Home Intelligence department wanted to know why Philby converted. Their concern, paralleling Hope-Gill's, was that Philby had converted to Wahhabism. So he was enquiring for the reasons for Philby's conversion. Such was the apparent concern in official circles that in the following February Andrew Ryan of the British Consulate in Jeddah wrote to the principal secretary of state for foreign affairs concerning the matter. Ryan was particularly concerned that there has been press speculation that Philby had become a confident of Ibn Saud himself and in so doing, had created the perception that the Saudis were being directed by the British: a dangerous accusation for the keepers of the holy places of Islam. Ryan admitted to the Secretary of State that there was indeed a relationship between Saud and Philby, but he denied that Philby had any connection to the British government policy in the area.

So it is clear that Philby's conversion had aroused considerable interest, not just within foreign policy circles but also further afield for the general public as well, following articles about him appearing in *the Pioneer* and *Daily Herald* (September 3, 1930).[21]

Several aspects of the concerns raised by British officials are intriguing, but as there is nothing further written about the underlying nature of their concerns, we will need to be content with simply asking the questions rather than getting the answers. The key question is why the conversion of one man should stir up such concern? There are many who convert to and from Islam in the United Kingdom and in the United States and very few of them make headlines, other than when one of them either becomes involved with Jihad or becomes a key spokesperson on behalf of their new faith. In that latter respect, the conversions of Professor Tim Winter at Cambridge and the former special advisor to Ronald Reagan, Robert Dickson-Crane must rank as key strategic conversions in the West. Yet Philby, other than the fact that he used to be a diplomat, had very little to recommend him. It was maybe the simple fact of, what appeared to be a relatively novel occurrence, which prompted so much attention to be brought to bear on him at a time when the British were heavily engaged in the Middle East and so the region was very much in public consciousness. Moreover, since his conversion appears to have been protest, rather than spiritual, it drew negative attention to the British activity in the region, something which they were keen to avoid.[22] It seems therefore that British concern about Philby's conversion centered around the potential implications that might arise as far as his loyalties were concerned. Accusations of being a traitor had been made in the British press concerning the expressed dual loyalty of Marmaduke Pickthall during the First World War and even before the war, as Ron Greaves observes, "Going Turk" was a phrase which was used to describe not only those who converted to Islam but, by implication also became potential traitors by virtue of their rejection of "Britishness."[23]

In the context of this book therefore, it is clear that, in the minds of British officials during the pre–Second World War era, there was a correlation between change of faith and a potential for change of loyalty to state. The freedom to convert, therefore, while not limited by the instruments or agencies of the state, drew suspicion.

Alexander Russell Webb

The conversion to Islam of the US diplomat Mohammed Alexander Russell Webb does not appear to have created the same form of concern in relation to loyalty in for the US government as Philby's conversion had within British government circles.

Webb's conversion was a final step along a path that had begun with his original rejection of Christianity at a relatively early stage in his life. The area where he had grown up in New York was a hotbed of religious searching and this restless spirituality appears to have made a deep impression on Webb, prompting him to become a Theosophist and to convert to Buddhism in 1881.[24] He traveled to India in order to discover more about non-Christian faiths and, when he traveled to India he began to study more about Islam from the Muslims who were also members of the Theosophical Society. He also corresponded with Mirza Ghulam Ahmed, founder of the Ahmadiyya movement. That study and correspondence prompted Webb to conclude that Muhammad had been given special and secret teaching, known only to a special few and, in the light of that, Islam was the faith through which the ancient wisdom of Theosophy was most profoundly manifest. This conversion was therefore not initially to mainstream Islam but to a metaphysical or philosophical adjunct of it. However, he converted to Sunni Islam once he had moved to the Philippines to become America's consul to that country.[25]

Yet his spiritual and physical journey did not end there, for he resigned from his post in Manila after only three years and, in conjunction with Moulvi Hasan Ali (among others) began to make arrangements for missionary trips to the United States which he made in 1893 in New York, publishing a book *Islam in America* (1893) as he did so.[26] He also published a pro-Muslim (and pro-Ottoman) newspaper called *Moslem World*.

Webb struggled to attract converts and, even though he was the only Muslim to attend the World Parliament of Religions in 1893, his ministry continued to attract donors. He moved to New Jersey and continued to be active in mission to the end of his life.[27]

As a person therefore, Webb was clearly man fascinated with discovering what the world outside of Europe and America had to offer and, as such, he was very much in tune with the times in which he was living: the Victorian period saw the explosion of numerous spiritual movements, such as the aforementioned Ahmadiyyas, as well as the Spiritualists, and the Baha'i. At the same time, with the traveling opportunities afforded to aristocratic (and middle-class) Westerners, there was a general fascination with the Orient. Webb's context was one in which such exploration was not unusual. But, given that Webb became a missionary for Islam back to America following his conversion, and the fact of his official connections as a Consul, one might have expected the American government to have been more concerned about him than they appear to have been. Yet, there is no record of the kind of discussion among US officials in that period as there was among British officials in relation to Philby's conversion and activities.

Why was that?

There are a number of potential explanations and it is worthwhile noting that Webb was asked to become a Consul after he had converted, rather than being in government and then converting as Philby had done.

First, the context of the era was important: it was a time of spiritual searching generally and so Webb's spiritual evolution was not unusual for the period. Furthermore, in the United States, Islam neither had the immediacy of the connection with piracy that was prevalent in the early nineteenth century, nor the connection with terrorism which some branches of Islam have today. Nor did it have the connection of dual loyalty to another ruler as the British had in relation to the Ottomans in the First World War. America too had been untouched by the growth of the pan-Islamic ideology which had been spreading across the British colonies in North Africa and South Asia.[28]

Second, Webb was contracted to government service after his conversion, so there must have been no concerns about his loyalty to the United States even though he had changed religious affiliation. Although it is interesting to note that his religious views did have one specific outworking in relation to some Protestant missionaries who were desiring the US Consulate to defend their interests as they developed their work on the Federated States of Micronesia. Webb instead recommended to the State Department that their interests should not be defended, and Umar Abdullah notes that Webb had no love for missionaries. This is an interesting statement given that he went on to be a missionary himself, but it must be assumed that Webb did not like the fact that the missionaries were seeking to spread a message which, in his view, was wrong, and so took his opportunity to limit the potential impact they might have otherwise had if the United States had lent its protection to them.[29]

Finally, Webb's correspondence with US officials reveals that, while they were interested in his religious journey, they were not really interested in his religious affiliation so much as they were wanting to make use of his valuable experience of the world. As a journalist Webb had been an enthusiastic supporter of Cleveland's candidacy for the Presidency and so, when he became President, Cleveland was happy to appoint Webb to a post in which Webb's preexisting knowledge of the Orient, and his loyalty to Cleveland, could be put to good use. And, although it was principally trade which interested the US authorities about the Philippines, there was also growing unrest which, as was mentioned in chapter 2, eventually led to rebellion. Someone with knowledge and understanding of the region, and of the issues that were involved was therefore invaluable to the United States.[30]

In this context, therefore, the contrast between the British and US government reactions to the conversion to Islam of someone who was working for them is interesting to note in terms of the divergence between them. Even with taking into account the differences in historical context between the two incidents, it is noticeable that the overriding issue for the British was not about religion adherence itself but about the potential shift in loyalty that it might bring. Whereas, for the United States, Cleveland's knowledge that Webb was loyal to him personally meant that he felt assured that Webb would work in the interests of America as a whole.

FORCED CONVERSION AND RELIGIOUS FREEDOM

British India

Of all the aspects of conversion and evangelism which were of greatest concern to governments, especially in the light of the aforementioned Proclamation of religious freedom in the British Empire in 1858, was the specter of having to deal with forced conversion. So when the Mapilla rebellions in Malabar took place and accusations of forceable conversion to Islam were made, the British government was obliged to investigate.[31] In a memo marked "Secret" in 1922, concerns were raised about issue of Hindus who had been forced to convert to Islam in Malabar. According to the memo, those converts now wanted to now revert back to Hinduism.[32]

Interestingly enough it is the plight of those wanting to revert back to their faith which was of greatest concern to the officials. The British were concerned about the reaction of fanatical Muslims in the area who, they believed, were likely to kill those reverting back. There was the belief that some Muslims might be open holding off, but there was the sense that others might have to be locked away. Secretary Graham believed that, given those concerns, only a fatwa from the authorities in Mecca itself would have been enough to contain the desire of the Mapillas to attack the reverts. A telegram on the issue dated February 11, 1922, from Viceroy, Foreign and Political Affairs Department in New Delhi showed that a keen interest in the event was being taken at the highest levels of government for it reiterated that those wanting to revert, both Hindus and others, were forcibly converted to Islam during the Mapilla rebellion.[33] The telegram ends with a request to mention to Hussein, Sharif of Mecca about the issue with a suggestion that a fatwa be produced saying that forcible conversion to Islam is illegal in Islam which "(can) only be wiped out by allowing converts freely and fearlessly to rejoin their own faith."[34] In reply, C. W. Gwaynne, of the Jeddah office, said that having consulted they do not feel that obtaining a fatwa is a good idea because there is no guarantee that the fatwa would say the things they desire and furthermore, that the very fact of using the Meccan 'Ulama would encourage Indian Muslims to look outside of India for guidance. Gwaynne's conclusion was that they must settle the matter locally.[35]

It is clear that the British took this matter very seriously, not from the standpoint of religious freedom necessarily but from an awareness that there were competing interests which had to be placated if they did not want riots from either Muslims or Hindus. Furthermore, the incident took place within the wider context of the aftermath of the First World War, and the advocacy from Indian Muslims on behalf of the defeated Ottoman Caliph-Sultan that had included accusations of anti-Muslim bias as manifested in the perceived harsher treatment of Ottoman ruler as against that of the defeated Kaiser. It is likely therefore that this wider concern was also informing British attitudes to the Mapilla rebellion accusations and that, therefore, there was a strong desire for the sake of their wider geostrategic interests, not to see the incident enflame public opinion among any of the British imperial subjects.[36]

Further internal Government of India correspondence stated that they had consulted T. E. Laurence about this as well as consulting T. W. Arnold's *The Preaching of Islam*. One piece of advice they were given (it doesn't say from whom) suggested that those wanting to revert might be moved to a different location. Even so, the Secretary of State, over the course of a conversation between a Mr. Grafftey Smith and the Grand Qadi of Mecca, on February 22, had raised the general question of whether forcible conversion to Islam was legal in Islam. He was "emphatically assured" that it was not.[37] This therefore provided the British government with a way out of a situation which they were profoundly uncomfortable at having to deal with. Effectively, the assurance provided them with legitimate grounds for not having to pursue the issue further from a cohesion perspective.

CONCLUSION

This selection of incidents drawn from history gives the reader some insight into the variety and impact of the social upheavals being caused by the changes in faith that were occurring all the time. The advice being received by the British with regards to forcible conversions, as we have seen, perhaps gives a slightly lopsided view of views on conversion from an Islamic point of view but, from a policy perspective, does display a desire to receive expert advice into their thinking. It is clear that there was a general suspicion of the motives behind conversion to Islam by the British government in the Philby case that was not seen in the US engagement with the conversion of Webb.

In the British case, this concern probably stemmed from a combination of the belief that conversion to any religion in the modern world was somewhat strange and the concern that conversion to certain forms of Islam, in this case Wahhabi, would bring with its security implications. In that context, therefore, it was not so much the conversion to Islam that was the issue but rather the potential shift in loyalties which that might involve.

So, in relation to the overarching theme of the book, these incidents show that the concerns of governments around issues of conversion were not about the conversion to Islam itself but rather the potential implications which might arise from them, either in relation to the change in loyalty which might follow on from the conversion, or the destabilization of social cohesion which might arise from evangelism, or from the potential for radicalization which might arise from conversion to specific denominations within Islam. Therefore, the correspondence suggests that there was no official concern about conversion to Islam as a faith as such but rather, a concern about its implications and about a specific ideology within it.

NOTES

1. Darwin, *Unfinished Empire*, p. 191.
2. All the correspondence relating to this issue can be found in file CAB 37/1, 1880. F47–112.
3. See Lewis, *Modern Turkey*, pp. 111–115.
4. *Census of the British Empire: 1901*. Great Britain Census Office. 1906, pp. xvi & xviii. Muslims constituted 24 percent of the total Imperial population and approximately 33 percent of the total Muslim population at that time.
5. Sean Oliver-Dee, *Muslim Minorities and Citizenship*, pp. 11–35.
6. CAB 37/1, 1880. F109.
7. See Eleanor Tejirian and Reeva Simon, *Conflict, Conquest and Conversion: Two Thousand Years of Christian Missions in the Middle East*. New York: Columbia University Press, 2012; Inger Okkenhaug (2015) "Christian Missions in the Middle East and the Ottoman Balkans: Education, Reform and Failed Conversions, 1819–1967," *International Journal of Middle East Studies* Vol. 47, Iss. 3, pp. 593–604; Akram Khater (2011) "New Faith in Ancient Lands: Western Missions in the Middle East in the Nineteenth and Early Twentieth Centuries," *Journal of Social Science and Missions* Vol. 24, Iss. 2–3, pp. 304–309; J. Herbert Kane, *A Concise History of the Christian World Mission: A Panoramic view of Missions from Pentecost to the Present*. Grand Rapids (MI): Baker Books, 1978, pp. 101–112 and 137–144; Adrian Hastings, *The Church in Africa, 1450–1950*. Oxford: Clarendon Press, 1996.
8. Oliver-Dee, *The Caliphate Question*, pp. 43–90.
9. Ibid., p. 18. Appears to be quoting al-Bukhari, Vol. 1, Book 59, Hadith 716.
10. Ibid., F5.
11. Fromkin, *The Peace to End All Peace*, pp. 424–432.
12. PZ 817/1922, F4.
13. Ibid.
14. IOR L/PS/15/1654, F3.
15. Bruce Clark discusses the wider context of European views on the Ottomans and Turkey in (2012) "Shifting Western Views on Turkey," *Asian Affairs* Vol. 43, Iss. 2, pp. 193–203. See also Nazim Cicektakan, *Great Britain and the Ottoman Empire: British Discourses on the Ottomans 1860–1878*. Unpublished PhD Thesis, University of Essex, 2014; Fahriye Yildizeli, *W.E. Gladstone and British Policy towards the Ottoman Empire*. Unpublished PhD Thesis, University of Exeter, 2016.
16. Muhammed Ally, *History of Muslims in Britain*. Unpublished Master's Thesis, University of Birmingham, 1981.
17. IOR L/PS/15 file 1654, F4.

18. Much of the fascination about Islam in the British aristocracy arose from the opportunities to travel to Egypt, Turkey and elsewhere. For example, Lady Evelyn Cobbold spoke of feeling a "Muslim at heart" and was the first British woman known to have performed the Hajj. She had spent much time in Egypt with her father, the Earl of Dunmore who was an explorer, as she grew up. See Jamie Gilham, *Loyal Enemies: British Converts to Islam 1850–1950*. London: Hurst and Co, 2014.

19. IOR L/PS/15 file 1654, F6.

20. Ibid.

21. IOR L/PS/15 file 1654, F7-9.

22. Robert S.G. Fletcher, *British Imperialism and the "Tribal Question": Desert Administration and Nomadic Societies, 1919–1936*. Oxford, New York: OUP, 2015, pp. 133–182.

23. Ron Greaves (2017) "Abdullah Quilliam (Henri De Léon) and Marmaduke Pickthall: Agreements and Disagreements between Two Prominent Muslims in the London and Woking Communities," in Geoffrey Nash (ed), *Marmaduke Pickthall: Islam and the Modern World*. Leiden: Brill, 2017. See also Ron Geaves, *Islam in Victorian Britain: The Life and Times of Abdullah Quilliam*. Leicester: Kube Press, 2019.

24. Umar Abdallah, *A Muslim in Victorian America: The Life of Alexander Russell Webb*. New York: Oxford University Press, 2006.

25. Ibid., p. 37

26. Ibid., pp. 71–79.

27. Richard Seager (ed), *The Dawn of Religious Pluralism: Voices from the World Parliament of Religions, 1893*. La Salle: Open Court Press, 1993.

28. Azmi Ozcan, *Pan-Islamism: Indian Muslims, the Ottomans and Britain, 1877–1924*. Leiden: Brill, 1997. See also Qureshi, *Pan-Islamism*, pp. 9–87; Benjamin Hopkins (2014) "Islam and Resistance in the British Empire," in David Motadel (ed), *Islam and the European Empires*. New York, Oxford: OUP, 2014; Landau, *The Politics of Pan-Islam*.

29. Abdallah, *Muslim in Victorian America*, p. 110.

30. Alexander Russell Webb to State Department, *Dispatch–Manila to Washington DC*, October 3, 1893.

31. This discussion is found in IOR/PS/11/211, PZ 657.

32. Secret, February 1, 1922, S A Graham, Acting Chief Secretary to the Gov of Madras to Secretary to the Gov of India, home department entitled "Mapilla Rebellions. Forcible Conversions."

33. IOR/Ps/11/211, PZ 657, F12.

34. Ibid.

35. Department Secretary to the Government of India, March 13, 1922.

36. Fromkin, *The Peace to End All Peace*, pp. 45–72.

37. British Agency in Jeddah, May 27, 1922, Major W E Marshall (British Agent and Consul) to Lord Curzon, Secretary of State for Foreign Affairs, London.

Chapter 7

Education

The place of Muslim education within British and US education systems has been a focus for debate over the past decade particularly. This has arisen partly from concerns over the nature of what has been taught in madrassas from the non-Muslim populations, to the impact of secular liberal education on Muslim children for Muslim parents. Given the importance of education in shaping successive generations in relation to not simply their ability to access the workplace, but in relation to their ability to form citizens whose outlook helps shape society, education is a key area of policy. For that reason, British and US government officials have taken substantial interest in this key policy area. This interest has manifested itself into two broad fields: first, the nature of what is being taught in Madrassas in the United States and United Kingdom and second, what understandings of Islam as a faith should be developed within the educational systems in these two countries.

During the imperial period, education became an important field of conflict between the brand of secular education which the British East India Company, and then British government sought to impose on the subcontinent and Muslims who wanted to protect themselves from what many saw as the pernicious influence of liberal Western education.[1] This resistance to liberal education had two principal incarnations, the first was the Dar ul-Uloom established at Deoband in India in 1866 and the second was Aligarh University (full name Madrassat ul-Uloom Musalmanan i-Hind) which was established in 1875. The Dar ul-Uloom at Deoband was established by two leading Indian 'ulama, Muhammad Qasim Nanotvi, Rasheed Ahmed Gangohi and Syed 'Abid Husayn for the specific purpose of providing both Islamic education but also the preservation of Islamic culture. In her history of Islamic revivalism in British India Barbara Metcalf locates the development of the Deobandi school within the wider stream of antiimperialist Muslim consciousness which grew exponentially with the inception of direct rule by the British government in 1858.[2] It was a movement which was quickly so successful that it franchised over much of the Subcontinent to the extent that twenty-nine schools were affiliated to the original Dar ul-Uloom by 1900.[3]

The Aligarh University model was somewhat different, although its ideological foundations were not dissimilar. The key contrasts between Aligarh and Deoband were in the social status of its pupils and its ultimate aim: for, whereas Deoband was principally a school for middle and lower-class South Asians, Aligarh was both founded and funded by Muslims drawn from the elites of South Asian society, such as Mohammad Ali Mohammed Khan (Raja of Mahmudabad) and Aga Khan III.[4] Furthermore, the ultimate aim for Aligarh was to ensure that Muslim students were able to compete in the very competitive jobs market for the Indian civil service in order to help maintain and develop Muslim influence in government. Deoband was not interested in preparing its pupils for the workplace and instead its focus was the preservation of what the founders and successive principals have seen as the "preservation of Islamic culture."[5]

This twin-track approach to Islamic education continues to this day in relation to the development of Muslim faith schools in the UK and America at secondary, or high school age, as well as in tertiary education. As of September 2015, there were 6,817 state-funded faith schools in England. The majority were primary schools; 6,182 (37% of all state-funded primaries). There were twenty-three state-funded Muslim faith schools.[6]

Leaving aside the arguments about the principle of having state-funded (or independent) religiously funded schools of any faith within a liberal educational system, this chapter will analysis correspondence between officials in Britain and in America in relation to what the correspondence reveals about their perceptions of, concerns about, and questions relating to, Islam in the educational system of both countries. It will do so through the lens of correspondence around the founding of the Zakariya School for girls in 1980 in the UK, along with anti-Americanism concerns in principally overseas madrassas from the 1990s onward.

ISLAM, MUSLIMS, AND THE BRITISH EDUCATIONAL SYSTEM

The question of Islamic schools in the UK was discussed by the British government in the 1980s in relation to the development of the Zakariya School for Girls. The school had been started as a private school by the musician and convert to Islam "Cat Stevens" (Yusuf Islam) in the early 1980s before it acquired faith school status and became able to take advantage of the financial awards that were available for such schools. The discussions which had led to the school being granted academic status within the English education system are contained in file ED172/578/9 and it is interesting to note that the religious aspect of the school was given relatively little attention in the discussions. Instead the focus was on safeguarding issues such as facilities for pupils, the lack of properly trained teachers and lack of integration.[7]

The requirement for Zakariya was located within a far wider discussion about separate education for Muslim girls which had been raging since the early 1980s. Not only were there concerns that integration into the state education would undermine the children's Islamic identity, there was a concern that what they perceived as the sexually permissive culture would also impact on the girls especially. In his book *Infidel* Humayun Ansari traces the flow of this discussion and includes a number of remarkable statistics among which is the claim that 98 percent of Muslims desired separate education for Muslim girls.[8] The desire push for the establishment of Zakariya can be seen in that context.

Indeed, in order to attain that status Zakariya had an extension built which allowed for sports facilities. Very little comment was made on the curriculum in the correspondence and it transpired that this lack of oversight was not just seen in the curriculum itself but in the pupils as well. For when the author Hanif Kureishi visited the school in 1985 he found that not only was the school lacking any female pupils (they were all male), but they also had educational materials which were entirely about the Qur'an and Islam, rather than including other elements of Western education.[9] It was an extraordinary failure of oversight which was mirrored once again more recently in the UK with the eventual discovery of the so-called Trojan Horse affair, where a number of schools in Birmingham were found to have been systematically taken over by Muslims who were seeking to exclude all other ideologies and perspectives.[10]

This speaks to the lack of concern expressed about the "need for" separate education for Muslim girls (or boys).

Reports such as *Guide to Religious Education in a Multi-Faith Community* which was first published in 1974 (and revised in 1983) expressed little concern about the integration aspects of the issue. This is surprising given the long history that the British had already had in relation to claims for separate Islamic education which stretched back into imperial days as has already been noted. This desire for separate education, expressed as necessity, for the preservation of culture, does not appear to have been questioned in British files.

The issue came to the fore once again in the UK in 2014 when an anonymous letter was sent to the Birmingham City Council containing serious accusations of deliberate attempts to "take over a number of schools in Birmingham and run them on strict Islamic principles."[11] The letter and the investigation which it launched provoked a public outcry with claim and counterclaim being made both about the events themselves and the Islamophobic language which was generated from that public debate.[12] For the purposes of this book however, the truth or otherwise of the case is not of central importance. What is of importance is the perception that British officials and politicians (rather than the public) had of Islam and Muslims from the revelations.

The first thing to note is that the schools were in Birmingham catchment areas which had a high number of South Asian Muslim background families. For that reason, a cultural environment in which Islam was more normative than it would be in a rural parish would be entirely natural. Second, as was seen with the Zakariya school in Yorkshire, Muslim faith schools had been part of the British educational landscape for decades and, during the days of the British Empire, schools which were deliberately and clearly run by and for Muslims such as the Dar ul-Uloom in Deoband were part of the educational landscape as well.

For those reasons the issue was therefore not that a school was being run according to any doctrinal stream of Islam, but that schools which were state-run and therefore supposed to be secular in nature, both in relation to culture and curriculum, were not being operated as such. Moreover, the letter and subsequent investigations found evidence that there had been deliberate attempts to exclude non-Muslims from teaching at the school and to operate systems of gender segregation which were not in keeping with guidelines on gender interaction in education.[13] The Clarke report stated that the investigation had

> revealed a sustained and coordinated agenda to impose upon children in a number of Birmingham schools the segregationist attitudes and practices of a hardline and politicized strand of Sunni Islam.[14]

Since that report was published and matters have been moved toward prosecutions and other actions resulting from the Clarke report recommendations, some teachers and governors have been banned but there has also been significant counterargument from advocates who argued that the actions of those involved in the schools in question were deliberately misrepresented. Moreover, the case against a number of the staff collapsed due to what were described as "improprieties on behalf of lawyers acting for the National College of Teaching and Leadership."[15]

But, while the truth of the matter concerning the Trojan Horse Affair is important in its own right, the key issue for this book is that the revelations it produced had an impact in Whitehall. For the affair provided concrete evidence (rather than vague insinuations) in the minds of officials and politicians, that there were Muslims who were seeking to pursue a deliberate agenda of Islamification (whether that be the defense of Muslim communities from secular influence, or the deliberate attempt to increase Islamic influence through the education system). Rumors of Islamification agendas and accusations of separatist mindsets among some Muslim communities which had been growing for more than two decades could have been dismissed as Islamophobia, or scaremongering by British politicians and officials for lack of evidence.[16] The Trojan Horse Affair was important insofar as it appeared to give hard evidence of the presence of such activities.

Anti-British Sentiment at Al-Azhar

On December 27, 1956, the governor of Uganda sent a telegram to the Secretary of State for Education in Whitehall suggesting that a Muslim Institute for Higher Education be set up, paid for by the British government, specifically for the purpose of training Imams as no such provision currently existed.[17] But the subtext of the desire was articulated in a letter early in the new year in which the Secretary of State's private secretary, Miles Hann warmly welcomed the idea of an institute which would counter the influence of Al-Azhar. Their concern was not about the form of Islam that was being taught at Al-Azhar, it was the rather the fact that Al-Azhar was known to be teaching anti-British sentiment and anti-Western feeling more broadly that was the issue. This was not surprising in the context of the fact that the Suez Crisis had been concluded only a month before this correspondence. Anti-British (and French) feeling was bound to be running high in a context where British troops had been sent to seize control of the recently state-owned canal.[18]

Yet it is interesting to note that the correspondence does not specifically contextualized the recent events around Suez but instead discusses longer-term concerns. Several of the responses to the idea are of interest insofar as they show the extent of a British alarm at Egyptian influence over Nigeria and other African States, but at its heart, the key importance for us was that it demonstrated that Western powers, even in the early Cold War, we're not so interested in the form of Islam that was being propagated, but rather concern about whether the message being received by Muslims via those who were teaching the teachers was pro or anti-Western.[19] Indeed, such was the level of naivety which proliferated among Western officials that many expressed the view that Islam was close to collapsing outright anyway, but, while it still existed, the message that was given should be positive about the west.[20] It was one of the clearest articulations of the desire for secularization made in a differing cultural context found in British files.

Professor Serjeant of SOAS university was sent on a scouting expedition to ascertain whether such an institution was viable and his report, which said "no," appears to have been the critical factor in preventing the idea gaining any further traction.[21]

This correspondence evidences the framework within the British government appeared to be working in relation their attitude to and understanding of Islam and the strategic role of major Islamic (in this case Sunni) institutions. For, the concerns being expressed around Al-Azhar are not primarily focused upon the impact of its ideology per se but instead, how that ideology might cause Britain (in this case) to lose strategic influence in West Africa.

Summary

The investigations and correspondence around the Birmingham schools, Al-Azhar and the Zakariya school shows consistency in relation to a lack of interest (or understanding) of the ideology being espoused but a concern about the strategic impact of perceived anti-British sentiment. As such, the issue was not the place of state, or even private religiously funded and operated educational establishments in the UK (or the Empire-Commonwealth or beyond) as a matter of principle but rather what was being taught and the protection of the students in the school's care. In relation to perceptions about Islam and Muslims therefore, the files, by their very silence on the matter on the inherent nature of Islamic education, strongly suggest that British officials had no concerns about Islamic education as a whole but had instead, concerns about the impact of what was being taught in some institutions in relation to separatism.

ISLAMIC EDUCATION AND AMERICA

The growth of Islamic education in America has been a very recent phenomenon. For that reason, little material on internal US government attitudes to US education in the country (as opposed to abroad), is publicly available. This section will therefore focus on a couple of snippets of information that are available, and cautiously extrapolate from those fragments, some sense of the US government's attitude to Muslim education in the United States and overseas.

In America, according to the 2011 report produced by the Institute for Social Policy and Understanding (ISPU) there are approximately 32,000 Muslim children in Islamic schools in the United States. The ISPU report estimates that there are approximately 850,000 Muslim children in the United States, which means that (assuming the accuracy of the figures) about 3.8 percent of Muslim children are being educated in Islamic schools at present. As the report highlights, this percentage represents a far lower figure for private school attendance than the national average (10%). It is worthwhile highlighting that the vast majority of those Islamic schools have opened since 9/11 (85%) and 55 percent are less than six years old or less.[22] This is an indication of the speed of growth in Islamic education in the United States.[23]

This growth in Islamic education within the United States has come at a time when the place of religious education in America has become increasingly hotly contested within the broad discussion of faith-state relations.

Symptomatic of that wider tension were the notes in the guidelines that were published for public schools in 2003 which included provision for the allowing of religious conversation but the forbidding of coercion into religious activity of any kind.[24] This guidance itself suggests a general, rather than Islam-specific concern around the potential for religious inculcation into students and it is important to note that guidance is deliberately generalized in its language around religion rather than identifying specific concerns with specific faiths. As such, the document is clearly seeking to show itself to be even-handed, but it suggests also the relative lack of confidence (constitutionally and religious knowledge) in engaging with an issue which has the potential to both interfere in state-run educational systems and cross the constitutional boundaries of state-faith interaction. As has been seen elsewhere in this book, that divide has been blurred at different points for very pragmatic reasons, such as seeking to respond to radicalization issues in the War on Terror, the Iranian Revolution and the issues manifested in seeking to encourage investment in Islamic economics. But, nevertheless, the question of federal engagement with religious issues of any kind remains highly sensitive and frequently confused as was observed by Walter Dellinger, Assistant Attorney General in his testimony to the Judiciary Committee of the Senate in October 1995.[25] Writing back in 2000, James Fraser makes the point that

> God's place within the public schools of the United States has been debatable, and subject to controversy, for as long as there have been public schools. In Colonial America, religion played a central role in the schools of every colony, but the understanding of religion differed substantially from colony to colony. With the coming of Nationhood and the separation of church and state on the federal level, the public school was pressed into service as the new as a new kind of national church, commissioned to create and carry the common culture and morality of the nation.[26]

He goes on to predict the increasing polarization of debate around the place of faith in public education which has characterized twenty-first-century American public debate. Insightful though Fraser's analysis is though, he fails to observe in this summation that the "understanding of religion differed substantially from colony to colony" was all still based within the Christian tradition.[27] Therefore, while differences certainly existed, there was a common cultural starting point in the early colonies and right through to mid to late nineteenth century when, it could be argued that, the failed "Blaine Amendment" to the constitution was symptomatic of the shift of public education away from normative Protestantism in educational (and wider) public culture.[28]

The growth of Islamic education in the United States is therefore coming at a time when this ongoing contest around religion and education continues and therefore brings an added dimension to it.

One Muslim academy school which has established a reputation for providing high-quality education within a religious context is the al-Ghazaly Academy and High School (AGA) in Jersey City.

On May 21, the AGA became the first school in New Jersey to be awarded accredited status by the AdvancED accrediting agency. According to their website they have sent graduates to all the Ivy League colleges and stated that many of their students have gone on to be doctors, engineers, and academics.[29]

Given their level of success it seems clear that the AGA is keen to encourage their students to be engaged with the culture around them and are happy for their graduates to attend non-Islamic tertiary institutions. At the same time it is clear also that the school places a high value on the Islamic part of this Islamic school with all pupils doing Qur'an, Arabic Language and Islamic studies as well as the traditional secular subjects such as Maths, Science, and Literacy.[30] Quite what is taught within any of these subject and whether any instruction about other faiths is given under the banner of "social science" is impossible to say. But on the surface at least, core content is being covered along with the explicitly Islamic framework.

The AGA's mission statements reads:

> Al-Ghazaly School holds a simple mission, grounded in the strengths of our Islamic heritage and spiritual beliefs: to develop highly educated, responsible, and active students with an interest in the pursuit of knowledge in all its forms.[31]

It therefore highlights that it has taken great pains to provide an education which will permit their graduates to enter "mainstream" American society. However, while all this is both encouraging from a broad integrationist point of view, one concern does remain.

The AGA is one of three schools which are all owned and run by the Islamic Education Foundation of New Jersey which was first formed in 1984. Since then it has become affiliated with the Islamic Schools League of America (ISLA), an organization which has links to the Muslim Brotherhood affiliate, the Islamic Society of North America (ISNA).[32] At least one member of the founders of the ISLA is also a current member of the ISNA: Karen

Keyworth and the Imam of the Mosque which is connected to the AGA, Farghal Ali, was recorded giving a sermon in May 2016, during the siege in Aleppo in which he enjoined his listeners to defend the city against

> the infidel Rafidites [Shiites], the atheist communists, the hateful Crusaders, and the evil vipers from the Jews.[33]

Given the nature of the ideology which is behind the school's organizational body therefore, it would be important to know what is being taught in, for example, the classes on American History, which are cited as part of the AGA's curriculum. Yet, no publicly available information suggests that the AGA is the subject of investigation. This does not mean that state officials at the educational board are either ignorant or are sanguine about what is happening at the AGA, but the apparent lack of investigation suggests that, at the very least, no alarms have been expressed about the AGA's curriculum content.

The apparent lack of investigation from educational officials could be due to a number of explanations ranging from ignorance or lack of time and resources through awareness, but a lack of confidence with dealing with the issue, to complicity: an awareness and tacit endorsement of the sentiment being expressed. Of course the latter is extremely unlikely, but the lack of action is troubling in the context of child protection and is, at the very least, suggestive of either naivety or complacency about the potential long-term impact the inculcation of such perceptions might have, including radicalization of the type that will be discussed in the following chapter. To that end, the characterization of concerns about what is taught in K-12 Islamic schools as xenophobic, as Sabith Khan and Shariq Siddiqui argue misses the point that accountability is required from the curriculum of any educational institution and that, if views are being expressed which run contrary to the values of that state, then investigation is not only appropriate but obligatory.[34]

Turning from Islamic schools to the teaching of Islam within the public education system in the United States, there have been a number of incidents in recent years which have shone a light on the way Islam is understood and portrayed. These incidents are interesting from a number of perspectives, but, for the purposes of this book, it is worthwhile briefly touching on a couple of them because they speak to the wider perception of Islam in the United States, as well as providing background for the comments about the issues which have emerged from White House administrations. But before citing these examples, it is worthwhile pausing to note that a false report in April 2017 stated that the Supreme Court had ruled that the teaching of sharia in schools was unconstitutional.[35] At the time of writing, that vote has not yet taken place, but the very fact of the report and the worries that it encapsulates speaks to an issue in US schools concerning what should and should not be taught about Islam (or any other faith) within the public school system.

The first, widely reported issue concerning the teaching of Islam in public schools in the United States we will highlight concerns the decision of the Board of the Unified San Diego School District (BUSDSD) to cooperate with CAIR in teaching some aspects of sharia in classrooms in their district.[36] The decision had been taken as part of an initiative which was seeking to combat Islamophobia that was highlighted in a CAIR report on Californian education published in 2015.[37]

In coming to this decision, the BUSDSD appeared to working within the spirit and letter of the guidelines laid out in the US Department of Education's action plan on combatting religiously based discrimination. The initiative, published in 2016, included new guidelines for educational establishments, an updated form for civil rights complaints and a website to provide easy access to information for religious discrimination issues.[38] The then Assistant Secretary for Civil Rights, Catherine Lharmon commented on the need for the new initiative:

> We will continue to work with schools and communities to stop discrimination and harassment so that all students have an equal opportunity to participate in school no matter who they are, where they come from or which faith, if any, they subscribe to.[39]

Both Lharmon's comments and those of Kevin Beiser, Vice President of the BUSDSD show that for federal officials and school district officers, the place of Islam and Muslims in US education was not just a matter of ensuring a rounded education about different faiths within the public education system but also about the protection of minorities. For Beiser's comments especially linked the defense of learning about sharia in San Diego's schools to initiatives around LGBTQ issues some years previously.[40]

There were misgivings expressed about CAIR as an organization having the authority to go into schools in San Diego to teach on aspects of Islam and there was also wider concern expressed about the principles of relationships between government bodies and any religious organization. As was discussed earlier, this had been a far longer-running issue.

When a parents group filed a lawsuit in San Diego over the matter, the judge in the suit ordered that internal correspondence relating to the matter had to be provided to the court and that material revealed a lack of understanding of who CAIR were as well as little understanding of the messages contained in the portfolio of books and materials they had ordered for distribution in San Diego schools.[41] It therefore could be argued that the BUSDSD had failed in their duty of care to do due diligence on potential collaborative partners. Moreover, it was clear that their concerns about combatting discrimination rose above the need to ensure that the materials presented to pupils were appropriate.

But while their actions can be criticized on these grounds, the aspiration for inclusivity in a rapidly changing social and cultural context is entirely appropriate. Southern California has taken in over 25,000 refugees over the past four years and the BUSDSD appears to have been seeking to shape a local school curriculum which aimed to be culturally friendly.[42] The inclusion of teaching about sharia was seen as a part of that move toward inclusivity.

But the incident raises important questions about what inclusivity should mean in practice?

For example, the BUSDSD-CAIR project included proposals for the adoption of Islamic holidays into the calendar. It also included the requirement for staff training on Islamic culture, including a stipulation that staff also advocate for Muslim culture (however that is defined) as well as being supplied with social science and history materials for teaching purposes. These initiatives would appear to step over the line from inclusivity, to the promotion of one faith. Moreover, the studies done by Liz Jackson on the teaching about Islam in US schools post-9/11 leads to legitimate questions about the necessity for additional materials as she found that the materials on Islam were neutral in tone, even matter of fact, rather than bias against the faith.[43]

Whatever can be reasonably framed as inclusivity work, or crosses into cultural promotion will doubtless be a matter of debate for decades to come. In the meantime, and in response to the criticism it received, the BUSDSD downgraded its relationship with CAIR to an advisory relationship rather than a partnership and has also taken on other advisory relationships with non-Muslim organization. Notably, the American Defense League: a Jewish civil rights organization.[44]

The second issue concerning teaching about Islam in US public schools developed around a worksheet about sharia given to pupils at a school in Indiana. Parents of seventh-grade children at Highland Hills middle school in New Albany, Floyed County raised objections to the worksheet which included a passage which was reputedly written by a woman living in Saudi Arabia called "Ahlima" who expressed her sense of good fortune at living under sharia law in Saudi Arabia. "Ahlima" was looking forward to becoming the second wife of the man she was about to marry and goes on to explain that even though westerners see Muslim women as oppressed for wearing coverings, she believes that Western women are immodest in the way they dress.[45]

One might assume that such a lesson would have been the product of a Saudi-based institution, or groups such as CAIR or the ISNA but that was not the case. Instead, it was the creation of a Christian woman called Sharon Coletti, President of "InspirEd Educators," who said that she created the worksheet to match the requirements of the local education board. The same worksheet had originally been used in 2011 at a school in Smyrna, Georgia where it had also attracted great controversy.[46]

In response to criticism Coletti argued that she was trying to create a worksheet which engendered a sense of the perspective of those who live with sharia and that the views expressed on the worksheet were those she had seen on a television interview with a young Saudi woman shortly before she came to produce the worksheet.

Critics of the worksheet described it as "propaganda" adding that

> the way that the worksheet is left would be like describing how effective Hitler was at nationalizing Germany and creating patriotism but leaving out that he slaughtered 6 million Jews.[47]

The school district said it was reviewing the material, as would be its usual policy in any case where school assignments were the subject of criticism.

In many ways the story is a relatively minor one insofar as it looks as if the material's provider had good intentions, even if she was very naïve about what she was producing. Her intention had been to provide food for thought which would begin a discussion. A review of the company's website and the other educational materials they offer shows that there are a number of class lessons on aspects of Islamic history and culture, including the "Shi'a-Sunni split," "Artifact Project on the Middle East," "The Impact of Zionism on Israel" and a unit entitled "Dubai City and Traditional Muslim Culture." So there is clearly an interest in the Middle East and some of the issues surrounding it along with units about aspects of Muslim life. However, there is no suggestion either on their website, or in their published company accounts that there is any connection with Gulf funding.

The minutes of the meeting of the New Albany Floyd County School Board (NAFCSB) held on January 9, 2017, which dealt with this issue reveal that the members of the board, in the much the same spirit as that of the BUSDSD, were keen to defend the worksheet on the grounds of encouraging greater understanding of Islam.[48] This, in turn, they hoped, would encourage a lessening of negative perceptions of that faith, particularly in relation to seeking to understand what sharia really is. In taking this principled approach the NAFCSB were assisted by the comments of renowned Muslim academic, Professor Asma Afsaruddin (who lectures on Islam in the Department of Near Eastern Languages and Cultures at Indiana State University) She said that there was a lot of misunderstanding of sharia which was playing into the concerns of the parents and went on to characterize sharia as a broad ethical code. She added that interpretation of the sharia could change over time and so can the rules derived from it—just as attitudes and laws about slavery in the United States did. "Notions of democracy and women's rights and human rights are actually now being derived from the Sharia in Muslim-majority societies."[49]

Afsaruddin (who is also a Fellow of the Berkley Centre for Religion, Peace and World Affairs) has written extensively in the field of Islamic political theology. Her books include *Contemporary Issues in Islam* (2015), *Striving in the Path of God: Jihad and Martyrdom in Islamic Thought* (2013), and *Islam, the State and Political Authority: Medieval Issues and Modern Concerns* (2011). In all of them there is some discussion of sharia and it is clear from the arguments she makes in all three (along with her other articles and books), that her comments concerning Highland Hills school were in line with a carefully thought out position.[50]

Whether one agrees with Afsaruddin's characterization of sharia or not, the incident highlighted once again that the events in San Diego and New Albany both came about because the educational boards were concerned about discrimination, rather than about seeking understand the truth about sharia (in this instance) or other aspects of the doctrines and practice of Islam. As such, it could be argued that focus therefore within official circles regarding Islam in the United States was more on the positive projection of the faith, rather than the critical assessment of its pros and cons. When understood within this framework therefore, the actions of both the BUSDSD and the NAFCSB show that both boards were working within the rubric on religious discrimination outlined in the 2016 US Department of Education initiative on religious discrimination cited earlier.

So there is therefore significant tension and debate going on within the United States concerning the content, scope remit of teaching about Islam in the country as well as the nature of what is being taught at Islamic schools. A debate which, in government terms, is being framed within discrimination context.

Inside US government circles, there has been significant concern, over a long period of time, being expressed about the teaching about America and the rest of the world in religious schools in Muslim-majority states. This has mainly been in the context of concerns about anti-American feeling and radicalization questions and in many ways parallel the specific concerns that the British expressed about the influence of Al-Azhar in the 1950s. Indeed, such has been the level of concern that an episode of the highly regarded US political drama *The West Wing* included dialogue in which the prickly head of Communications, "Toby Zeigler," in an argument about the language of a foreign policy speech about to be given by the President "Josiah Bartlett," shouted:

thousands of madrassas teaching nothing, nothing, but the Qur'an and to hate America: who do we see about that? . . . I want those kids to at least look at a globe, be exposed to social sciences, history. Some literature...[51]

"Toby's" frustration was the expression of some concerns which had been felt in real administrations for many years. Indeed, the remarks discussed in chapter 2 by President H. W. Bush also reflected that concern. The basis for this concern can be found in Stephen Brooks's book about US diplomacy and the problem of anti-Americanism. In the book Brooks cites a number of studies and quotes from prominent jihadis concerning the anti-American (anti-Western) content of their classes. By way of example, he quotes Shea and Al-Ahmed's studies of materials in Saudi madrassas which found that

> students are being taught that Christians and Jews and other non-Muslims are "enemies" of the true believer, and, to befriend and show respect only to other true believers, such as Wahabbis. These Saudi state textbooks propound a belief that Christians and Jews and other unbelievers have united in a war against Islam that will ultimately end in the complete destruction of such infidels.[52]

This survey provided anecdotal proof of a dynamic which some believe is prevalent throughout the parts of the world which have Muslim governments. Yet Brooks was quick to point out that, perhaps contrary to expectations and beliefs, there had not been evidence found in Pakistan of the same kind of systematic anti-American, or anti-Western indoctrination.[53] However, Brook's evidence was contradicted by that of Dr. Alex Alexiev, who presented his findings at the Hearing of the Subcommittee on Terrorism, Technology and Homeland Security in 2003. Dr. Alexiev was, at that time was a Senior Fellow at the Center for Security Policy and he argued that

> you are talking about an absolutely astounding amount of money being spent for the specific purpose of promoting, preaching Wahhabi hatred. / They have used this amount of money to take over mosques around the world, to establish Wahhabi control of Islamic institutions, subsidize extremist madrassas in South Asia and elsewhere, control Islamic publishing houses. They currently control probably four-fifths of all Islamic publishing houses. And spend money, a lot of it, on aggressive proselytizing, apart from direct support of terrorism. / What have they achieved for that money? I would submit to you that they have achieved quite a bit. To give you just one example, in Pakistan there are roughly 10,000 extremist madrassas that are run by Deobandi allies of the Wahhabis, and the Deobandis are very similar in their ideology to the Wahhabis. They currently teach, according to Pakistan sources, between one and 1.7 million children, essentially to hate. They do not get much schooling in any subject that is not related to Islamic activities. / It is important to know that of these at least 1 million children, 15 percent are foreigners. So it is not just Pakistan that is affected

by the fact that tens of thousands, hundreds of thousands of kids are taught how to hate, and graduate from these madrassas without any useful education that could be used in the marketplace, but perfectly prepared for a career in jihad and extremist activities. 16,000 of them, for instance, are Arabs that are taught in these schools. / As a result, Pakistan is very close to being a dysfunctional country.[54]

Perhaps, therefore, the issue of anti-Americanism in education is focused more tightly around the Middle East than the rest of the parts of the world where there are Muslim-majority states. In the short term this probably is a reflection of the imposition of various dictatorships bypassed US governments in the region in order to provide secure mineral resources. For example, Dilip Hiro details the support provided to the Shah of Iran and Saudi Arabia, as well as other states in the MENA region.[55] However, in the shorter term, the creation of Israel and the writings of the Egyptian and Muslim Brotherhood ideologue Sayyid Qutb (the second highest-selling Muslim author after Maududi), have probably been more of a contributing factor to anti-Americanism.[56] In his book *The America I have Seen* (1951) which he wrote following his time studying in Colorado, Qutb assessed the American culture which he saw around him and concluded that its influence was pervasive and pernicious. As such, it was something to be rejected: especially what Qutb saw as the lax attitudes to relations between men and women which he observed as well as Jazz, which he was, apparently, particularly disturbed by.[57]

However, whatever the truth as far as systematic educational anti-American indoctrination in the Middle East and other Muslim-majority states, there can be no doubting the depth of anti-American feeling across multiple regions as starkly displayed in this sobering opening to Gentzkow and Shapiro's 2004 article concerning anti-Americanism in the Muslim-majority parts of the globe:

> America has an image problem. Only 1 percent of people surveyed in June 2003 in Jordan or the Palestinian Authority expressed a favorable opinion of the United States. Favorability ratings elsewhere in the Middle East were almost all below 30 percent. Osama bin Laden was amongst the top three leaders most often trusted to "do the right thing" by survey respondents in Indonesia, Jordan, Morocco, Pakistan and the Palestinian Authority (Pew Research Center, 2003).[58]

So, whether anti-Americanism is the result of state inculcation or not, the problem of anti-Americanism is certainly clear and apparent for the US public and policymakers alike to see.[59] Indeed, Cifci and Tezcur's 2016 fascinating study on the impact of Anti-Americanism on Muslim's perceptions of other states in the Middle East strongly suggests that connections with America also lower the esteem felt by Muslims for other Muslim states who are seen to be too closely allied to the United States. For example, Iran's opposition to the United States was a significant factor in her higher rating in the data analysis they did.[60]

This anti-American feeling, whether inculcated through teaching as evidenced in Saudi Arabia, or through a broader buildup of resentment which had been the result of the factors described earlier, has been a source of concern both in terms of international relations policy and domestic policy considerations.

CONCLUSION

From a policy perspective, both the case of the Zakariya school in the UK and the AGA in the United States highlight the relative lack of oversight being exercised over the curriculum content found in some faith-based Islamic schools. This lack of oversight is, to some degree, consistent with the desire not to limit free speech in a liberal democratic context and does connect to questions of religious freedom.[61] However it also raises important questions about the scope of the oversight role of governments on both sides of the Atlantic for, while concerns about the schools focused on the welfare of the children in the physical sense, there appeared to be a lack of engagement with the content of the curriculum.[62]

In the United States, it was interesting to note that the core concern of education staff and officials was around discrimination rather than critical engagement with ideologies. This probably reflected the limited scope for religious engagement of any kind for the government-mandated in the US constitution, yet, as was seen in the chapter on Economics, this has not prevented US administrations from exhorting the benefits of Islamic financing.

In both countries there was a high level of concern about the teaching taking place at schools in Muslim-majority countries along with the growing influence of certain institutions and the ideology they espouse. This concern was couched in terms of geostrategic considerations rather than ideological considerations.

In terms of the overall consideration of this book, therefore, officials and educationalists displayed less interest in seeking to understand the doctrines of Islam in relation to how they impacted their own contexts and more interest in the social impact of perceptions of Islam in the public realm. This is consistent with the overarching desire of governments to maintain and improve harmonious, cohesive societies, but it did open officials to potentially naïve choices about the partners they chose in order to facilitate that cohesion. And, from the perspective of what engagement with Islam in the realm of education contributed to the perception of the faith within government; the impression is that Islam is not only discriminated against but also the potential source of strong identity-focused segregationist agendas.

NOTES

1. See Ali Qadir (2013) "Between Secularism's: Islam and the Institutionalization of Modern Higher Education in Mid-Nineteenth Century British India," *British Journal of Religious Education* Vol. 35, Iss. 2, pp. 125–139. See also Robert Invermee, *Secularism, Islam and Education in India, 1830–1910*. London, New York: Routledge, 2015; Peter Gottschalk, *Religion, Science and Empire: Classifying Hinduism and Islam in British India*. Oxford, New York: OUP, 2012.

2. Barbara Metcalf, *Islamic Revival in British India: Deoband, 1860–1900*. Princeton: Princeton University Press, 2014, p. 87.

3. Metcalf, *Deoband*, p. 126, p. 134.

4. Gail Minault and David Lelyveld (1974) "The Campaign for a Muslim University 1898–1920," *Modern Asian Studies* Vol. 8, Iss. 2, pp. 145–189.

5. Invernee, *Secularism, Education and Islam in India*, pp. 19–40; and Shan Muhammad, *Education and Politics: From Sir Syed to the Present Day: The Aligarh School*. New Delhi: APH Publishing Corporation, 2002.

6. Robert Long and Paul Bolton, *Faith Schools: FAQs*. House of Commons Briefing Paper Number 06972. October 14, 2015.

7. ED/172/578/9. F2.

8. Ansari, *Infidel*, pp. 326–335.

9. Hanif Kureishi, *Collected Essays*. London: Faber and Faber, 2011, pp. 44–46.

10. Anon, "Trojan Horse Report Finds 'Aggressive Islamist Ethos' in Schools," *BBC News*, http://www.bbc.co.uk/news/uk-england-birmingham-28349706.

11. Peter Clarke, *Report into Allegations Concerning Birmingham Schools Arising from the "Trojan Horse" Letter*. HC 576. London: HMSO, 2014, p. 5. The original letter with its attachments can be found at Annex 2 of the report.

12. The public debate was centered around two broad narratives with the vast majority of responses in the public domain falling somewhere between the two: either that what had happened in Birmingham was not only verifiable, but was also just the tip of the iceberg, or that the claims were highlighted exaggerated and deliberately designed to stoke fear and prejudice. One of the more balanced responses (tending toward the latter rather than the former) was an article published three years after the story initially broke by Samira Shackle, "Trojan Horse: The Real Story behind the Fake "Islamic Plot" to Take Over Schools," *The Guardian*, September 1, 2017.

13. See Clarke, *Allegations Concerning Birmingham Schools*, pp. 33, 35–36, 39–46.

14. Ibid., p. 48.

15. John Holmwood, "Investigate the Birmingham Trojan Horse Affair," www.opendemocracy.net October 2, 2018.

16. The course and potential impact of the Trojan Horse Affair are analyzed in John Holmwood and Therese O'Toole, *Countering Extremism in British Schools? The Truth about the Birmingham Trojan Horse Affair.* Bristol: Polity Press, 2018. See also Shamin Miah, *Muslims, Schooling and Security: Trojan Horse, Prevent and Radical Politics.* London: Palgrave MacMillan, 2017.

17. SSA513/05 F1.

18. The events and impact of them are analyzed in Derek Varble's *The Suez Crisis.* New York: Rosen Publishing, 2009.

19. See J.A. Hail, *Britain's Foreign Policy in Egypt and Sudan 1947–1956.* Reading: Ithaca Press, 1996.

20. Ibid., F18.

21. Ibid., F103.

22. See Karen Keyworth, *Islamic Schools of the United States: Data-Based Profiles,* May 18, 2011, https://www.ispu.org/islamic-schools-of-the-united-states-data-based-profiles/.

23. This is discussed in Yvonne Haddad, Farid Senzai and Jane Smith, *Educating the Muslims of America.* Oxford, New York: OUP, 2012.

24. The searchable website for the US Department of Education makes for fascinating reading in relation to these guidelines. http://www2.ed.gov/policy/gen/guid/religionandschools/prayer_guidance.html.

25. Walter Dellinger, "Religious Expression in Public Schools," Testimony before the Committee on the Judiciary of the United States Senate, October 25, 1995, p. 1.

26. James Fraser, *Between Church and State: Religion and Public Education in a Multicultural America.* New York: St. Martin's Press, 2000, p. 3.

27. Ibid., p. 243.

28. See Donald Drakeman, *Church State and Original Intent.* Cambridge, New York: CUP, 2010, pp. 87–89.

29. AGA website is at http://www.iefnj.org/.

30. See http://www.iefnj.org/OurSchools/AlGhazalyHighSchool/Curriculum.aspx.

31. Ibid.

32. See Lorenzo Vidino, *The New Muslim Brotherhood in the West.* New York: Columbia University Press, 2010, pp. 172–176.

33. Cynthia Farahat (No Date) "Islamists with Direct Ties to Terrorists Lobby Congress," https://www.meforum.org/MiddleEast Forum/media/MEFLibrary/Muslim-Advocacy-Day-Dossier.pdf.

34. Sabith Khan and Shariq Siddiqui, *Islamic Education in the United States and the Evolution of Muslim Non-Profit Institutions.* Cheltenham, Northampton (MA): Edward Elgar Publishing, 2017. "Introduction" p. 1.

35. Anon, "Supreme Court Sides with Trump—This Changes Everything," www.usapoliticstoday.com, April 7, 2017. The report has since been removed from the website.

36. Jim Kouri, "San Diego School Board: CAIR to Teach Your Kids Sharia Law," www.newswithviews.com, April 20, 2017.

37. Douglas Ernst, "San Diego School District to Create Muslim Safe Spaces, Boost Islam Lessons to Combat Bullying," *The Washington Times,* April 6, 2017.

38. Anon, "US Department of Education Takes Action to Address Religious Discrimination," *US Department of Education Press Office Release.* July 22, 2016. https ://www2.ed.gov/about/offices/list/ocr/ religion.html.

39. Ibid.

40. Beiser's opinions were quoted in Elliot Spagat, "San Diego Schools Defend Effort to Fight Islamophobia," *The Philadelphia Tribune*, April 30, 2017.

41. Citizens for Quality Education, San Diego et al v San Diego Unified School District, Case 3:17-cv-01054-BAS-JMA, February 20, 2018. All the evidence, including the internal correspondence can be found at https://www.fcdflegal.org/wp-content/uploads/2018/02/QE-SD-v-SDUSD-Memo-P.I.-Index-of-Exhibits_2.pdf.

42. Further data on immigration to California can be found at the website of the Public Policy Institute of California. Hans Johnson and Sergio Sanchez (No Date) "Just the Facts: Immigrants in California," https://www.ppic.org/publication/immigrants-in-california/.

43. Liz Jackson (2011) "Islam and Muslims in US Public Schools since September 11, 2001," *Journal of Religious Education* Vol. 106, Iss. 2, pp. 162–180.

44. Meghan Burks, "Judge Considers Injunction against Anti-Islamophobia Program in San Diego Schools," www.kpbs.org July, 18, 2018.

45. Kirsten Clark "Worksheet on 'Sharia Law' Irks School Parents," www.courier-journal.com, January 17, 2017.

46. Ibid.

47. Ibid., quote of Dean Holt, one of the protesting parents.

48. The board meeting minutes can be found at http://www.nafcs.k12.in.us/wpcontent/uploads/2017/02/minutes-of-1-9-17.pdf.

49. Clark "Worksheet."

50. See Asma Afsaruddin, *Contemporary Issues in Islam.* Edinburgh: Edinburgh University Press, 2015; *Striving in the Path of God: Jihad and Martyrdom in Islamic Thought.* Oxford, New York: OUP, 2013; (ed), *Islam, the State and Political Authority: Medieval Issues and Modern Concerns.* New York: Palgrave Macmillan, 2011.

51. The quote and surrounding contextual discussion can be found at https://www.youtube.com/watch?v=iZYs2UpLYAI.

52. Nina Shea and Ali al-Akhmed's findings were updated in 2009 and 2011. The collected knowledge and evidence of their work was then included in a Committee on Foreign Affairs Hearing on July 19, 2017. Published as "Saudi Arabia's Troubling Educational Curriculum": *Hearing before the Subcommittee on Terrorism, Non-Proliferation and Trade of the Committee on Foreign Affairs, House of Representatives, One Hundred and Fifteenth Congress, First Session.* Dated July 19, 2017, Serial Number 115-46. https://www.gpo.gov/fdsys/pkg/CHRG-115hhrg263 12/pdf/CHRG-115hhrg26312.pdf. See also Stephen Brooks, *Anti-Americanism and the Limits of Public Diplomacy: Winning Hearts and Minds?* Abingdon, New York: Routledge, 2016.

53. Brooks, *Hearts and Minds,* p. 49.

54. Testimony of Alex Alexeiv, "Hearing before the Subcommittee on Terrorism, Technology and Homeland Security of the Committee on the Judiciary," *United States Senate,* 108th Congress, June 26, 2003, pp. 15–19.

55. Hiro, *Cold War in the Islamic World,* Chapter 3.

56. The impact of the creation of Israel on Muslim perceptions of the United States are discussed in a number of books including Steven Kull, *Feeling Betrayed: The Roots of Muslim Anger at America*. Washington DC: Brookings Institute Press, 2011. However, it is worthwhile noting that, although the US state to recognize Israel, there were many "Arabists" in the US State Department who favored the Arabs, such as Loy Henderson. See Robert Kaplan, *The Arabists: The Romance of an American Elite*. New York: The Free Press, 1993. See also William Pugh, *American Encounters with Arabs: The "Soft Power" of US Diplomacy in the Middle East*. Westport (CT): Greenwood Publishing, 2005.

57. John Calvert (2000) ""The World is an Undutiful Boy!": Sayyid Qutb's American Experience," *Islam and Christian-Muslim Relations* Vol. 11, Iss. 1, pp. 87–103.

58. Matthew Gentzkow and Jesse Shapiro (2004) "Media, Education and Anti-Americanism in the Muslim World," *Journal of Economic Perspectives* Vol. 18, Iss. 3, pp. 117–133.

59. The evidence of that knowledge is covered in this chapter, but it is also worth noting that Gentzkow and Shapiro quote surveys on American public respondents which also suggest the same level of distrust and dislike. Ibid., p. 117.

60. Sabri Ciftci and Gunes Tezcur (2016) "Soft Power, Religion and Anti-Americanism in the Middle East," *Foreign Policy Analysis* Vol. 12, Iss. 3, pp. 374–394.

61. While it is an important and not unrelated issue to this book, religious freedom is such a complex policy question that it could constitute a separate publication and, were it to be included in this book, could potentially have served as a distraction from its core analysis. Two helpful books in the understanding the issues raised by "religious freedom," especially in recent years, both of which are by Roger Trigg's *Equality, Freedom and Religion*. Oxford: OUP, 2012 and *Religious Diversity: Philosophical and Political Dimensions*. Cambridge: CUP, 2014.

62. This issue is given extensive treatment in Maureen O'Neill, *Muslim Mothers: Pioneers of Islamic Education in America*. Unpublished PhD thesis, College of Notre Dame, Maryland, 2010; Hakim Rashid and Muhammad Zakiyyah (1992) "The Sister Clara Muhammad Schools: Pioneers in the Development of Islamic Education in America," *Journal of Negro Education* Vol. 61, Iss. 2, pp. 178–185; Innes Bowen, *Medina in Birmingham, Najaf in Brent: Inside British Islam*. London: Hurst and Company, 2014.

Chapter 8

Radicalism

Of all the arenas of Anglo-US engagement with Islam this book engages with, it is the issue of radicalization which is the most high profile. The 9/11 and 7/7 attacks, along with a number of smaller deadly incidents, have ensured that concerns about the impact of radicalization have required an ongoing policy response from the United States, United Kingdom, and other Western governments. As was noted back in the Introduction, concerns about the impact of radicalization have been an important factor in the election of Donald Trump and the British "Brexit" vote in 2016. Indeed, the setting up of the US Department of Homeland Security and inauguration of the UK's CONTEST strategy can be directly traced to policy concerns around radicalization, homegrown terrorism, and lately, the "foreign fighter" phenomenon.

This chapter will assess the American and British government's responses to Islamic Extremism (IE) from 2000 to the present day by analyzing their Countering (Violent) Extremism (C(V)E) strategies and using that analysis as a basis to discuss what the British and US governments have, either by public speech, or implicit messaging in their policies, understood about Islam and Muslims.

Before discussing the policy responses themselves it is worthwhile noting that the very use of the term "Islamic Extremism" has revived echoes of the discussion in chapter 2 in which we saw that leaders in both the United States and United Kingdom sought to find language which separated the faith of Islam from the actions of the terrorists in the 9/11 era.[1] This process has been all the more important in relation to homegrown terrorism as any discussion of an inherent link between the faith and the actions of those calling themselves "jihadis" would have a direct implication for Muslim citizens in those countries.[2] In the political world, therefore, politicians have fought hard to ensure that any concerns they raise about the possible presence of jihadis in their countries are very carefully couched.

In the academic world similar dynamics have emerged. These debates around the connection (if any) between the faith of Islam and the actions of "jihadis," while happening in a distinct space away from the public and policy rhetoric which defines the political sphere are not detached from it. This is because academics have frequently been called upon to lend their expertise to policy discussion in this sphere perhaps even more than others. This is not a new phenomenon; as has been seen in previous chapters, eminent experts such as Bernard Lewis, Thomas Arnold, and Robert Serjeant (among others) were called upon to lend their advice over the decades, indeed centuries, past.

Any discussion of the perceptions of academics on IE generally would be far too complex to discuss here; however, a sense of the diversity of opinion can be seen in the fact that, for example, Githens-Mazer and Lambert argue that any suggestion of a link between terrorism incidents or extremist ideologies and the religion of "Islam" was "exestentializing red herrings that are prone to miss the point."[3] Other eminent scholars of Islam such as John Esposito (whose testimony to Congress in 1980 was discussed in chapter 3) have sought a more nuanced views rather than binary ones, arguing that religion is one among a number of motivations of those calling themselves "jihadis" while, at the same time highlighting the fact that the actions are perpetrated by a comparatively small number of Muslims and that anti-Americanism of the kind that was seeking to be addressed by successive US presidents in chapter 2 and by government officials in chapter 7 was also a highly significant factor.[4]

It's worth noting that outside of the Anglo-American milieu that this book is focused upon, other leaders in states that have suffered jihadi attacks such as Germany's Angela Merkel and France's then-president Francois Hollande have taken slightly differing approaches to suggesting that there might be any link between the faith of Islam and the activities of the terrorists. For example, in a speech at the Munich Security Conference in February 2017 Angela Merkel specified that "Islam was not the source of terrorism."[5] Yet, Francois Hollande was less keen to make such a decisive separation between the faith and the actions of the terrorists. Instead he used the term "Islamic Terrorism" after the attack in Nice and made a speech in which he exhorted French Muslims to take steps to ensure that extremism did not find any foothold in their communities, particularly in relation to the preaching in some French mosques.[6]

Across the academic and political world therefore, the issue of homegrown "jihadism" has heightened an already delicate debate around questions of loyalty and compatibility between Islam and Western democracies in which there remain multiple competing perspectives. Therefore, as this chapter explores the perceptions of US and British policymakers in this vital arena, it is worthwhile remembering the underlying security implications that accompany them.

US AND BRITISH COUNTER-EXTREMISM STRATEGIES

CONTEST[ED]: British Counter-Extremism Initiatives

The British government adopted CONTEST and its four strands of work (Prevent, Pursue, Protect, Prepare) in 2003 and published a version for public review in 2006.[7] At its heart was the belief in the need to separate community work from counterterrorism work.

Even though, following review, the strategy was recast in 2011 to engage more directly with extremist ideologies (and despite changes in government which had differing philosophical perspectives), this core separation of community work from intelligence-led work has remained. This is not to say that Muslim communities have necessarily felt this to be the case: criticisms that the community—based element of the strategy was really simply a cover for intelligence work have remained.[8] But, the strategy has sought to delineate between the two from the outset.

There had been an earlier attempt to deal with terrorism post-9/11 when emergency laws were passed to allow for indefinite detention without trial, but they were successfully challenged as contrary to Human Rights in 2004.[9] Yet it was the attacks on 7/7 and 21/7 that threw into sharp focus the need for a strategy to engage specifically with homegrown extremism. It was this need which gave rise to CONTEST, the new Counter Terrorism Strategy with its four workstreams: Protect, Prepare, Prevent, and Pursue.[10] It has been the "Prevent" element which has been the cornerstone of the community-based element of the CE strategy and it is this element which will be the focus of the discussion here rather than the intelligence-led elements.

The Prevent strategy became the purview of the Department for Communities and Local Government under the auspices of the Home Office.[11] In addition to the community-based approaches government developed, new legislation was introduced making it a criminal offense to glorify terrorism and extending the grounds for proscription of an organization. This action enabled the UK government to add a number of organizations to proscription lists including Hizb ut-Tahrir and pursue legislation which would allow for the closure of places of worship which were fermenting extremism. At the same time, the taking of British citizenship had added to it, the requirement to attend a citizenship ceremony. The most controversial aspect of these measures was the move to extend periods of pretrial detention: a measure which had profound implications for the principles established in the Habaeus Corpus Act (1689).[12]

What eventually emerged as the Counter Terrorism Act (2006) set a new limit of 28 days detention without trial and created the new, and rather ill-defined offense of "encouraging terrorism" as well as endorsing the New Labor government's grounds for widening proscription criteria.[13] Not surprisingly, criticism of the lack of clarity in the Bill's language and the difficulties with implementation they posed meant that the law was deemed counterproductive by commentators and academics alike.[14]

Chapter 2 already quoted the publicly stated feelings of British prime ministers on terrorist-related issues up to David Cameron. Their remarks showed that there had been a shift in thinking around perceptions of the link between some of the ideologies embedded within Islam and the actions of terrorists who described themselves as "jihadis" within government circles. This internal shift was publicly manifest in the statement made following the review of the previous Labor government's Prevent strategy in 2011, when the then Home Secretary Theresa May announced

> [T]he Prevent programme that we inherited from the previous Government was flawed. It confused Government policy to promote integration with Government policy to prevent terrorism. It failed to tackle the extremist ideology that not only undermines the cohesion of our society, but inspires would-be terrorists to seek to bring death and destruction to our towns and cities. In trying to reach out to those at risk of extremism, funding sometimes even reached the very extremist organizations that Prevent should have been confronting. We will not make the same mistakes.[15]

Leaving aside the validity or otherwise of Theresa May's statement about the perceived flaws of the previous government's approach to the issue, this shift toward an attempt to create an explicit strategy to confront the root ideologies behind extremism, rather than simply seeking to engage with the socioeconomic problems which could also provide a pathway to extremism, marked a distinct break from the previous strategy and strongly suggested a shift in policymaker's thinking about engaging with radicalization issues. As part of that reorientation, the language of counter-extremism was shifted from "Countering Violent Extremism," to simply "Countering-Extremism."[16] Jeffrey Bale of the Terrorism Research Initiative argued that this change had been too slow in coming and that, targeting the ideology should have been an integral element of the Prevent strategy from the beginning.[17] Nevertheless, whether judged as too slow or not, this subtle, but important change in language suggests that there appears to have been a growing realization within Whitehall that those who were grooming the extremists had to be using ideological arguments to persuade their followers to not only kill but be willing to die in the process.

It seems therefore that policymakers in the UK have developed their analysis of the causes of radicalization over the past decade. This evolution has been characterized by a slow but steadily move away from a complete disassociation of the Islamic faith from the acts of those claiming to fight in its name, to a more nuanced position which acknowledges that not all Muslims understood their faith in the same way and, therefore, cannot all be held responsible for those actions. As such, one could posit that the emerging perception of Islam which has developed over the period in British government circles was one that understood that there were multiple competing ideological streams within the faith, some of which lend themselves more naturally to what have been termed "extremist activities" than others.

This evolution in thinking has been underpinned with recent studies on the drivers behind "extremism" and "radicalization." Perhaps the most significant of these was that done by the highly regarded British defense think tank, the Royal United Services Institute (RUSI) in 2015. It sought to capture the current debate in the CVE field in their chapter which surveyed hypotheses on the drivers of extremism.[18] Although it engaged with international, rather than homegrown extremism, and although it was engaging with generic extremism, rather than specific ideological extremisms, the paper was valuable as it sought to offer differing weights to each of the factors which have been associated with fostering, or driving extremism. In the review (which was commissioned by the British government's Department of International Development) hypotheses were cited and then given a grading which related to whether the hypothesis was supported by evidence. Hypotheses "3" and "4" respectively dealt with religious and identity search, both of which were categorized as "strongly supported" in the evidence. Other hypotheses with "strongly supported" caveats were "government failure to provide welfare and health," "absence of peace and security which leads people to grasp any offer of stability," and "discrimination along religious or ethnic fault lines."[19] What order of priority any of these had in relation to one another was not discussed, but the list of drivers (or factors) RUSI cited would certainly have been familiar to the vast majority of people working in the CVE field. It was in the light of their analysis of the principal drivers in IE that RUSI proposed a model of extremism factors along with an intervention model designed to combat the development of extremism.

The briefing paper on counter-extremism policy for the British Houses of Parliament summarized the British government's approach thus:

> Since the terrorist attacks in New York on 11 September 2001, the UK's approach to combating terrorism has evolved from focusing on the threat posed

by foreign nationals affiliated with Al-Qaida and related groups, to the threat from "home grown" terrorists. In recent years, government policy has increasingly sought to confront the underlying causes of terrorist behavior, including extremist ideologies.[20]

Whether this revised approach will produce more success in terms reducing, even ending, the threat posed by Islamic extremism remains to be seen, but it is clear that attempts since 2015 and the election of the Conservative government have stalled. This is partly due to external factors, such as the policy demands of Brexit but also because of the lack of agreement on the definition of "extremism" as proposed in legislation.

START[ED]: US Counter-Extremism Initiatives

American problems with "homegrown terrorism," or Islamic extremism materialized later than in the UK, although homegrown "extremism" in terms of right-wing and survivalist incidents had seen standoffs between lone citizens or groups, and law enforcement officers for decades. Incidents such as the Oklahoma Bombing by Timothy McVeigh in 1995 had been the most high-profile attack in a long line which, it could be argued, stretched back into the early years of the Republic.[21] In relation to Islamic extremism specifically, even before the World Trade Center attacks and 9/11, there had been concerns expressed about Islamic extremism in the shape of the Nation of Islam.

A secret memorandum sent to the White House administration of Richard Nixon in 1972 expressed concern at a report that the Nation of Islam (NoI) had reached an agreement with the Libyan government for an interest-free loan of $3 million to fund its activities.[22] In the memorandum the NoI was described as a "radical black organization." before going on to describe its views, internal political disunity and its developing ties with Libya.[23] The memorandum was written in the context of recent (at that time) reports of a shootout between a group of armed black Muslims and police in Louisiana. The *New York Times* carried a very vivid description of the incident on January 16, 1972, which reported the Mayor of Baton Rouge's accusation that the participants were black Muslims from Chicago.[24] In April the same year a police officer was shot and fatally wounded in front of a NoI mosque in Harlem, New York.[25] Notwithstanding the potential for the stories to have been embellished and distorted, it is not surprising that John Dean's memo in February 1972 should have used that description. Furthermore, in the context of this book these incidents, although very isolated clearly helped lay a perception in the minds of American officials that homegrown manifestations of Islam had the potential to be subversive force, whether it took an armed form or not.

Yet, remarkably perhaps, twenty years later, one of Elijah Muhammed's sons, Warith Deen Muhammed, became the first Muslim to offer prayers on the Senate floor.[26]

The evolution of this shift in political perception from "radicals" to "establishment" is remarkable and points to the fact that the term "radical," or "extremist" is generally predicated on both the perceptions of an administration and pervading public attitudes of what are considered appropriate (or not) attitudes toward society and state. In this it is reminder of one of the themes of the first chapter of this book: the cultural and political shift within both America and Britain over the period covered in *Courting Islam*.

Moving on to post-9/11 "Islamic Extremism," the US approach to homegrown extremists, as with the British strategy, has focused on a community-based approach to engagement with extremism. The US government's strategy, first announced under President Obama in 2011, has been specifically directed against "Violent Extremism" (VE) and has maintained that stance even with the change in administration. The three core elements of the strategy have been first, "Building Awareness": which is a federally coordinated and directed program of equipping state and local institutions in the drivers of, and signs of, extremism.[27] Second, "Countering Extremist Narratives" which is defined as offering alternative narratives to those being inculcated by extremist groomers and third, "Emphasizing Community-Lead Intervention" which seeks to encourage and empower communities to make interventions themselves to prevent any member of their community being drawn into extremism.[28]

The strategy has had two fundamental premises: that communities themselves provide the best hope for finding solutions to the IE problem and that, countering (CVE) is best done at a local level so that the most appropriate solutions can be found. That being said, the post of CVE Coordinator at the Department of Homeland of Security (DHS) was created in 2011which strongly suggests, despite the accent upon locally driven solutions in the strategy, central government has become an important player in CVE efforts.[29] However, this role has been as a facilitator and expertise-provider for local efforts, rather than making the issue a centrally managed effort.

Three local pilot schemes have been created in cities across the United States to test the model: Los Angeles, Boston and the Twin Cities. The choice of each of these three is interesting given that both the Great Lakes area and New York both have very sizable (and more established) Muslim populations. However, the Department of Justice website cites these cities' "existing achievements with community engagement" as the reason why they were chosen for the initial scheme although there has been some question as to the measures of success of the scheme.[30] For example, Erroll Southers argued that the Los Angeles program has fallen into the same problems as have bedeviled the UK Prevent program: that, rather than encouraging cooperation, it has instead caused suspicion of the program's motivations.[31] This concern was echoed and expanded upon in a briefing note with policy recommendations written by Robert McKenzie, Visiting Fellow in US Relations with the Muslim World at Foreign Policy's Centre for Middle East Policy (which was addressed to whomever was to be the winning candidate of the then forthcoming US presidential election). He had two principal concerns. First, that

> the Obama administration's domestic CVE policy has strained relations with an entire religious community, in large part because its policy perceives American Muslims through a security lens.[32]

His second concern was that, even five years (at his time of writing) into the policy initiative, there had been little research or evidence produced on the drivers of extremism which, in his eyes hampered CVE initiatives from the outset.[33]

For both McKenzie and Southers therefore, the net results of the pilot programs had been the increase in suspicion of the government program's aims, rather than the increase in cooperation in fighting IE that had been the program's goal. Their observations concerning the results of the government program were borne out in separate studies done by Esseissah and Kleinmann.[34]

Just before the US presidential election in 2016, two documents were published by the Department of Homeland Security: *Security Strategy for Countering Violent Extremism* and *Strategic Implementation Plan for Empowering Local Partners to Prevent Violent Extremism in the United States* (SIP-PVE).[35] (Dept Homeland Security, 2016) The Security strategy, as the name suggests, focused upon the intelligence elements of CVE, whereas the SIP-PVE focused on community engagement. It reiterated the fundamental and consistent consensus on both sides of the Atlantic that "resilient communities" were the best preventative force in CVE. In this context, the DHS contended that it was the protection of civil rights and liberties which built the kind of trust that would enable communities to resist those who would seek to divide and lead people into extremism.[36] The three facets of that strategy were essentially the same as had been articulated in 2011: research and analysis, Engagement and Technical Assistance, Interventions and Communications and Digital Strategy and the tone of the strategy appeared to be geared toward "wooing" or "courting" the communities through a combination of propaganda and making efforts to show that they were being treated the same as other communities.

An essential element of the strategy remained the offering of grants to local community organizations engaged in CVE work at grassroots level and while the fundamentals of the DHS strategy have remained the same even with the change of president, it is the groups who have been funded which is being reviewed. Until such time as that review process is completed, the funding has been frozen.

There have been reports that the administration of President Trump is planning to change the CVE's name to "Countering Islamic Extremism," but no official confirmation of that has been made.

At state level however, the most high-profile outworking of the counterterrorism activity has been seen in the coverage of the New York Police Department's Zone Assessment Unit (ZAU).

The ZAU was originally named The Demographics Unit when it was established in 2003 by Lawrence Sanchez (a CIA officer seconded to NYPD). Its aim was to identify the mundane locations where terrorists could blend into society and continue their activities without the risk of the kind of exposure that would come from living in a more integrated area.[37] Officers and detectives looked for hot spots of radicalization which, when kept under observation might give the police an early warning about impending terrorist activity. The ZAU typically comprised about a dozen members and focused its operations on twenty-eight, what they termed, "ancestries of interest." According to the online New York magazine portal www.NYMag.com,

> Nearly all were Muslim. There were Middle Eastern and South Asian countries such as Pakistan, Iran, Syria, and Egypt. Former Soviet states like Uzbekistan and Chechnya were included because of their large Muslim populations. The last "ancestry" on the list was "American Black Muslim."[38]

Members of the unit went out to befriend Muslim-owned businesses with the aim of getting a sense of Muslim feelings about America and its foreign policy. Over time the ZAU was able to build up a thorough picture of the patterns of life among Muslim communities in the city. They were able to establish "where Albanian men played chess in the afternoon, where Egyptians watched soccer and where South Asians played cricket" in order to tap into intelligence gathering seams.[39]

However, for all the intelligence gathered (and the two lawsuits endured), the unit's activities did not generate a single useful lead according to the NYPD themselves. Perhaps this was due to the fact that there were some severe misunderstandings of North American Muslim culture(s). For, in the long chapter by Apuzzo and Goldman last summer, an unnamed police official defended the eavesdropping activities in the mosques particularly by saying that

> it [mosque] plays a bigger role in society and its day-to-day activities. They pray five times a day. They're [Muslims] there all the time. If something bad is going

to happen, they're going to hear about it in the mosques. It's not as sinister as it sounds. We're just going into the mosques. We just want to know what they're saying.[40]

Yet the numbers don't back up the strategy. According to Ahmed Nassef, the cofounder and editor in chief of MuslimWakeUp.com, less than 7 percent of American Muslims attend mosque regularly (compared with 38% of American Christians who attend church weekly). Furthermore, it has been recognized even by Imams themselves that many (if not most) of their colleagues are very out of touch with their congregations.[41] So the idea that the mosque is a good place to find out about upcoming plots is somewhat misguided, although it is also only fair to point out that the ZAU also went to bars, cafes and shops for information.

New York police commissioner Bratton ended the ZAU activities and his decision, although undoubtedly motivated in part by the negative press the program was receiving, could also be seen as part of a cultural shift away from the intelligence-led counterterrorist activity that has characterized the past decade, to a more cooperative Counter Radicalization strategy. The NYPD's spokesperson, Stephen Davis said that

> In the future, we will gather that [terrorist] information, if necessary, through direct contact between the police precincts and the representatives of the communities they serve.[42]

In many ways this community-based prevention strategy makes common sense in relation to the fact that the NYPD scheme appears to have had no discernible advantages intelligence-wise. However, the reporting suggests that underlying the change in tactics was not a search for improved preventative measures but rather concerns about improving relations with Muslim communities who had been complaining about the operation. Just before the decision to close the operation in New York was made, Commissioner Bratton had met with representatives from the Muslim communities (on what basis they were representing all Muslims in the city is another question) and other senior staff. One of the representatives, Linda Sarsour of the Arab-American Association of New York said

> The Demographics Unit [initial title for the ZAU] created psychological warfare in our community.[43]

The two lawsuits that had been filed against the ZAU's activities also expressed the bad feeling that the practice engendered.

Though a desire to "reach out" to Muslim groups with a more open approach to Counter Radicalization which incorporates the communities rather than simply investigates them has merit, there is a danger inherent in this changed tactic which is not difficult to discern. It lies in the deepening of distrust of Muslims for authorities at a time when those who would seek to radicalize Muslims argue that the only form of legitimate government is an Islamic one.[44] Thus, whatever one might say to counter the arguments of such radicalizers, the core fact remains that actions such as those of the New York Police Department (and other Police departments in North America), increase the sense of Muslim's dislocation from society at the same moment when its legitimacy is being questioned.[45]

Clearly, policing in a democratic state cannot involve the same tools as those employed by a totalitarian one if it is to retain any semblance of moral authority. Yet the difficulty for US intelligence officials grappling with the specter of terrorist fermentation and a set of communities who are deeply distrustful of the societies around them is how to encourage integration in the long-term without permitting multiple terrorist atrocities in the short term. Yet, perhaps the most damaging aspect of this work, certainly from the point of view of this book at least, was that it sent the overwhelming signal that their perceptions of Islam and Muslims was that the Muslim communities within New York could not be trusted to root out the problem peoples and ideologies themselves.

The RUSI chapter cited earlier referenced the USAid analysis of extremism factors found in their paper *Guide to the Drivers of Violent Extremism* which refutes the idea of socioeconomic factors as key drivers to extremism and unpacks instead the what it sees as the seven political drivers of extremism.[46] Its conclusions were:

> There can be no general theory about why and how the turn to VE occurs, because the answer to that question will vary from one setting to another. A detailed and nuanced understanding of the context, therefore, represents the first step toward the development of adequate policy responses to stem the flow of volunteers into VE organizations, deter community support for those organizations, and/or create an environment that makes it harder on them to operate.[47]

This analysis, which was done at national and international level clearly takes a different view to the one which the NYPD took and therefore is a good example of the diversity of opinion within the US government both of the relationship between the faith of Islam and the jihadis, as well as the perception of the willingness to Muslim communities to engage with the problem. However, although the differences in perception between USAid and the NYPD are being discussed here, it can be confidently asserted that this diversity of opinion also exists within other branches of both US and British administrations.

ANALYZING THE DIFFERENT APPROACHES AND THEIR PERCEPTIONS OF ISLAM

There are really two main differences between the American and British engagements with IE. First, the United States' approach to C(V)E issues has highlighted international cooperation in a way that is generally absent in the British strategy. For example, the White House briefing paper on the 2015 CVE summit highlighted UN statutes on countering extremism as well as the Global Counterterrorism Forum's workshop *Raising Community Awareness to Address the Foreign Fighter Phenomenon* (2015).

This emphasis on the international dimension is almost certainly due to the fact that the initial threats to the United States from Islamic extremism of the post-Cold War era had manifested internationally: the perpetrators of 9/11 were not US citizens, whereas the perpetrators of 7/7 were British citizens. The United States did not experience a homegrown IE incident until the attacks of Nadal Hasan and Carlos Bledsoe in 2009. Indeed, for the United States the whole issue of IE had, with the exception of the isolated incidents relating to the NoI in 1972, generally been confined to overseas right up until the 1990s. For, such expressions as there had been of IE on the international stage had been in Iran and Afghanistan. As such they were far distant from the United States. Even the hijacking epidemic in the 1970s and 1980s had been outside the United States and the motives of the terrorists had been issues-driven, such as Israel-Palestine, rather than being perpetrated in the name of the religion itself. Indeed, one of the earliest expressions of terrorism in the context of Arab Nationalism was Harakyat al-Wataniyin al-Arabiyin (ANM) which was founded in Beirut by Palestinian Greek Orthodox Christians.[48]

Furthermore, the numbers of Muslim immigrants to the United States were tiny and so even Islam as a religious presence was relatively limited in the United States in a way that it was not in the UK, where significant numbers of Muslim migrants had been arriving since the Second World War.

The second difference between the US and UK policy approach has been the connection between intelligence gathering and community engagement. For, the United States located the central hub for its Prevent program within the Department of Homeland Security, whereas the UK sought to ensure that there was an administrative gap between the intelligence and community elements of their Prevent strategy. Whatever the real connections (if any) between the community and intelligence elements of the CVE policy in either the United States or United Kingdom, the UK strategy did, at least on the surface, seek to separate the two elements.

That being said though, it is important to note that the accusations of spying and victimization from the perspective of the Muslim communities have been levelled at both programs. So there must be a question mark over the extent to which this location of the Prevent hub in the Department of Homeland Security has made much of a difference in terms of perception?

As has been seen, both the United States and United Kingdom have adopted almost identical approaches to C(V)E. And, while both sides of the Atlantic can point to successes in terms of plots foiled through community cooperation this major benefit should not be confused with success in relation to measurable decreases in the adoption of Islamic extremism ideology and dissemination of extremist material within those communities. In other words, "success" here defined can be measured in relation to community cooperation, rather than measurable decreases in those adopting extremist ideologies.[49]

In the United States, the administration of President Trump is going through a process of reevaluation which may produce a shift in CVE policy while the drive to combat extremism in the UK has been stifled by at least one factor within current CVE policy, and a number of external political priorities (principally Brexit).

CONCLUSION

Ever since the terrorist attacks on 9/11 and 7/7, policymakers have been faced with a series of uncomfortable choices about engaging with communities who are suspicious of them and yet remain key allies in the struggle against terrorist elements. Over this period, therefore, the experiences which US and British officials have had with the differing facets of the issue of "Islamic Extremism" and "Radicalization" have evolved differing perceptions of Islam and Muslim communities.

The PVE and surveillance strategies which have been adopted on either side of the Atlantic have been notable for their lack of success in relation to preventing extremism as the numbers of Muslims going to fight for Islamic State can testify too. But at a deeper level it has had the long-term impact of enhancing fear and distrust between Muslim and non-Muslim communities in both countries. Figures from surveys of public opinion done in Britain and the United States have shown that public distrust of Muslims is deepening rather than reducing.[50] What is more, that distrust is turning to anger at the lack of effective response (as they see it) coming from the governing classes. This is also leading to an increasing polarization, driven by cries of "Islamophobia" by some Muslims, and equally loud anti-Muslim cries (which are principally focused around the effects of immigration) by others.[51]

For officials on both sides of the Atlantic therefore, the long-term effect of "Islamic Extremism" has been that among officials and politicians, a conscious effort has had to be made to seek to avoid seeing Islam and Muslim citizens as a potentially disrupting force.

In 2010 Paul Thomas argued that the Preventing Violent Extremism (PVE) strategy in the UK had achieved little except "othering" Muslims, "predictably creat[ing] envy and suspicion from other communities."[52] Furthermore, as Charlotte Heath-Kelly argues, although the strategy has analyzed the production of the radicalization discourse to explore its performance as a form of risk governance there are legitimate questions about its suitability as a methodology for rooting out radicalization. But, leaving that aside, to date Prevent's outworking on both sides of the Atlantic has been the increasing separation and suspicion of Muslims rather than the growing inclusion and prevention which had been its aim.[53]

These concerns and criticisms were echoed by Imran Awan in his 2012 chapter in which he argued that the PVE strategy, rather than helping to prevent radicalization, risked labeling the Muslim community as a "suspect" community.[54] The shift in focus since 2010 in the UK, and latterly within the administration of President Trump (although it was already shifting before that) suggests that Awan's assessment is accurate. The natural follow-on question then concerns whether the accusation of institutional "Islamophobia" which it implies can be upheld. An accusation which is likely to fuel the separatism developing between Muslim and non-Muslim communities rather than opposing it.[55]

Of course answering this serious discriminatory charge is important and delicate insofar as an affirmative answer implicitly impugns the motives of all officials on both sides of the Atlantic. It also assumes that the officials in question have a "phobia." That being the case, the answer to the charge must be negative for, as the analysis here, and indeed throughout the book is seeking to explore, the attitudes of policymakers in the United States and Britain toward Islam have not been created in a vacuum. They have been the result of long interactions.

NOTES

1. In using the term "Islamic Extremism" the chapter is implicitly acknowledging that the "extremists" believe their actions to be an expression of their faith. See S. Atran, "Mindless Terrorists? The Truth about ISIS is Much Worse," *The Guardian*, November 15, 2015.

2. It should also be noted that the ideological roots of the Sunni Islamic extremism are principally to be found in what has been labelled the "Salafi School" which is closely related to the "Islamic Fundamentalist" movement, both of which are utopian in nature and have both Shi'a and Sunni expressions. The key doctrines of the "Salafi School" are described within the other recognized denominations of Sunni Islam by

no lesser publication than *The Muslim 500* which is published by the Royal Islamic Strategic Studies Centre in Amman, Jordan. (The same center which was behind *The Common Word* initiative published in 2007.) This is important because naming the "Salafi" and "Islamic Fundamentalism" schools within the section entitled "The House of Islam" confirms that they are considered legitimate interpretations of the faith. See S. Abdullah Scheifer (Chief Editor), *The Muslim 500 (2018): The World's 500 Most Influential Muslims.* Amman: The Royal Islamic Strategic Studies Centre, 2017, p. 14.

3. J. Githens-Mazer and R. Lambert (2010), "Why Conventional Wisdom on Radicalization Fails: The Persistence of a Failed Discourse," *Journal of International Affairs* Vol. 86, Iss. 4, pp. 889–901.

4. See, for example, John Esposito, *Unholy War: Terror in the name of Islam.* Oxford, New York: OUP, 2003.

5. T. Keinzle, 'Merkel "Islam is not the Source of Terrorism," *Al Jazeera*, February 18, 2017. See also, Guido Steinberg, *German Jihad: On the Internationalization of Islamist Terrorism.* New York: Columbia University Press, 2012.

6. As reported in Tim Hume and Lauren Said-Moorhouse, "Hollonde: Republic Must Create 'Islam of France' to Respond to Terror Threat," www.edition.cnn.com, September 8, 2016. See also Giles Kepel, *Terror in France: The Rise of Jihad in the West.* Princeton and Oxford: Princeton University Press, 2017.

7. Raffaello Pantucci (2010) "A Contest to Democracy? How the UK has Responded to the Current Terrorist Threat," *Democratization* Vol. 17, Iss. 2, pp. 251–271.

8. V. Dodd, "Government Anti-Terrorism Strategy 'Spies' on Innocent," *The Guardian*, October 16, 2009.

9. P. Thomas, *Responding to the Threat of Violent Extremism.* London: Bloomsbury Academic, 2012, pp. 3–9.

10. *Terrorism Act.* HM Government, 2006.

11. T. Cantle, *The Prevent Strategy: A Guide for Local partners in England.* HMRC, 2010, p. 5, http://www.tedcantle.co.uk/publications/039%20CLG%20Prevent%20Guide%20guide%20for%20local%20partners%202008.pdf.

12. J. Beckman, *Comparative Legal Approaches to Homeland Security and Anti-Terrorism.* Aldershot: Ashgate, 2007, p. 76.

13. S. Marchant (2010) "An Ambiguous Response to a Real Threat: Criminalizing the Glorification of Terrorism in Britain," *The George Washington International Law Review* Vol. 42, Iss. 1, pp. 123–157.

14. C. Pantazis and S. Pemberton (2009) "From the 'Old' to the 'New' Suspect Community: Examining the impacts of Recent UK Counter-Terrorist Legislation," *British Journal of Criminology* Vol. 49, Iss. 5, pp. 646–666.

15. Hansard, *House of Commons.* June 7, 2011. c52.

16. Home Office, *Cm 8092.* June 2011.

17. Jeffrey Bale (2013) "Denying the Link between Islamist Ideology and Jihadist Terrorism 'Political Correctness' and the Undermining of Counterterrorism," Terrorist Research Initiative, Leiden University, Vol. 7, Iss. 5, http://www.terrorismanalysts.com/pt/index.php/pot/article/view/290/html.

18. H. Allen, Andrew Glazzard, Sasha Jesperson, Sneha Reddy-Tumu and Emily Winterbotham (2015) "Drivers of Violent Extremism: Hypotheses and Literature Review," p. 116, www.rusi.org.

19. Ibid.

20. J. Dawson and S. Godec, *Counter Extremism Policy: An Overview*. HOC Briefing Paper No. 7238, June 23, 2017.

21. See George Michael, *Confronting Right Wing Extremism and Terrorism in the USA*. New York, London: Routledge, 2003.

22. John Dean to Al Haig, Memorandum "Possible Libyan Funding of the Nation of Islam" dated February 3, 1972, Department of State EO, 12958.

23. Ibid.

24. Ton Nordheimer, "The Police Advanced; The Blacks Waited" January 16, 1972. An archived copy of the *New York Times* article can be found at https://www.nytimes.com/1972/01/16/archives/the-police-advanced-the-blacks-waited-race-relations.html.

25. The incident is discussed in Vincent Cannato, *The Ungovernable City: John Lindsay and his Struggle to Save New York*. New York: Basic Books, 2001, pp. 484–488.

26. Eric Lincoln, *The Black Muslims in America*. Michigan: Grand Rapids, 1994, p. 265.

27. White House (2011) *Empowering Local Partners to Prevent Violent Extremism*, https://obamawhitehouse.archives.gov/sites/default/files/empowering_local_partners.pdf.

28. Ibid.

29. George Michael gathers localized, on the ground accounts of participants in order to assesses the strengths and weaknesses of the strategy so far in *Extremism in America*. Tampa (FL): University of Florida Press, 2015.

30. Department of Justice (2015) "Pilot Programs are Key to Our Countering Violent Extremism Efforts," https://www.justice.gov/archives/opa/blog/pilot-programs-are-key-our-countering-violent-extremism-efforts.

31. E. Southers, "The U.S. Government's Program to Counter Violent Extremism Needs an Overhall" (Op Ed), *The Los Angeles Times*, March 21, 2017.

32. R. McKenzie, "Countering Violent Extremism in America: Policy Recommendations for the next President," https://www.brookings.edu/research/countering-violent-extremism-in-america-policy-recommendations-for-the-next-president/, October 18, 2016.

33. Ibid.

34. K. Esseissah, *The Increasing Conversion to Islam since 9/11: A Study of White American Muslim Converts in Northwest Ohio*. Dissertation, Bowling Green State University, 2011; K. Kleinmann (2012) "Radicalization of Homegrown Sunni Militants in the United States: Comparing Converts and Non-Converts," *Studies in Conflict and Terrorism* Vol. 35, Iss. 4, pp. 278–297; J. Galonnier (2015) "The Radicalization of Muslims in France and the United States: Some Insights from White Converts to Islam," *Social Compass* Vol. 62, Iss. 4, pp. 570–583.

35. Department of Homeland Security, *Security Strategy for Countering Violent Extremism* and *Strategic Implementation Plan for Empowering Local Partners to Prevent Violent Extremism in the United States* (2016), https://www.dhs.gov/sites/default/files/publications/NSCITF% 20CVE%20Report.pdf.

36. Ibid., p. 3.

37. Matthew Apuzzo and Adam Goldman, "Inside the Spy Unit that NYPD Says doesn't Exist," www.ap.org, August 31, 2011.

38. Adam Goldman and Matthew Apuzzo, "The NYPD Division of Un-American Activities," http://nymag.com/news/features/nypd-demographics-unit-2013-9/, August 25, 2013.

39. Matthew Apuzzo and Joseph Goldstein, "New York Drops Unit Which Spied on Muslims," *The New York Times*, April 15, 2014.

40. Apuzzo and Goldman, "Spy Unit."

41. As discussed in Zareena Grewal, *Islam is a Foreign Country*. New York: University of New York, 2013, pp. 286–289.

42. Ibid.

43. Ibid.

44. This is discussed in Alan Richards *Socio-Economic Roots of Radicalism? Towards Explaining the Appeal of Islamic Radicals*. Washington DC: Diane Publishing Co., 2003, pp. 27–41.

45. There is a useful discussion of these issues in Jack Boulton (2103) "Defining the Enemy: Myth and Representation in the War on Terror," *vis-à-vis: Explorations in Anthropology* Vol. 12, Iss. 1.

46. G. Denoeux and L. Carter, *Guide to the Drivers of Violent Extremism*. Washington DC: USAid, 2009; S. Lukes (2005) "Power and the Battle of Hearts and Minds," *Millennium: Journal of International Relations* Vol. 33, Iss. 3, pp. 477–493.

47. Ibid., p. 491.

48. B. H. Vincent, *Bombers, Hijackers, Body Scanners and Jihadists*. New York: Xlibris, 2012, p. 407.

49. Figures for the number of terrorist plots disrupted through the cooperation of Muslim communities are virtually impossible to attain. A number of chapters in the media have hinted at foiled plots on both sides of the Atlantic through police-community cooperation, but how many of the (for example) sixty plots said to have been foiled in the US between 9/11 and April 2013 (Boston Marathon Bombing) have been the result of community intervention and how many were due to purely intelligence work is not clear (Heritage Foundation, 2013).

50. Mona Chalabi, "How Anti-Muslim Are Americans? Data Points to Extent of Islamophobia," *The Guardian*, December 8, 2015.

51. George Morgan and Scott Poynting, *Global Islamophobia: Muslims and Moral Panic in the West*. Ashgate, 2012 is a very informed discussion of the nuances of this growing dynamic.

52. Paul Thomas (2010) "Failed and Friendless: The UK's 'Preventing Violent Extremism' Programme," *The British Journal of Politics & International Relations* Vol. 12, Iss. 3, pp. 442–458.

53. Charlotte Heath-Kelly (2013) "Counter-Terrorism and the Counterfactual: Producing the 'Radicalization' Discourse and the UK PREVENT Strategy," *The British Journal of Politics & International Relations* Vol. 15, Iss. 3, pp. 394–415.

54. Imran Awan (2012) "I Am a Muslim Not an Extremist": How the Prevent Strategy Has Constructed a "Suspect" Community," *Politics & Policy* Vol. 40, Iss. 6, pp. 1158–1185.

55. This is discussed in Therese O'Toole, Daniel Nilsson DeHanas and Tariq Modood (2012) "Balancing Tolerance, Security and Muslim Ein the United Kingdom: The Impact of the 'Prevent' Agenda," *Critical Studies on Terrorism* Vol. 5, Iss. 3, pp. 373–389.

Conclusion

Lawrence Pintak's recently published book about America and Islam sees a fundamental antagonism between America and the religion of Islam which he blames on what he perceives to be the scaremongering of American politicians.[1] Yet, the evidence presented in this book would suggest that there are legitimate, long-term reasons why policymakers in America and Britain would have reason to be cautious about their relationships with Muslim peoples and regimes. Furthermore, the evidence here would suggest further that the relationships have been surprisingly free of antagonism in the context of the deep-rooted civilizational differences that lie at the roots of their differing worldviews and that this cautious working relationship has lasted for over a century for a number of consistent reasons, even in the face of changing geopolitical and cultural circumstances.

At the beginning of this book the proposal was advanced that the experiences of American and British governments with differing aspects of policy engagement and cultural interaction have taught them that while Islam and Muslims could be valuable allies, they were also a potential threat. But, while these concerns were continued to be present throughout the period in question, the correspondence also showed that these concerns have played and continue to play a secondary role compared to the broader, and ultimately decisive, fact that, for a host of strategic and economic reasons, both countries have needed the goodwill and cooperation of Muslims and Muslim-majority states. Moreover, the policy culture in the United States and Britain has also seen a marked shift and that shift has impacted the way that Islam and Muslims are perceived in policymaking circles. Indeed one might argue that the patterns of relationship between the Anglo-US sphere and the Muslim majority areas of the world have not changed at all: concerns about loyalty, economic interdependence, political turbulence, and periodic violence have been constants in the relationship throughout the period this book covers and it is only the composite elements which shift. What has shifted far more over the period is how those events are viewed and talked about in policymaking circles. In this, the impact of the philosophical changes discussed in chapter 1 are clear; no longer are Islamic cultures and Muslims themselves talked about as "others," but as fellow stakeholders in common goals (however those are defined). Over the course of the last two centuries Britain first, and now America, have lost confidence in the value of their civilizations and have sought to invite the diaspora peoples of those they formerly looked down upon to help shape a new future which includes also a new narrative about the past.

The perception of Islam and Muslims therefore has changed not because Muslims have changed (although it seems clear that theologically the faith of Islam is experiencing its own Reformation at present), but because the incidents and events which have characterized the relationship are talked about differently.

The relationship between "Islam" as represented by the states and diaspora peoples that claim adherence to that faith, and that of the policymakers of the Anglosphere, have been largely dichotomous in the sense that a deep suspicion of one another which has continued throughout the period in differing forms has not prevented interaction for potential benefit. Perhaps the miracle of the relationship between Islam and the US-British sphere is that it has continued at all given the violence (and little else) which marked the relationship for so long before the last 200 years. As such, in this long-term context, it could be argued that the relationship between US-British policymakers and Muslims has seen a marked improvement over the past century, despite the continuation of the concerns which have characterized the relationship before.

Of course it is important to reiterate that this book is not trying to say that this suspicion has not been characteristic of all interactions between all policymakers and all Muslims at all times in all places. Indeed, as was discussed in the chapter on conversion and proselytizing, St. John Philby and Alexander Russell Webb, although unusual in their conversion to Islam for their day, were certainly not unusual in their fascination with the "Orient." Moreover, in both the State Department and the Foreign and Commonwealth Office, there were generations of officials who had a deep interest in, and affinity for, Muslim peoples and interests.[2] Indeed, as was highlighted in that same chapter, the British aristocracy, particularly in the late nineteenth and twentieth centuries, were fascinated by the "Orient": a fascination which led some to convert to Islam.[3]

If this book had been engaging with the day-to-day encounters which went on throughout the imperial period between peoples of all faiths, then it would have been making a strong case for the possibility of friendly US-British-Muslim relations because, at a business and personal level, such relationships certainly existed and, in many cases, flourished.⁴ However, this book has been focused upon the perceptions of Islam that developed and were shaped in the minds of leaders and officials who engaged with Muslims and Islam as the manifestation of a doctrinal entity at a formal level.

Inevitably, such interactions missed the casual personal flavor of other nonofficial engagements and so, therefore, it would be reasonable to argue that the perceptions that were built up in the US and British governments were skewed. However, it is in the realms of policy and government that the actions of US and British governments have been characterized by Muslims as seeking to destroy Islam rather than at the personal level. This book has therefore sought to provide a window into the perspectives that might, from the outside, have looked as if the United States and Britain were seeking to destroy Islam.

Indeed, instead of evidencing a desire to destroy Islam, the evidence instead has suggested that US and British governments have very clearly shown that they regard engagement with Islam and Muslims as a matter of strategic importance. That, whatever the private views of officials and leaders, there has been no evidence at all that there is any desire to destroy Islam or any other faith. Instead, the correspondence has shown a marked desire to avoid religious issues whenever possible for fear of the cohesion issues that will arise from doing so. Moreover, as the discussion in chapter 3 (Foreign Affairs) evidenced, the general perception of Islam, especially in the Cold War period, was that it was a valuable source of regional stability. For that reason, the Cold War became another period in which, for strategic reasons, regimes of states that had an Islamic state religion became important strategic partners against the Soviets.

The consistent theme running through this book, therefore, is that Britain and America needed Muslims and Islam to be onside for a host of policy and strategic reasons which shifted and evolved over the course of the past two centuries but which did not alter the fundamental pattern of the need for goodwill from a US-British perspective. This dynamic was manifested in the overwhelming majority of incidents the book discusses but is perhaps most clearly seen in the chapters on foreign policy goals and economics. The use of Muslim sentiment against an aggressor, whether it be during the Indian Rebellions of 1857–1858, the attempt to create an anti-Soviet Bloc in the early Cold War, or in relation to the arming of the Mujahidin in the Afghanistan in the 1980s, was a strategy which was both understandable and successful in the short term. However, it was based upon a conception that Islam could somehow be controlled and the further (and wider) lack of understanding of how important religious perspective was (and is) outside of the West.

This observation is the basis for the contention that, for all its engagement with differing states and peoples who could all be described as Islamic, and despite the expertise upon which they drew from inside the academy and policymaking circles (especially intelligence agencies), there was a surprising underestimation of the power that Islam as an expression of faith had to move and motivate actions. These perceptions have meant that, for example, issues of Islamic extremism have, until very recently, been spoken of as short-term rather than long-term ways. The perfect example of this was the 2015 British government's "Counter Extremism" strategy which posited that the problems which are today characterized as "Islamic Extremism" (or some variant of that) are located in writings which had their origins in the twentieth century: names such as al-Banna, Maududi, and Qutb.[5] These ideologues were indeed vitally important in helping to formulate many of the ideas behind modern extremism, but its roots, as the term "Salafi" shows, go back far beyond that into Islamic history.

The problem of mis-casting "Islamic Extremism" as a short-term problem rather than the accumulation of long-term drivers (along with the short-term triggers such as poverty or US-British foreign policy) is that a short-term solution will, therefore, seem not only possible but appropriate. This leads to unrealistic expectations of dealing with the issue as well as failing to comprehend the scale of the problem.

One of the outworkings of the failure to understand the long-term nature of the issues is the somewhat weak attempts at messaging both about Islam to British and American non-Muslim citizens and about the benevolence of these countries toward Islam as was seen in chapters 3 and 5—messages which were, by their very nature, short-termist, rather than long-termist. For, as we have seen, from the post–Second World War period, both Britain and America have sought to curry favor with Muslim diaspora peoples, as well as with the governments of Muslim states, by a range of propaganda and intelligence activities. Notable among them was the granting of £100,000 by the British government in 1940 to build what have become Regents Park Mosque and the East London Mosque in Whitechapel. As this incident and other incidents such as the opening of the Islamic Centre in Washington by President Eisenhower in 1957 showed, the accent of both governments was upon developing a narrative of Islam and the West which encouraged Muslims to feel like they could belong and encourage the wider populations to feel that Islam did not represent a threat to them. It also meant that, when Muslims were stirred up for any reason, both governments became nervous and sought to deal with whatever was upsetting Muslims as quickly as possible. This was seen in the incidents described in chapter 5 around the cartoons in the British newspaper in the late nineteenth and twentieth centuries.

Perhaps the closest that either the US or British governments have come to fulfilling the charge often levelled at it by Muslims, that of seeking to destroy Islam, lies in the attitudes of the "Controntationalists" discussed in chapter 3. However, even there, their expectation, rather than desire, was of a confrontation in the manner that Huntington proposed. Moreover, even at the height of the British Empire (for example), when, for a short time, the British were relatively unassailable, they showed a marked reluctance to encourage large-scale evangelism to Muslims in an attempt to convert them and try, therefore, to somehow end the faith. As chapter 6 showed, rather there was a marked reluctance to give Christian missionaries the freedom to evangelize, especially in areas deemed holy to the faith of Islam, such actions, other than seeking to seek the peace, clearly displayed the underlying assumption that there were areas which were "Muslim" and that therefore needed to be protected or preserved as such.

When it came to issues of radicalization and revolution both the US and British governments were keen to show that they understood that there were differing denominations within Islam and that the activities of Islamic extremists only formed a tiny minority among the global House of Islam. Nevertheless, as the attacks have continued since 9/11 on both sides of the Atlantic, there has been a shift in the language being used from British and US leaders from the complete separation of any connection between the faith of Islam and the actions of the terrorists, to a cautious criticism of the ideologies that are seen to motivate such actions. As such, it has been a refined, and carefully phrased, critique which has moved away from the somewhat insulting stereotyping which had characterized the writings of nineteenth-century leaders like Adams and Gladstone. But while these characterizations are to be rightly condemned for their generalizations and characterizations, it is also worth remembering that, as this book has sought to show, those viewpoints were not incubated in a vacuum. They were based on interactions that lead to perceptions and, while the reporting of events such as the Bulgarian Massacre were certainly sensationalized, that does not mean that they did not happen. Moreover, British and US officials had been given reasons, by Muslims in authority such as the ambassador of Tripoli why the actions of the Barbary pirates, for example, could be justified within a religious or doctrinal framework. It is little wonder therefore that such stinging assessments were made.

Of course, there have been numerous occasions when policy goals have taken precedent over the desires of Muslim states, or diaspora peoples. Perhaps the most pertinent example of that was the ongoing support for the creation and maintenance of the state of Israel as well as the recent (temporary) "Travel Ban" imposed by President Trump, or the support of dictatorships in the Middle East in the Cold War period, or the invasion of Iraq and the ongoing "meddling" in the Middle East. Furthermore, there can be no doubt that both Britain and America have deliberately sought to manipulate and contain Islam, such as in the First World War period and in the Raj. Indeed, attempts have been made to create a "theology" of Islam which is comparable with a passive identity of belonging, rather than of activism for the sake of cohesion and geostrategic considerations such as the anti-Soviet Muslim-bloc proposal.[6]

Therefore while there are legitimate criticisms that can be made of US and British policies in the Muslim-majority world and among Muslim diaspora communities it would not be appropriate to put them in the same category of aggression as a charge of "seeking to destroy Islam" would engender. Moreover, there is no group of any religious or ethnic constituency which has no legitimate grounds for complaint about some historical, or current, government action (whether Western or non-Western).

In the wider context, therefore, could it perhaps be said that, on balance, geostrategic considerations have meant that Muslim concerns and opinions have been taken into account more than any other religious or ethnic group?

To be able to justify such a hypothesis based upon that question, there would need to be studies to be done on other religions and ethnic groupings and so it is not possible to answer that here. However, what can be said with some confidence is that Muslim states and diasporas have been and continue to be voices whose opinions carry a lot of weight within the corridors of Washington DC and Whitehall.[7]

What's more, as has been seen, shifting cultural and political frameworks within the United States and Britain have also changed the perceptions of Islam as a faith. Or, maybe, just changed the way that Islam is talked about. In that context, the growing emergence of Post-Secularism as a political theory, with its desire to incorporate non-Christian, especially Islamic, elements into Western political theory, is likely to take that process of changing perception on further.[8] What that will mean as far as changing the culture of the interstate and diaspora relationships is yet to be seen, but given that Post-Secular theory contains within it a fusion of Islamic and Western philosophical constructs, it will probably serve to lessen the official cultural distrusts which have been evidenced in this book.

Looking forward, therefore, there are reasons to believe that the deep-rooted distrust which goes back to the advent of Islam and the founding of "Christendom" in the eighth century is likely to gradually dissipate.[9] Yet centuries of distrust and suspicion have not prevented mutually beneficial efforts being made to engage one another and, as Islamic political philosophies become embedded within Western political thinking, and increasing numbers of Muslims on both sides of the Atlantic enter government service and attain senior roles, those enmities will probably continue to dissipate.

Yet familiarity will not be the only factor in deciding the future relationship. For, it seems clear that much of the transatlantic engagement with Islam will depend on a number of interconnected geostrategic factors.

First, and perhaps of most strategically important given that it impacts the other issues highlighted here, the effects of Gulf oil flows stopping would be seismic. Indeed, given that America, Canada, and Israel (among others) have also discovered (and begun to tap) substantial natural gas and oil reserves, reducing Minority World dependence on Gulf-produced minerals, there is a very real possibility that the flow of funds to all the Gulf states will be substantially reduced.[10] In so doing, this would not only undermine financial stability but would have significant political impact.[11] This could be offset or mitigated with the increased flow of sharia finance products, as was discussed in chapter 4, and the development of tourism, but these revenues would not compare to the oil wealth they currently enjoy, nor would they offset the reduction in political influence that the ending of oil extraction would also entail.

Second, given both the rise in radicalization of Muslims and the growing backlash from right and center-right parties in Britain and the United States there is a growing likelihood that some significant incident or incidents against Muslim communities will happen in the not-too-distant future.[12] As and when that happens, the capacity of governments across the Atlantic to deal with frustrations of non-Muslims while maintaining their engagement with diaspora Muslims will be vital.

These factors are an important facet of the developing relationship and perception of Islam in the West generally, and within policymaking circles. But, as revivalism is worked out within the House of Islam in the years to come, the path forward at an official level will be set by the interplay of perception and need on both sides.

Necessity and desire have perpetuated the relationship independently of perception. So, while a growing understanding of the specific streams within the House of Islam that are likely to be of security concern has embedded itself in policymaking circles, the fundamental cultural and political differences between the US-Britain and Muslim communities and regimes will be a source of tension for many years to come. As such, while the "courting of Islam" has been a consistent policy theme in both American and British administrations over a century and a half that is not to say that the interactions have been a signal of closer relations. That is likely to come organically, as described earlier, rather than through official engagement.

NOTES

1. Lawrence Pintak, *America and Islam: Soundbites, Suicide Bombs and the Road to Donald Trump*. London, New York: I.B. Tauris, 2019.

2. Leslie McLoughlin, *In a Sea of Knowledge: British Arabists in the 20th Century*. London: Ithaca Press, 2002. See also Kaplan, *The Arabists*.

3. For a more detailed history of this, see Jamie Gilham, *Loyal Enemies: British Converts to Islam, 1850–1950*. Oxford, New York: OUP, 2014.

4. See, for example, Hugh Goddard, *A History of Christian Muslim Relations*. Edinburgh: Edinburgh University Press, 2000.

5. HM Government, *Counter Extremism Strategy*. Cm 9148, HMSO, October 2015, p. 21.

6. The work which eventually produced the declaration of the British Empire as "dar al-Islam" would be one example of that. See H. Enyat, *Modern Islamic Political Thought*. Basingstoke: Macmillan Education, 1982, p. 57.

7. One aspect of this influence would be the work of lobbyists in both capitals. Measuring the impact of lobbyists is difficult as the world of political influencing continues to be cloaked in fog, but articles such as Kaja Borchgrevink's (2017) "NGOization of Islamic Charity: Claiming legitimacy in Changing Institutional Contexts," *VOLUNTAS: International Journal of Voluntary and Nonprofit Organizations*, pp. 1–23, doi: 10.1007/s11266-017-9892-7 offer insight into the growth of their impact. See also, Aysha Khan and Lauren Markoe, "Muslims on Capitol Hill Learn How to Lobby," www.religionnews.com, May 2, 2017.

8. Hent de Vries and Lawrence Sullivan (eds), *Political Theologies: Public Religions in a Post-Secular World*. New York: Fordham University Press, 2006, remains the one-volume repository for this emerging school of political thought.

9. The founding of "Christendom" is vividly described in Tom Holland's *Millennium*. London: Little Brown, 2008. That narrative is expanded and contextualized within the longer story of "Christendom" in the same author's new work *Dominion: The Making of the Western Mind*. London: Little Brown, 2019. See also, Christopher Wickham, *Medieval Europe: From the Breakup of the Western Roman Empire to the Reformation*. New Haven (CT): Yale University Press, 2017, pp. 61–79.

10. The geo-strategic impacts of energy changes are analyzed in Meghan O'Sullivan, *Windfall: How the New Energy Abundance Upends Global Politics and Strengthens American Power*. New York: Simon and Schuster, 2017.

11. Gawdat Bahgat (2011) "Israel's Energy Policy: Regional Implications," *Middle East Policy Council* Vol. XVIII, Iss. 3.

12. The shootings in Norway and New Zealand are suggestive of a worrying direction of travel and it seems clear that, while there have not been shootings of this type seen in either Britain or the US thus far, there has been a rise in attacks on Muslims in both countries. Given the relatively vague definitions given to "hate crimes," statistics can perhaps distort the true extent of anti-Muslim acts, but there can be little doubt that incidents against Muslims are on the rise. For America, see Maya Berry and Kai Wiggins, "FBI Stats on Hate Crimes are Scary. So What's Missing?" www.edition.cnn.com, November 14, 2018. For the UK, see Vikram Dodd, "Anti-Muslim Hate Crimes Soar in the UK after Christchurch Shootings," *The Guardian*, March 22, 2019.

Bibliography

Abdallah, Umar, *A Muslim in Victorian America: The Life of Alexander Russell Webb*. New York: Oxford University Press, 2006.

Abed, George, 'Middle Eastern Oil Producers Still Have Strong Hand.' *Financial Times*, April 5, 2017.

Adelson, Roger, *London and the Invention of the Middle East: Money, Power and War, 1902–1922*. New Haven (CT): Yale University Press, 1995.

Afsaruddin, Asma, *Contemporary Issues in Islam*. Edinburgh: Edinburgh University Press, 2015.

———, *Striving in the Path of God: Jihad and Martyrdom in Islamic Thought*. Oxford, New York: Oxford University Press, 2013.

——— (ed), *Islam, the State and Political Authority: Medieval Issues and Modern Concerns*. New York: Palgrave-Macmillan, 2011.

Ahmed-Ullah, Roe and L. Cohen, 'American Muslims Divided.' *Chicago Tribune*, September 20, 2004.

Aksakal, Mustafa (2011) 'Holy War Made in Germany? Ottoman Origins of the 1914 Jihad.' *War in History* Vol. 18, Iss. 2, pp. 184–199.

Alexeiv, Alex, Testimony, 'Hearing before the Subcommittee on Terrorism, Technology and Homeland Security of the Committee on the Judiciary.' *United States Senate*, 108th Congress, June 26, 2003, pp. 15–19.

Ali, Ameer, *Letter to Sir Arthur Hirtzel*, March 14, 1927, India Office Records, File L/PS/12/883.

Allen, H., Andrew Glazzard, Sasha Jesperson, Sneha Reddy-Tumu and Emily Winterbotham (2015) 'Drivers of Violent Extremism: Hypotheses and Literature Review.' www.rusi.org.

Ally, Muhammad, *History of Muslims in Britain*. Unpublished Master's Thesis, University of Birmingham, 1981.

Angell, Norman, *The Great Illusion*, Originally published 1910, Republished and updated 1933. Ithaca (NY): Cornell University Press, 2011.

Anon, 'Bank of London and the Middle East Launches as London Based Islamic Bank.' *AME Info*, July 9, 2008.

———, 'Halal Laws in the USA.' December 29, 2014. https://halaltransactions.word press.com/2014/12/29/halal-laws-in-the-usa/.

——— (No Date) 'History of the Special Relationship.' https://uk.usembassy.gov/our-relationship/policy-history/.

———, 'Islamic Finance's Global Surge Remains a Missed Opportunity for Banks in the US and Canada.' www.theconversation.com, March 6, 2015.

———, 'Islamic Finance in the UK.' *Islamic Finance Home*, December 19, 2003.

———, 'Manhattan Tower Secures $219million in Shari'a Compliant Financing.' *Financial Times*, June 21, 2016.

———, 'Tony Blair: Islamic Extremists' Ideology Enjoys Support of Many Muslims.' *The Guardian*, October 6, 2015.

———, 'UK's Brown Backs Islamic Finance.' *BBC News*, June 13, 2006.

——— (July 22, 2016) 'US Department of Education Takes Action to Address Religious Discrimination.' *US Department of Education Press Office Release*. https://www2.ed.gov/about/offices/list/ocr/religion.html.

Ansari, Humayun, '"A Mosque in London Worthy of the Tradition of Islam and Worthy of the Capital of the British Empire" The Struggle to Create Muslim Space 1910–1944.' In Susheila Nasta (ed), *India in Britain: South Asian Networks and Connections, 1858–1950*. London, New York: Palgrave Macmillan, 2013, pp. 80–95.

———, *The Infidel Within: Muslims in Britain since 1800*. London: Hurst and Company, 2008.

Apuzzo, Matthew and Joseph Goldstein, 'New York Drops Unit Which Spied on Muslims.' *New York Times*, April 15, 2014.

———, and Adam Goldman, 'Inside the Spy Unit that NYPD Says Doesn't Exist.' *Associated Press*, August 31, 2011.

Arnold, James, *The Moro War: How America Battled a Muslim Insurgency in the Philippine Jungle 1902–13*. New York: Bloomsbury, 2011.

Atran, S., 'Mindless Terrorists? The Truth about ISIS is Much Worse.' *The Guardian*, November 15, 2015.

Austin, Allan, *African Muslims in Antebellum America: Transatlantic Stories and Spiritual Struggles*. New York: Routledge, 1997.

Awan, Imran (2012) '"I Am a Muslim Not an Extremist": How the Prevent Strategy Has Constructed a "Suspect" Community.' *Politics & Policy* Vol. 40, Iss. 6, pp. 1158–1185.

Aydin, Emil, 'The Question of Orientalism in Pan-Islamic Thought: The Origins, Content and Legacy of Transnational Muslim Identities.' In Sucheta Mazumdar, Vasant Kaiwar and Theirry Labica (eds), *From Orientalism to Post-Colonialism: Asia, Europe and the Lineages of Difference*. Abingdon: Rutledge, 2010, pp. 107–128.

Ayers, Thomas (2005) 'Six Floors of Detainee Operations in the Post-9/11 World.' *Parameters* Vol. 35, p. 35. Testimony to joint Senate Select Committee on Intelligence and the House Permanent Select Committee on Intelligence hearing, September 26, 2002.

Ayyub, Rana (2015) 'Exploring Perceptions of Non-Muslims towards Halal Foods in the UK.' *British Food Journal* Vol. 117, Iss. 9, pp. 2328–2343.

Azumah, J.A., *The Legacy of Arab-Islam in Africa: A Quest for Inter-Religious Dialogue*. New York: Oneworld Publications, 2001.

Bahadurk, Syed Ahmed Khan, *The Causes of the Indian Revolt*. Benares: Medical Hall Press, 1873.

Bahgat, Gawdat (2011) 'Israel's Energy Policy: Regional Implications.' *Middle East Policy Council* Vol. XVIII, Iss. 3.

Bailey, Tom and Valentina Gentile (eds), *Rawls and Religion*. New York: Columbia University Press, 2014.

Bale, J.M. (2013) 'Denying the Link between Islamist Ideology and Jihadist Terrorism "Political Correctness" and the Undermining of Counterterrorism.' *Terrorist Research Initiative*, Leiden University Vol. 7, Iss. 5. http://www.terrorismanalysts.com/pt/index.php/pot/article/view/290/html.

Barber, Steve (2011) 'The "New Economy of Terror": The Financing of Islamist Terrorism.' *Global Security Studies* Vol. 2, Iss. 1, pp. 38–51.

Barclay, Christopher, *Religious Slaughter*, House of Commons Library SN/SC/1314, June 11, 2011.

Beckman, J., *Comparative Legal Approaches to Homeland Security and Anti-Terrorism*. Aldershot: Ashgate, 2007.

Beliles, Mark and Jerry Newcombe, *Doubting Thomas? The Religious Life and Legacy of Thomas Jefferson*. New York: Morgan James Publishing, 2015.

Bentley, Michelle and Jack Holland, *Obama's Foreign Policy: Ending the War on Terror*. New York, London: Routledge, 2014.

Berry, Maya and Kai Wiggins, 'FBI Stats on Hate Crimes are Scary. So What's Missing?' www.edition.cnn.com, November 14, 2018.

Beyers, Jan, Rainer Eising and William Maloney (2008) 'Researching Interest Group Politics in Europe and Elsewhere: Much We Study, Little We Know?' *West European Politics* Vol. 31, Iss. 6, pp. 1103–1128.

Biglari, Mattin (2016) '"Captive to the Demonology of the Iranian Mobs": US Foreign Policy and Perceptions of Shi'a Islam during the Iranian Revolution, 1978–79.' *Diplomatic History* Vol. 40, Iss. 4, pp. 579–605.

Blair, Tony, 'True Britishness.' March 28, 2000. https://www.theguardian.com/uk/2000/mar/28/britishidentity.tonyblair.

Blewett, Timothy, Adrian Hyde-Price and Wyn Rees, *British Foreign Policy and the Anglican Church: Christian Engagement with the Contemporary World*. Aldershot: Ashgate Publishing, 2011.

Bluestein, Adam, 'Bringing a Muslim Culinary Tradition Mainstream.' www.inc.com, May 3, 2012.

Borchgrevink, Kaja (2017) 'NGOization of Islamic Charity: Claiming Legitimacy in Changing Institutional Contexts.' *VOLUNTAS: International Journal of Voluntary and Nonprofit Organizations*, pp. 1–23.

Boulton, Jack (2013) 'Defining the Enemy: Myth and Representation in the War on Terror.' *vis-à-vis: Explorations in Anthropology* Vol. 12, Iss. 1, pp. 12–22.

Bouwen, Pieter (2002) 'Corporate Lobbying in the European Union: The Logic of Access.' *Journal of European Public Policy* Vol. 9, Iss 3, pp. 365–390.

Bowen, Innes, *Medina in Birmingham, Najaf in Brent: Inside British Islam*. London: Hurst and Company, 2014.

Boyd, Julian (ed), *The Papers of Thomas Jefferson, Vol. 9, 1 November 1785–22 June 1786*. Princeton: Princeton University Press, 1954.
Boyle, Michael (2008) 'The War on Terror in American Grand Strategy.' *Journal of International Affairs* Vol. 84, Iss. 2, pp. 191–209.
Brock, Michael and Eleanor (eds), *Herbert Asquith Letters to Venetia Stanley*. Oxford, New York: Oxford University Press, 1982.
Bronson, Rachael, *Thicker than Oil: America's Uneasy Partnership with Saudi Arabia*. New York, Oxford: Oxford University Press, 2008.
Brooks, Stephen, *Anti-Americanism and the Limits of Public Diplomacy: Winning Hearts and Minds?* Abingdon, New York: Routledge, 2016.
Bukhari, Muhammad and Muhammad Khan, *The English Translation of Sahih Al-Bukhari with the Arabic Text*. Baltimore (MD): Al- Saadawi Publications, 1996.
Burke's, Kathleen, *Old World, New World*. London: Abacus, 2009.
———, *Lion and the Eagle: The Interaction of the British and American Empires 1783–1972*. London, New York: Bloomsbury Press, 2018.
Burkett, John and Frederick Leiner, *The End of Barbary Terror: America's 1815 War Against the Pirates of North Africa*. Oxford, New York: Oxford University Press, 2006.
Burks, Meghan, 'Judge Considers Injunction against Anti-Islamophobia Program in San Diego Schools.' www.kpbs.org, July 18, 2018.
Bush, George W., 'Remarks.' Islamic Center, Washington DC, September 17, 2001. https://www.presidency.ucsb.edu/documents/remarks-the-islamic-center-washington.
———, 'Address to a Joint Session of Congress and the American People.' September 20, 2001. http://www.whitehouse.gov/news/releases/2001/09/20010920-8.html.
———, 'Interview.' Good Morning America, December 14, 2003. https://www.youtube.com/watch?v=UGu0-kTi3Eg.
Bush, George (Snr), 'Interview with Middle Eastern Journalists.' March 8, 1991. Transcript. https://www.presidency.ucsb.edu/documents/interview-with-middle-eastern-journalists.
Cabinet Office, *Minutes*, June 29, 1989, File 128/94/3.
———, *Minutes*, August 14, 1940, File OS/323/12.
Calhoun, Craig, Mark Juergensmeyer and Jonathan van Antwerpen (eds), *Rethinking Secularism*. Oxford, New York: Oxford University Press, 2011.
Calvert, John (2000) '"The World is an Undutiful Boy!": Sayyid Qutb's American Experience.' *Islam and Christian-Muslim Relations* Vol. 11, Iss. 1, pp. 87–103.
Cameron, David, 'Extremism.' Transcript. Ninestiles School, Birmingham, July 20, 2015. https://www.gov.uk/government/speeches/extremism-pm-speech.
Cannato, Vincent, *The Ungovernable City: John Lindsay and His Struggle to Save New York*. New York: Basic Books, 2001.
Cantle, Ted and Eric Kaufmann, 'Is Segregation Increasing in the UK?' November 2, 2016. http://tedcantle.co.uk/wp-content/uploads/2013/03/099-Is-Segregation-Increasing-in-the-UK-Cantle-and-Kaufmann-Open-Democracy-Nov-2016.pdf6.
Carey, S. Peace, *William Carey*. New York: Wakeman Trust, 2008.
Carter, Denise (2016) '(De)constructing Difference: A Qualitative Review of the "Othering" of Muslim Communities, Extremism, Soft Harms and Twitter

Analytics.' *Journal of Behavioral Sciences of Terrorism and Political Aggression* Vol. 9, Iss. 1, pp. 21–36.

Cattelan, Valentino, *Islamic Finance in Europe: Towards a Plural Financial System*. London: Edward Elgar Publishing, 2013.

Cecil, Robert (Lord Salisbury) to Austen Layard, Letter, September 4, 1879, Cabinet Office, file 37/1.

Census Bureau (US), 'United States Census Bureau: Quick Facts.' June 3, 2018. https://www.census.gov/quickfacts/fact/table/US/PST045218.

Chalabi, Mona, 'How Anti-Muslim are Americans? Data Points to Extent of Islamophobia.' *The Guardian*, December 8, 2015.

Chamberlain, A., 'Belligerent Rights at Sea and the Relations between the United States and Great Britain.' 26 October 1927, C.P. 258(27), CAB 24/189.

Chisholm, Archibald, *The First Kuwait Oil Concession: A Record of Negotiation, 1911–1934*. London: Frank Cass, 1975.

Chozik, Amy and Steve Eder, 'Foundation Ties Bedevil Hillary Clinton's Presidential Campaign.' *The New York Times*, August 20, 2016.

Churchill, Winston, *The Story of the Malakand Field Force* (First published 1898). London: Bloomsbury Academic, 2015.

Cicektakan, Nazim, *Great Britain and the Ottoman Empire: British Discourses on the Ottomans 1860–1878*. Unpublished PhD Thesis, University of Essex, 2014.

Ciftci, Sabri and Gunes Tezcur (2016) 'Soft Power, Religion and Anti-Americanism in the Middle East.' *Foreign Policy Analysis* Vol. 12, Iss. 3, pp. 374–394.

Citizens for Quality Education, San Diego et al v San Diego Unified School District, Case 3:17-cv-01054-BAS-JMA, February 20, 2018. https://www.fcdflegal.org/wp-content/uploads/2018/02/QE-SD-v-SDUSD-Memo-P.I.-Index-of-Exhibits_2.pdf.

Clark, Bruce (2012) 'Shifting Western Views on Turkey.' *Asian Affairs* Vol. 43, Iss. 2, pp. 193–203.

Clark, Kirsten, 'Worksheet on "Sharia Law" Irks School Parents.' www.courier-journal.com, January 17, 2017.

Clarke, Peter, *Report into Allegations Concerning Birmingham Schools Arising from the "Trojan Horse" Letter*. HC 576. London: Her Majesty's Stationary Office, 2014.

Cleary, Edward and Allen D. Hertzke (eds), *Representing God at the Statehouse: Religion and Politics in the American States*. Lanham (MD): Rowman & Littlefield, 2006.

Clinton, Bill, 'Remarks to the Jordanian Parliament.' Amman, Jordan. Transcript. October 26, 1994. https://www.presidency.ucsb.edu/ws/index.php?pid=49373&st=islam&st1.

Cocco, F., 'How Many Foreign Fighters have Joined Islamic State.' www.theweek.co.uk, June 24, 2015.

Coen, David and Jeremy Richardson (eds), *Lobbying the European Union: Institutions, Actors and Issues*. Oxford, New York: Oxford University Press, 2009.

Coffee, Kevin (2008) 'Cultural Inclusion, Exclusion and the Formative Role of Museums.' *Museum Management and Curatorship* Vol. 23, Iss. 3, pp. 261–279.

Colley, Linda, *Britons: Forging the Nation, 1707–1837*. New Haven (CT), London: Yale University Press, 1992.

Compton, Wilson, to Mr. Bruce, January 13, 1953, State Department, File IIA:IPO:GHDamon:bv.
Conlon, Kevin and Kristine Sgueglia 'Two Shot Dead after They Open Fire at Mohammed Cartoon Event in Texas.' www.cnn.com, May 4, 2015.
Crawford, Sue and Laura Olson (eds), *Christian Clergy in American Politics*. Baltimore (MD): The John Hopkins University Press, 2001.
Curtis IV, Edward (ed), *The Columbia Sourcebook of Muslims in the United States*. New York: Columbia University Press, 2008.
Daddow, Oliver (2013) 'The Use of Force in British Foreign Policy: From New Labour to the Coalition.' *The Political Quarterly* Vol. 84, Iss. 1, pp. 110–119.
Dalrymple, William, *The Last Mughal: The Fall of Delhi, 1857*. London: Bloomsbury, 2006.
Damon, G.H., to Richard Sanger, *Memorandum*, April 2, 1952, file Department of State, File 511.80/4-252, CS/Y.
Dard, A.R., *Letter to the Secretary for Home Affairs*, August 26, 1925, India Office Records, File L/PJ/6/1911.
Darwin, John, *Unfinished Empire: The Global Expansion of Britain*. London: Penguin, 2013.
Dathan, Matthew, 'Revealed: The Buildings across Westminster Governed by Sharia Law – Including Admiralty House, Once Home to Members of the Royal Family and Sea Lords.' *The Daily Mail*, March 3, 2016.
Davis, Robert, *Christian Slaves, Muslim Masters: White Slavery in the Mediterranean, the Barbary Coast and Italy, 1500–1800*. London: Palgrave MacMillan, 2003.
Dawisha, Adeed, *Arab Nationalism in the Twentieth Century: From Triumph to Despair*. Princeton (NJ): Princeton University Press, 2016.
Dawley, Alan, *Changing the World: American Progressives in War and Revolution*. Princeton: Princeton University Press, 2003.
Dawson, J. and S. Godec, *Counter Extremism Policy: An Overview*. House of Commons Briefing Paper No. 7238, June 23, 2017.
Dean, John, to Al Haig, *Memorandum* 'Possible Libyan Funding of the Nation of Islam.' February 3, 1972, Department of State EO, 12958.
Dearden, Lizzie, 'Theresa May's Government Condemned for Driving "More Austerity and More Racism" after the Integration Review.' *The Independent*, December 6, 2016.
Decaro, Louis, *On the Side of My People: A Religious Life of Malcolm X*. New York: New York University Press, 1996.
Dellinger, Walter, Testimony, 'Religious Expression in Public Schools.' *Committee on the Judiciary of the United States Senate*, October 26, 1995.
Denoeux, G., and L. Carter, *Guide to the Drivers of Violent Extremism*. Washington DC: USAid, 2009.
Department of Education (US), SSA513/05.
———, 'Guidance on Constitutionally Protected Prayer in Public Elementary and Secondary Schools.' February 7, 2003. http://www2.ed.gov/policy/ gen/guid/religionandschools/prayer_guidance.html.
Department of Homeland Security (2016) *Security Strategy for Countering Violent Extremism and Strategic Implementation Plan for Empowering Local Partners to*

Prevent Violent Extremism in the United States. https://www.dhs.gov/sites/default/files/publications/NSCITF%20CVE%20Report.pdf.

Department of Justice (2015) 'Pilot Programs are Key to Our Countering Violent Extremism Efforts.' https://www.justice.gov/archives/opa/blog/pilot-programs-are-key-our-countering-violent-extremism-efforts.

Department of State, U.S. Chargé, London to Secretary of State for Foreign Affairs, March 29, 1932, File E1549/121/91.

Department of Treasury, 'Islamic Finance 101: Conference Program.' University of Harvard, November 6, 2008. http://www.saneworks.us/uploads/news/applications/7.pdf.

de Vries, Hent and Lawrence Sullivan (eds), *Political Theologies: Public Religions in a Post-Secular World.* New York: Fordham University Press, 2006.

Dienow, Jessica and Mark Donfred, *Searching for Cultural Diplomacy.* Oxford: Berghahn Books, 2010.

Dilanian, Ken, 'Why Won't Obama Say Radical Islam?' www.nbcnews.com, June 13, 2016.

Dirks, Nicholas, *The Scandal of Empire: India and the Creation of Imperial Britain.* London, Cambridge (MA): Belknap Press, 2006.

Dodd, Vickram, 'Government Anti-Terrorism Strategy "Spies" On Innocent.' *The Guardian*, October 16, 2009.

———, 'Anti-Muslim Hate Crimes Soar in the UK after Christchurch Shootings.' *The Guardian*, March 22, 2019.

Doyle, Mark, *Communal Violence in the British Empire: Disturbing the Pax.* London: Bloomsbury, 2017.

Drakeman, Donald, *Church State and Original Intent.* Cambridge, New York: Cambridge University Press, 2010.

Dressler, Markus (2015) 'Rereading Ziya Gokalp: Secularism and Reform of the Islamic State in the Late Young Turk Period.' *International Journal of Middle East Studies* Vol. 47, Iss. 3, pp. 511–531.

Dunne, Timothy and Christian Reus-Smit, *The Globalization of International Society.* Oxford, New York: Oxford University Press, 2017.

Eide, Elizabeth and Risto Kunelius, *Transnational Media Events: The Mohammad Cartoons and the Imagined Clash of Civilizations.* New York: Coronet, 2008.

Eisenhower, Dwight, *Remarks.* Washington DC, Islamic Center, June 28, 1957. https://www.whitehousehistory.org/press-room/press-fact-sheets/u-s-presidential-visits-to-domestic-mosques.

Elkholy, Abdo, *The Arab Moslems in the United States.* New Haven (CT): College and University Press, 1966.

Enyat, Hamid, *Modern Islamic Political Thought.* Basingstoke: Macmillan Education, 1982.

Ernst, Douglas, 'San Diego School District to Create Muslim Safe Spaces, Boost Islam Lessons to Combat Bullying.' *The Washington Times*, April 6, 2017.

Esposito, John, *Unholy War: Terror in the Name of Islam.* Oxford, New York: Oxford University Press, 2003.

———, Testimony, *Hearing before the Subcommittee on Terrorism, Non-Proliferation and Trade of the Committee on Foreign Affairs, House of Representatives,*

One Hundred and Fifteenth Congress, First Session. July 19, 2017, Serial Number 115–46.

Esseissah, K., *The Increasing Conversion to Islam since 9/11: A Study of White American Muslim Converts in Northwest Ohio.* Dissertation, Bowling Green State University, 2011.

Evans, Laurence, *United States Policy and the Partition of Turkey, 1914–1924.* Baltimore: Johns Hopkins University Press, 1965.

Fair, C. Christine (2012) 'The US–Pakistan Relations after a Decade of the War On Terror.' *Contemporary South Asia* Vol. 20, Iss. 2, pp. 243–253.

Farahat, Cynthia (No Date) 'Islamists with Direct Ties to Terrorists Lobby Congress.' https://www.meforum. org/MiddleEast Forum/media/MEFLibrary/Muslim-Advocacy-Day-Dossier.pdf.

Fergusson, J., *Al-Britannia, My Country.* Milton Keynes: Bantam Press, 2017.

Fletcher, Robert, *British Imperialism and the 'Tribal Question': Desert Administration and Nomadic Societies, 1919–1936.* Oxford, New York: Oxford University Press, 2015.

Ford, Nancy, *Americans All! Foreign-Born Soldiers in World War I.* College Station (TX): Texas A&M University Press, 2001.

Foreign Office, U.S. Chargé, London to Secretary of State for Foreign Affairs, March 29, 1932, E1549/121/91, File 371/16001.

———, Eastern Section, *Third Quarterly Report on Islamic World*, October 1949, File 371/75047 (1019).

———, *Sir Luke (Colonial Office) to Sir Caccia*, August 22, File 1942371/24548.

Foreign Service Dispatch, 237.511.80/7-2753.

Fraser, James, *Between Church and State: Religion and Public Education in a Multicultural America.* New York: St. Martin's Press, 2000.

Fromkin, David, *The Peace to End All Peace: The Fall of the Ottoman Empire and the Creation of the Modern Middle East.* London: Phoenix Press, 2000.

Fukayama, Francis (1989) 'The End of History.' *The National Interest* Vol. 16, pp. 3–18.

Funk, Nathan and Abdul Aziz Said (2004) 'Islam and the West: Narratives of Conflict and Transformation.' *International Journal of Peace Studies* Vol. 9, Iss. 1, pp. 1–28.

Galonnier, J. (2015) 'The Radicalization of Muslims in France and the United States: Some Insights from White Converts to Islam.' *Social Compass* Vol. 62, Iss. 4, pp. 570–583.

Geaves, Ron, *Islam in Victorian Britain: The Life and Times of Abdullah Quilliam.* Leicester: Kube Press, 2019.

——— (2017) 'Abdullah Quilliam (Henri De Léon) and Marmaduke Pickthall: Agreements and Disagreements between Two Prominent Muslims in the London and Woking Communities.' In Geoffrey Nash (ed), *Marmaduke Pickthall: Islam and the Modern World.* Leiden: Brill, 2017.

General Headquarters, Middle East, *Minutes of Meeting with Amin Osman Pacha at British Embassy May 18, 1942*, File DS (E) 200/42.

Gentzkow, Matthew and Jesse Shapiro (2004) 'Media, Education and Anti-Americanism in the Muslim World.' *Journal of Economic Perspectives* Vol. 18, Iss. 3, pp. 117–133.

Gerges, Fawaz (2003) 'Islam and Muslims in the Mind of America.' *Annals of the American Academy of Political and Social Science* Vol. 588, pp. 73–89.

———, *America and Political Islam: Clash of Cultures of Clash of Interests?* Cambridge: Cambridge University Press, 1999.

Gerrard, Christopher and Alejandra Gutierrez (eds), 'Part X, A Wider Context: Trade and Exchange, Europe and Beyond.' In *The Oxford Handbook of Later Medieval Archaeology in Britain.* Oxford, New York: Oxford University Press, 2018, pp. 878–905.

GhaneaBassiri, Kambiz, *A History of Islam in America.* Cambridge, New York: Cambridge University Press, 2010.

Ghaznavi, Masood (1974) 'Recent Muslim Historiography in South Asia: The Problem of Perspective.' *Indian Economic and Social History Review* Vol. 11, Iss. 2–3, pp. 183–215.

Gilham, Jamie, *Loyal Enemies: British Converts to Islam 1850–1950.* London: Hurst and Co, 2014.

Gillespie, Dizzy and al Frazer, *To Be or Not–To Bop.* New York: Doubleday, 1974.

Githens-Mazer, J. and R. Lambert (2010) 'Why Conventional Wisdom on Radicalization Fails: The Persistence of a Failed Discourse.' *Journal of International Affairs* Vol. 86, Iss. 4, pp. 889–901.

Gladstone, William, *The Bulgarian Horrors and the Question of the East.* London: John Murray, 1876.

Goddard, Hugh, *A History of Christian Muslim Relations.* Edinburgh: Edinburgh University Press, 2000.

Godwin, Matthew and Thomas Raines, February 7, 2017. https://www.chathamhouse.org/expert/com ment/what-do-europeans-think-about-muslim-immigration.

Goldman, Adam and Matthew Apuzzo, 'The NYPD Division of Un-American Activities.' August 25, 2013. http://nymag.com/news/features/nypd-demographics-unit-2013-9/.

Gomez, Michael, *Black Crescent: The Experience and Legacy of African Muslims in the America.* Cambridge, New York: Cambridge University Press, 2005.

Goodhart, David, *The Road to Somewhere: The New Tribes Shaping British Politics.* London: Penguin, 2017.

Goody, Jack, *Islam in Europe.* London: Wiley, 2013.

Gordts, Elaine, 'Mohammed Cartoons: White House Questions 'Judgement' behind Charlie Hebdo Cartoons.' *The Huffington Post*, September 20, 2012.

Gottschalk, Peter, *Religion, Science and Empire: Classifying Hinduism and Islam in British India.* Oxford, New York: Oxford University Press, 2012.

Gould, Blake, *Islamic Finance in North America 2009* (No Date) Yassar Media. https://umgroup.ca/2019/06/yasaar-media-islamic-finance-in-north-american-2009/.

Graham, S.A., *Memorandum to Secretary to the Government of India*, February 1, 1922, India Office Records, File PS/11/211.

Great Britain Census Office, *Census of the British Empire: 1901*. London: Her Majesty's Stationary Office, 1906.
Green, John, *The Faith Factor: How Religion Influences American Elections*. Westport (CT): Praeger, 2007.
Grewal, Zareena, *Islam is a Foreign Country*. New York: University of New York, 2013.
Grinel, Klas (2018) 'Framing Islam at the World of Islam Festival, London, 1976.' *Journal of Muslims in Europe* Vol. 7, Iss. 1, pp. 73–93.
Guerrero, Javier (2017) 'Propaganda Broadcasts and Cold War Politics: The Carter Administration's Outreach to Islam.' *Journal of Cold War Studies* Vol. 19, Iss. 1, pp. 4–37.
Guidance Financial, March 25, 2015. https//:guidancefinancial.com.
Gunther, Sebastian, 'Education.' In Gerhard Bowering (Editor in Chief), *The Princeton Encyclopedia of Islamic Political Thought*. Princeton, Oxford: Princeton University Press, 2013.
Haddad, Yvonne, Farid Senzai and Jane Smith, *Educating the Muslims of America*. Oxford, New York: Oxford University Press, 2012.
———, 'Arab Muslims.' In Samer Abraham and Nabeel Abraham (eds), *Arabs in the New World: Studies on Arab American Communities*. Detroit (MI): Wayne State Press, 1983.
Hail, J.A., *Britain's Foreign Policy in Egypt and Sudan 1947–1956*. Reading: Ithaca Press, 1996.
Halliday, Fred, *The Middle East in International Relations: Power, Politics and Ideology*. Cambridge, New York: CUP, 2005.
Halman, Talat, 'Turks.' In Stephen Thernstrom (ed), *Harvard Encyclopedia of American Ethnic Groups*. Cambridge (MA): Harvard University Press, 1980.
Hart, Justin, *The Empire of Ideas: The Origins of Public Diplomacy and the Transformation of U.S. Foreign Policy*. Oxford, New York: Oxford University Press, 2013.
Hartman, Andrew, *A History of the Culture Wars: A War for the Soul of America*. Chicago: University of Chicago Press, 2015.
Hassan, Kabir and Michael Mahlknecht, *Islamic Capital Markets: Products and Strategies*. Oxford: Wiley, 2014.
Hastings, Adrian, *The Church in Africa, 1450–1950*. Oxford: Clarendon Press, 1996.
Hay, Rupert (1955) 'The Impact of the Oil Industry on the Persian Gulf Shaykhdoms.' *Middle East Journal* Vol. 9, pp. 361–392.
Heath-Kelly, Charlotte (2013) 'Counter-Terrorism and the Counterfactual: Producing the 'Radicalization' Discourse and the UK PREVENT Strategy.' *The British Journal of Politics & International Relations* Vol. 15, Iss. 3, pp. 394–415.
Heraclides, Alex and Ada Dialla, 'Intervention in the Greek War of Independence, 1821–32.' In *Humanitarian Intervention in the Long Nineteenth Century*. Manchester: Manchester University Press, 2015, pp. 105–133.
Her Majesty's Government, *Counter Extremism Strategy, Cm 9148*. London: Her Majesty's Stationary Office, 2015.
Higgins, Andrew and Maia De La Baume, 'Two Brothers Suspected in Killings were Known to French Intelligence Services.' *The New York Times*, January 8, 2015.

Hiro, Dilip, *Cold War in the Islamic World*. New York, Oxford: Oxford University Press, 2018.

———, *Iran under the Ayatollahs*. New York, London: Routledge, 2013.

Hirodin, Mohamed, *Letter to Lord Hamilton* (Secretary of State for India), February 17, 1896, India Office Records, File L/PJ/6547.

HM Government, 'Population of England and Wales.' August 1, 2018. https://www.ethnicity-facts-figures.service.gov.uk/uk-population-by-ethnicity.

Hobsbawn, Eric, *The Age of Empire: 1875–1914*. London: Abacus, 1989.

Hoing, Esther, 'You Might Be Eating Halal Meant and Not Even Know It.' *National Public Radio*, April 5, 2018.

Holbraad, Carsten, *The Concert of Europe: A Study in German and British International Theory*. London: Prentice Hall Press, 1970.

Holland, Matthew, *America and Egypt: From Roosevelt to Eisenhower*. Westport (CT): Praeger Publishers, 1996.

Holland, Tom, *Millennium*. London: Little Brown, 2008.

———, *Dominion: The Making of the Western Mind*. London: Little Brown, 2019.

Holmwood, John, 'Investigate the Birmingham Trojan Horse Affair.' www.opendemocracy.net, October 2, 2018.

———, and Therese O'Toole, *Countering Extremism in British Schools? The Truth about the Birmingham Trojan Horse Affair*. Bristol: Polity Press, 2018.

Home Office, *Prevent Strategy, Cm 8092*. London: Her Majesty's Stationary Office, 2011.

Housby, Elaine, *Islamic and Ethical Finance in the United Kingdom*. Edinburgh: Edinburgh University Press, 2013.

———, *Islamic Financial Services in the United Kingdom*. Edinburgh: Edinburgh University Press, 2011.

House of Commons Debate, June 7, 2011, *Hansard*. c52.

———, April 24, 2012, *Hansard*, pp. 823–5.

House of Commons Foreign Affairs Committee, *The UK's Relations with Saudi Arabia and Bahrain*, Fifth Report of Session 2013–14. Vol. 1, November 12, 2013.

Howell, Sally, 'Federation.' In Jocelyne Cesari (ed), *Encyclopedia of Islam in the United States*. Vol. 1. Westport (CT): Greenwood Press, 2007.

Huddle, Franklin, *The Future of Iran: Implications for the US*, INR, Iran Documents 01144, DSNA January 28, 1977.

Human Rights Council Resolution 16/18, April 12, 2011. https://www2.ohchr.org/english/bodies/ hrcouncil /docs/16session/a.hrc.res.16.18_en.pdf.

Hume, Tim and Lauren Said-Moorhouse, 'Hollonde: Republic Must Create "Islam of France" to Respond to Terror Threat.' www.edition.cnn.com, September 8, 2016.

Huntington, Samuel, *Who Are We? America's Great Debate*. New York: Free Press, 2004.

———, *The Clash of Civilizations and the Remaking of the World Order* (Originally published 1997). London, New York: Simon and Schuster, 2002.

Hurlock, Kathryn, *Britain, Ireland and the Crusades, c.1000–1300*. Basingstoke: Palgrave Macmillan, 2013.

Hurst, Steven, *Cold War US Foreign Policy: Key Perspectives*. Edinburgh: Edinburgh University Press, 2005.

Husain, Ed, *The House of Islam: A Global History*. London: Bloomsbury, 2018.

India Office Records, *Coatman Script*, File L/I/877.

Intelligence Bureau, Section F, *Memorandum: The Russian Moslems and the Bolsheviks*, (No Date) Foreign Office, File 141/587.

Invermee, Robert, *Secularism, Islam and Education in India, 1830–1910*. London, New York: Routledge, 2015.

Ipgrave, Julia, 'Inter Religious Relations and the English Model of Church Establishment in Nation and Parish.' In Wolfram Welbe, Katajun Amirpur, Anna Kors and Dorthe Vieregge (eds), *Religions and Dialogue: International Approaches*. Munster, New York: Waxman, 2014.

Ipgrave, Michael (2005) 'Anglican Approaches to Christian Muslim Dialogue.' *Journal of Anglican Studies* Vol. 3, Iss. 2, pp. 219–236.

Irfan, Harris, *Heaven's Bankers: Inside the Hidden World of Islamic Finance*. London: Hachette, 2014.

Islamic Education Foundation of New Jersey, 'Invest in Your Child's Future.' October 16, 2019. http://www.iefnj.org/.

Jackson, Liz (2011) 'Islam and Muslims in US Public Schools since September 11, 2001.' *Journal of Religious Education* Vol. 106, Iss. 2, pp. 162–180.

Jacobs, Matthew, *Imagining the Middle East: The Building of an American Foreign Policy, 1918–1967*. Chapel Hill (NC): University of North Carolina Press, 2011.

Jacobson, Jon, *When the Soviet Union Entered World Politics*. Berkley: University of California, 1994.

Jamal, Ameney, *Of Empires and Citizens: Pro-American Democracy or No Democracy At All?* Princeton: Princeton University Press, 2012.

James, Lawrence, *Raj: The Making and Unmaking of British India*. London: Abacus, 1997.

Johnson, Jenna, 'Donald Trump Would "Strongly Consider" Closing Some Mosques.' *The Washington Post*, March 20, 2017.

Johnson, Hans and Sergio Sanchez (No Date) 'Just the Facts: Immigrants in California.' https://www.ppic.org/publication/immig rants-in-california/.

Judd, Denis, *Empire: The British Imperial Experience from 1765 to the Present*. London: Fontana Press, 1997.

Kamran, Mehran, *The Middle East: A Political History since the First World War*. Berkley, Los Angeles: University California Los Angeles Press, 2005.

Kane, J. Herbert, *A Concise History of the Christian World Mission: A Panoramic View of Missions from Pentecost to the Present*. Grand Rapids (MI): Baker Books, 1978.

Kaplan, Robert, *The Arabists: The Romance of an American Elite*. New York: The Free Press, 1993.

Karoub, Jeff, 'McDonalds to Pay $700,000 To Settle Allegations that the Franchise Falsely Claimed Food Complied with Halal.' *The Huffington Post*, January 21, 2013.

Karpat, Kemal (1985) 'Ottoman Emigration to America.' *International Journal of Middle Eastern Studies* Vol. 17, Iss. 2, pp. 175–209.

Karsh, Efraim and Inari Karsh, *Empires of the Sand: The Struggle for Mastery of the Middle East (1789–1923)*. Cambridge (MA), London: Harvard University Press, 2001.

Kaufmann, Eric, *Shall the Religious Inherit the Earth? Demography and Politics in the 21st Century*. London: Profile Books, 2010.

———, *Whiteshift: Populism, Immigration and the Future of White Majorities*. London: Penguin, 2019.

Keinzle, T., 'Merkel "Islam is not the Source of Terrorism".' *Al Jazeera*, February 18, 2017.

Keohane, Joseph and Joseph Nye. *Power and Interdependence* (4th Edn). Boston: Longman, 2011.

Kepel, Giles, *Terror in France: The Rise of Jihad in the West*. Princeton and Oxford: Princeton University Press, 2017.

Keyworth, Karen, *Islamic Schools of the United States: Data-Based Profiles*, May 18, 2011. https://www.ispu.org/islamic-schools-of-the-united-states-data-based-profiles/.

Khan, Sabith and Shariq Siddiqui, *Islamic Education in the United States and the Evolution of Muslim Non-Profit Institutions*. Cheltenham, Northampton (MA): Edward Elgar Publishing, 2017.

Khan, Aysha and Lauren Markoe, 'Muslims on Capitol Hill Learn How to Lobby.' www.religionnews.com, May 2, 2017.

Khater, Akram (2011) 'New Faith in Ancient Lands: Western Missions in the Middle East in the Nineteenth and Early Twentieth Centuries.' *Journal of Social Science and Missions* Vol. 24, Iss. 2–3, pp. 304–309.

Kirby, Michael, *The Decline of British Power since 1870*. London and New York: Routledge, 2014.

Kirk, Andrew, *Civilizations in Conflict? Islam, the West and Christian Faith*. Oxford: Regnum Books International, 2011.

Klausen, Jytte, *The Cartoons that Shook the World*. New Haven, London: Yale University Press, 2009.

Kleinmann, K. (2012) 'Radicalization of Homegrown Sunni Militants in the United States: Comparing Converts and Non-Converts.' *Studies in Conflict and Terrorism* Vol. 35, Iss. 4, pp. 278–297.

Krämer, Gudrun, Denis Matringe, John Nawas and Everett Rowson, *Encyclopedia of Islam* (3rd Edn). Leiden: Brill, 2011.

Kull, Steven, *Feeling Betrayed: The Roots of Muslim Anger at America*. Washington DC: Brookings Institute Press, 2011.

Kuntzel, Matthias, *Jihad and Jew Hatred: Islamism, Nazism and the Roots of 9/11* (trans. Colin Meade). New York: Telos Press, 2007.

Lake, Anthony (1994) 'Building a New Middle East, Challenges for US Policy' address to the Soref Symposium of the Washington Institute of Near Eastern Policy, May 17, 1994, Department of State.

Landau, Jacob, *Pan Islamism: History and Politics*. London, New York: Routledge, 2015.

Layman, Geoffrey, *The Great Divide: Religious and Cultural Conflict in American Party Politics*. New York: Columbia University Press, 2001.

Leonard, Karen, *South Asian Americans*. Philadelphia (CT): Temple University Press, 1992.

Lewis, Bernard, *The Emergence of Modern Turkey* (3rd Edn). Oxford, New York: Oxford University Press, 2002.

Lincoln, Eric, *The Black Muslims in America*. Michigan: Grand Rapids, 1994.

Lukes, S. (2005) 'Power and the Battle of Hearts and Minds.' *Millennium: Journal of International Relations* Vol. 33, Iss. 3, pp. 477–493.

MacLean, Gerald and Nabil Matar, *Britain and the Islamic World, 1558–1713*. Oxford, New York: Oxford University Press, 2016.

—— (ed), *Britain and the Muslim World: Historical Perspectives*. Newcastle upon Tyne: Cambridge Scholars Publishing, 2011.

Makariev, Plamen (ed), *Islamic and Christian Cultures: Conflict or Dialogue*. Washington DC: The Council for Research in Values and Philosophy, 2001.

Malik, Kenan, *From Fatwa to Jihad: The Rushdie Affair and its Legacy*. London, New York: Atlantic Books, 2009.

Mallmann, Klaus M., and Martin Cuppers, *Nazi Palestine: The Plans for the Extermination of the Jews in Palestine*. New York: Enigma Books, 2010.

Marchant, S. (2010) 'An Ambiguous Response to a Real Threat: Criminalizing the Glorification of Terrorism in Britain.' *The George Washington International Law Review* Vol. 42, Iss. 1, pp. 123–157.

Markey, Daniel, *No Exit from Pakistan: America's Tortured Relationship with Islamabad*. Cambridge, New York: Cambridge University Press, 2013.

Massad, Joseph, *Islam in Liberalism*. Chicago, New York: University of Chicago Press, 1994.

Matar, Nabil, *Islam in Britain 1558–1685*. Cambridge: Cambridge University Press, 1998.

Mathew, Johan (2017) 'Specters of Pan-Islam: Methodological Nationalism and British Imperial Policy after the First World War.' *The Journal of Imperial and Commonwealth History* Vol. 45, Iss. 6, pp. 942–968.

Matthew, H.C., *Gladstone, 1809–1898*. Oxford: Oxford University Press, 1997.

Matthews, Mark, 'UK Statement at the Implementation of Council Resolution 16/18 On Combating Religious Intolerance.' February 14, 2017. https://www.gov.uk/government/news/ uk-statement-at-the-implementation-of-council-resolution-161 8-event-on-combating-religious-intolerance-hosted-by-universal-rights-group.

McCaffree, Kevin, *The Secular Landscape: The Decline of Religion in America*. New York: Palgrave Macmillan, 2017.

McCloud, Aminah, *African American Islam*. New York: Routledge, 1995.

McKenzie, R., 'Countering Violent Extremism in America: Policy Recommendations for the Next President.' October 18, 2016. https://www.brookings.edu/research/countering-violent-extremism-in-america-policy-recommendations-for-the-next-president/.

McKercher, B.J.C., *The Second Baldwin Government and the United States, 1924–29*. Cambridge: Cambridge University Press, 1984.

Mcleod, Kate, 'The Role Museums Play in Social Activism.' www.americansforthearts.org, August 2, 2017.

McLoughlin, Leslie, *In a Sea of Knowledge: British Arabists in the 20th Century*. London: Ithaca Press, 2002.
McMahon, Henry, *Minutes of the Meeting with m. Déclassé*, India Office Records, File L/PS/11/85.
Menon, Meena (2010) 'Chronicle of Communal Riots in Bombay Presidency (1893–1945).' *Economic and Political Weekly* Vol. 45, Iss. 47, pp. 63–72.
Metcalf, Barbara, *Islamic Revival in British India: Deoband, 1860–1900*. Princeton: Princeton University Press, 2014.
Miah, Shamin, *Muslims, Schooling and Security: Trojan Horse, Prevent and Radical Politics*. London: Palgrave MacMillan, 2017.
Michael, George, *Confronting Right Wing Extremism and Terrorism in the USA*. New York, London: Routledge, 2003.
Middel, Christoffel, 'The West Wing: Why the [sic] Islam is Without Guidance.' March 14, 2017. https://www.youtube.com/watch?v=iZYs2UpLYAI, November 29, 2018.
———, *Extremism in America*. Tampa (FL): University of Florida Press, 2015.
Milton, Giles, *White Gold*. London: John Murray, 2005.
Minault, Gail and David Lelyveld (1974) 'The Campaign for a Muslim University 1898–1920.' *Modern Asian Studies* Vol. 8, Iss. 2, pp. 145–189.
Morgan, George and Scott Poynting, *Global Islamophobia: Muslims and Moral Panic in the West*. Ashgate, 2012.
Motadel, David (ed), *Islam and the European Empires*. New York, Oxford: Oxford University Press, 2014.
Mujeeb, Muhammad, *The Indian Muslims*. Aligarh: Aligarh University Press, 1967.
Mukherjee, Sumita and Sadia Zulfiqar (eds), *Islam and the West: A Love Story?* Cambridge: Cambridge Scholars Publishing, 2015.
Mullin, Corinna (2011) 'The US Discourse On Political Islam: Is Obama's a Truly Post-'War On Terror' Administration?' *Critical Studies on Terrorism* Vol. 4, Iss. 2, pp. 263–281.
Munoz, Gema, *Islam, Modernism and the West: Cultural and Political Relations at the End of the Millennium*. London: I.B. Tauris, 1999.
NatCen Social Research, 'British Social Attitudes 31: Proud to be British.' 2014. http://www.bsa.natcen.ac.uk/media/38109/proud-to-be-british-data.pdf.
———, 'Church of England Numbers at Record Low.' September 7, 2018. http://www.natcen.ac.uk/news-media/press-releases/2018/september/church-of-england-numbers-at-record-low/.
National Security Council, *Memorandum to James Lay Jnr, Office of the President*, July 6, 1954.
Navidi, Sandra, *Superhubs: How the Financial Elite and their Networks Rule Our World*. New York: Nicholas Brealey Publishing, 2017.
Nevakivi, Jukka, *Britain, France and the Arab Middle East 1914–1924*. London: Athlone Press, 1969.
New Albany Floyd County School Board (NAFCSB), *Minutes of the Meeting*, January 9, 2017. http://www.nafcs.k12.in.us/wp-content/uploads/2017/02/minutes-of-1-9-17.pdf.

Nichols, Michelle, 'Muslims Believe US Goal to Weaken Muslims.' *Reuters*, April 24, 2007.

Nordheimer, Ton, 'The Police Advanced; The Blacks Waited.' *New York Times*, January 16, 1972. https://www.nytimes.com/1972/01/16/archives/the-police-advanced-the-blacks-waited-race-relations.html.

Nye, Joseph (2010) 'The Future of American Power: Dominance and Decline in Perspective.' *Foreign Affairs* Vol. 89, Iss. 6, pp. 2–12.

Office of the Prime Minister, Press Release: *Counter-Extremism Bill – National Security Council Meeting*, May 13, 2015. https://www.gov.uk/government/news/counter-extremism-bill-national-security-council-meeting.

Okkenhaug, Inger (2015) 'Christian Missions in the Middle East and the Ottoman Balkans: Education, Reform and Failed Conversions, 1819–1967.' *International Journal of Middle East Studies* Vol. 47, Iss. 3, pp. 593–604.

———, *Is the American Century Over?* Cambridge: Polity Press, 2015.

Oliver-Dee, Sean, *The Caliphate Question: British Government and Islamic Governance*. Lanham (MD): Rowman and Littlefield, 2009.

———, *Muslim Minorities and Citizenship: Authority, Communities and Islamic Law*. London, New York: I.B. Tauris, 2012.

Olson, Laura, 'Mainline Protestant Washington Offices and the Political Lives of Clergy.' In Robert Wuthnow and John H. Evans (eds), *The Quiet Hand of God: Faith-Based Activism and the Public Role of Mainline Protestantism*. Berkeley, CA: University of California Press, 2002, pp. 54–79.

——— and Edward Jelen, *The Religious Dimension of Political Behavior. A Critical Analysis and Annotated Bibliography*. Westport (CT): Greenwood Press, 1998.

———, *Filled with Spirit and Power. Protestant Clergy in Politics*. Albany (NY): State University of New York Press, 2000.

O'Neill, Maureen, *Muslim Mothers: Pioneers of Islamic Education in America*. Unpublished PhD thesis, College of Notre Dame, Maryland, 2010.

O'Toole, Therese, Daniel Nilsson DeHanas and Tariq Modood (2012) 'Balancing Tolerance, Security and Muslim Engagement in the United Kingdom: The Impact of the "Prevent" Agenda.' *Critical Studies on Terrorism* Vol. 5, Iss. 3, pp. 373–389.

Ozcan, Azmi, *Pan-Islamism: Indian Muslims, the Ottomans and Britain, 1877–1924*. Leiden: Brill, 1997.

Pantazis, C. and S. Pemberton (2009) 'From the "Old" to the "New" Suspect Community: Examining the impacts of Recent UK Counter-Terrorist Legislation.' *British Journal of Criminology* Vol. 49, Iss. 5, pp. 646–666.

Pantucci, Raphael (2010) 'A Contest to Democracy? How the UK has Responded to the Current Terrorist Threat.' *Democratization* Vol. 17, Iss. 2, pp. 251–271.

Parsons, Lynn, *John Quincy Adams – A Bibliography*. Lanham: Rowman and Littlefield, 1999.

Pelletreau, Robert (1994) 'Symposium: Resurgent Islam.' *Middle East Policy* Vol. 3, Iss. 2, pp. 1–21.

Pew Research Center, 'Social and Demographic Trends.' September 10, 2019. http://www.pewsocialtrends.org.

Philips, Melanie, 'It's Pure Myth that Islam is a Religion of Peace.' *The Times*, June 29, 2015.

Pintak, Lawrence, *America and Islam: Soundbites, Suicide Bombs and the Road to Donald Trump*. London, New York: I.B. Tauris, 2019.
Porter, Andrew, *Religion versus Empire? British Protestant Missionaries and Overseas Expansion, 1700–1914*. Manchester, New York: Manchester University Press, 2004.
Poston, Larry, *Islamic Da'wah in the West: Muslim Missionary Activity and the Dynamics of Conversion to Islam*. Oxford, New York: Oxford University Press, 1992.
Prasad, Bimla (1967) 'The Emergence of the Demand for India's Partition.' *International Studies* Vol. 9, Iss. 3, pp. 241–278.
Privy Council File 4/1.
Pugh, William, *American Encounters with Arabs: The "Soft Power" of US Diplomacy in the Middle East*. Westport (CT): Greenwood Publishing, 2005.
Qadir, Ali (2013) 'Between Secularism's: Islam and the Institutionalization of Modern Higher Education in Mid-Nineteenth Century British India.' *British Journal of Religious Education* Vol. 35, Iss. 2, pp. 125–139.
Quak, Johannes and Cora Schuh (eds), *Religious Indifference: New Perspectives from Studies on Secularization and Nonreligion*. Cham: Springer, 2017.
Qureishi, M. Naeem, *Pan-Islamism in British Indian Politics*. Leiden: Brill, 2011.
———, *Pan-Islam in British-Indian Politics: A Study of the Khilafat Movement, 1918–1924*. Leiden: Brill, 1999.
Rai, Milan, *7/7: The London Bombings, Islam and the Iraq War*. London: Pluto Press, 2006.
Raja, Raza, thoughtful article 'Why are Conspiracy Theories So Rife in the Muslim World.' *Huffington Post*, July 7, 2017.
Rashid, Hakim and Muhammad Zakiyyah (1992) 'The Sister Clara Muhammad Schools: Pioneers in the Development of Islamic Education in America.' *Journal of Negro Education* Vol. 61, Iss. 2, pp. 178–185.
Reisner, Christian, *Roosevelt's Religion*. Oxford: Clarendon Press, 1922.
Rice, Condoleeza, 'Remarks at the American University in Cairo.' June 20, 2005. https://2001-2009.state.gov/secretary/rm/2005/48328.htm.
Richards, Alan, *Socio-Economic Roots of Radicalism? Towards Explaining the Appeal of Islamic Radicals*. Washington DC: Diane Publishing Co., 2003.
Roosevelt, Theodore, *Fear God and Take Your Own Part* (Originally Published 1916). New York: Forgotten Book, 2017.
Rotter, Andrew, *Comrades at Odds: The United States and India, 1947–1964*. New York: Ithaca Press, 2000.
Rubin, Barry and Wolfgang Schwanitz, *Nazis, Islamists, and the Making of the Modern Middle East*. New Haven (CT): Yale University Press, 2014.
Rumpole, Horace, *Letter to Lord Curzon*, May 18, 1921, Foreign Office, File 371/6470.
Sadiq, Muhammad (1921) 'My Advice to the Muhammadans in America.' *Muslim Sunrise* Vol. 1, Iss. 2, p. 29.
Samei, Mohammed (2010) 'Neo Orientalism? The Relationship between the West and Islam in Our Globalized World.' *Third World Quarterly* Vol. 31, Iss. 7, pp. 1145–1160.

Sanders, David, *Losing and Empire, Finding a Role: British Foreign Policy since 1945*. Basingstoke: MacMillan, 1990.

Saunders, Liane, *The Motives Pattern and Form of Anglo-Ottoman Diplomatic Relations c1580–1661*. Unpublished PhD thesis, University of Oxford, 1993.

Scheifer, S.E. (Chief Editor), *The Muslim 500 (2018): The World's 500 Most Influential Muslims*. Amman: The Royal Islamic Strategic Studies Centre, 2017.

Seager, Richard (ed), *The Dawn of Religious Pluralism: Voices from the World Parliament of Religions, 1893*. La Salle: Open Court Press, 1993.

Seymour, Charles, *The Intimate Papers of Colonel House*. Boston: Houghton Mifflin, 1928.

Shackle, Samira, 'Trojan Horse: The Real Story behind the Fake "Islamic Plot" to Take Over Schools.' *The Guardian*, September 1, 2017.

Shah, Sonia, *Crude: The Story of Oil*. New York, London: Seven Stories Press, 2011.

Shehata, Samer, *Islamist Politics in the Middle East: Movements and Change*. New York, London: Routledge, 2012.

Shields, Charles, *The 1993 World Trade Center Bombing*. New York: Chelsea House Publishers, 2002.

Shleifer, James (2014) 'Tocqueville, Religion and Democracy in America: Some Essential Questions.' *American Political Thought* Vol. 3, Iss. 2, pp. 245–278.

Smart, W.A., *Memorandum*, General Headquarters, Middle East, October 10, 1942, File DS (E) 140/1.

———, *Memorandum*, General Headquarters, Middle East, November 11, 1942, File DS (E) 140/1.

Smith, Jane D., *Islam in America*. New York: Columbia University Press, 1999.

Sorensen, Georg, *Rethinking the New World Order*. London: Palgrave Macmillan, 2016.

Southers, Errol, 'The U.S. Government's Program to Counter Violent Extremism Needs an Overhall (Op Ed).' *Los Angeles Times*, March 21, 2017.

Styler, Catherine, *Barbary Pirates, British Slaves and the Early Modern Atlantic World, 1570–1800*. PhD Thesis, University of Pennsylvania, 2011.

Suleiman, Michael (1987) 'Early Arab Americans: The Search for Identity.' In Eric Hoogland (ed), *Crossing the Waters: Arabic-Speaking Immigrants to the United States before 1940*. Washington DC: Smithsonian Institution Press, 1987.

Summitt, April (2004) 'For a White Revolution: John F Kennedy and the Shah of Iran.' *Middle East Journal* Vol. 58, Iss. 4, pp. 560–575.

Tejirian, Eleanor and Reeva Simon, *Conflict, Conquest and Conversion: Two Thousand Years of Christian Missions in the Middle East*. New York: Columbia University Press, 2012.

Terrorism Act. London: Her Majesty's Government, 11th April, 2006.

Teye, Patrick, *Barbary Pirates: Thomas Jefferson, William Eaton, and the Evolution of U.S. Diplomacy in the Mediterranean*. Unpublished Master's Thesis, East Tennessee State University, 2013.

Thatcher, Margaret, 'Islamism is the New Bolshevism.' *The Guardian*, February 12, 2002.

Thomas, Paul (2010) 'Failed and Friendless: The UK's "Preventing Violent Extremism" Programme.' *The British Journal of Politics & International Relations* Vol. 12, Iss. 3, pp. 442–458.

Thomas, T., *Responding to the Threat of Violent Extremism*. London: Bloomsbury Academic, 2012.

Tinniswood, Adrian, *Pirates of Barbary: Corsairs, Conquests and Captivity in the 17th Century*. London: Vintage, 2011.

Tracy, Kimberly (2006) 'Islamic Finance: A Growing Industry in the United States.' *North Carolina Banking Institute* Iss. 355, pp. 29–31.

Trigg, Roger, *Equality, Freedom and Religion*. Oxford: Oxford University Press, 2012.

———, *Religious Diversity: Philosophical and Political Dimensions*. Cambridge: Cambridge University Press, 2014.

Trump, Donald, 'Speech to the Muslim World.' May 21, 2017. https://www.haaretz.com/ middle-east-news/read-in-full-transcript-of-trump-s-speech-to-the-muslim-world-1.5474977.

———, Campaign Rally Press Conference, Mount Pleasant, South Carolina, December 7, 2015. https://www.youtube.com/watch?v=hLgTF8FrYlU.

United States Code 1901–1907. *Humane Slaughter Act*. https://www.animallaw.info/statute/us-food-animal-humane-methods-livestock-slaughter.

Varble, Derek, *The Suez Crisis*. New York: Rosen Publishing, 2009.

Vidino, Lorenzo, *The New Muslim Brotherhood in the West*. New York: Columbia University Press, 2010.

Vincent, B., *Bombers, Hijackers, Body Scanners and Jihadists*. New York: Xlibris, 2012.

Walberg, Eric, *Postmodern Imperialism: Geopolitics and the Great Games*. Atlanta: Clarity Press, 2014.

Wald, Kenneth and Allison Calhoun-Brown, *Religion and Politics in the United States* (5th Edn). Lanham (MD): Rowman & Littlefield, 2010.

Warikoo, Niraj, 'Halal Food at KFC.' *Detroit Free Press*, March 30, 2008.

Watson, Adam, *The Evolution of International Society: A Comparative Historical Analysis*. London: Routledge, 1992.

Watson, Charlie and Ian Cooper, 'Five Whitehall Buildings Held by Wealthy Businessmen Now Operating under Sharia Rules.' *The Independent*, March 3, 2016.

Webb, Alexander Russell, to State Department, *Dispatch – Manila to Washington DC*. October 3, 1893.

White House (2011) *Empowering Local Partners to Prevent Violent Extremism*. https://obamawhitehouse.archives.gov/sites/default/files/empowering_local_partners.pdf.

Wickham, Christopher, *Medieval Europe: From the Breakup of the Western Roman Empire to the Reformation*. New Haven (CT): Yale University Press, 2017.

Wilson, Gramme, 'Young British Muslims Getting More Radical.' *The Daily Telegraph*, January 29, 2007.

Wise (2011) 'Islamic Revolution of 1979: The Downfall of American-Iranian Relations.' *Legacy* Vol. 11, Iss. 1, pp. 1–16.

Woodward, Ernest, *British Foreign Policy in the Second World War*. London: Her Majesty's Stationary Office, 1962.
Woolock, Nicola, 'No Interest-but a Surefire, Best Selling Hit.' *The Daily Telegraph*, November 15, 2003.
World Bank, 'GDP: 1960–2018.' https://data.worldbank.org/indicator/ny.gdp.mktp.cd? name_desc=true April 5, 2019.
World Evangelical Crusade, *Letter to William Batten* (British Agent, Jeddah), March 14, 1922, India Office Records, File L/PS/15/1654.
Wright, Denis, *The Persians amongst the English*. London: I.B. Tauris, 1985.
Wright, Theodore (1966) 'Muslim Education in India at the Crossroads: The Case of Aligarh.' *Public Affairs* Vol. 39, Iss. 1, pp. 50–61.
Yakub, Salim, *Containing Arab Nationalism: The Eisenhower Doctrine and the Middle East*. Chapel Hill (NC): University of North Carolina Press, 2002.
Yildizeli, Fahriye, *W.E. Gladstone and British Policy towards the Ottoman Empire*. Unpublished PhD thesis, University of Exeter, 2016.
Zyp, Victoria, *Islamic Finance in the United States: Product Development and Regulatory Adoption*. Master's Thesis, Georgetown University, 2009.

Index

9/11, 1, 6, 15, 39, 44, 45, 49, 51, 57, 68–72, 75, 76, 96, 133, 147, 149, 152, 153, 158, 162, 163, 169

Adams, John, 40, 41, 45, 53, 169
Ahmadiyya, 23, 96, 121

Barbary Pirates, 26–28, 30, 36, 37, 40, 46, 52, 53, 169
Blair, Tony, 12, 19, 49, 50, 54, 68
Brown, Gordon, 12, 83, 92
Bush, George, (Snr), 43, 140
Bush, George W., 44, 45, 46, 53, 54, 68, 69, 71, 72, 76

Caliph, 30, 58, 60, 74, 100, 101, 102, 110, 111, 114, 116, 123
Cameron, David, 50, 51, 55, 150
Churchill, Winston, 31, 47, 48, 54, 80, 102, 105
Clinton, Hilary, 53
Clinton, William (Bill), 43, 70
Cold War, 6, 7, 11, 17, 42, 43, 45, 57, 60, 63, 65, 68, 69, 70, 75, 105, 106, 112, 118, 131, 145, 158, 167, 169

culture, 1, 3, 7, 11, 24, 31, 32, 33, 42, 43, 46, 52, 63, 65, 77, 88, 91, 104–6, 108, 128, 129, 130, 133, 134, 137, 155, 170; culture war, 1, 11, 16, 17, 19

East India Company, 30, 32, 33, 34, 113, 127
Eisenhower, Dwight, 24, 42, 43, 53, 64, 75, 105, 112, 168
Esposito, John, 66, 67, 76, 148, 161

Gladstone, William, 46, 47, 54, 125, 169

halal, 24, 88, 89, 90, 93, 94. *See also* 'Sharia'
Huntington, Samuel, 19, 43, 69, 70, 169

India, 19, 30–37, 46, 47, 60, 62, 65, 74, 75, 80, 97–99, 100, 102, 103, 110–19, 121, 123, 124, 126, 127, 128, 137, 138, 143, 167
Iran, 25, 26, 43, 61, 64–68, 70, 72, 73, 75, 76, 104, 108, 133, 141, 142, 155, 158

Islam. *See* 'Muslim'

Jefferson, Thomas, 26, 36, 40, 41, 52, 53

Lausanne, Treaty of, 57, 58

Mapilla Rebellion, 123, 124, 126
May, Theresa, 150
Middle East, 14, 27, 29, 30, 35, 43, 49, 53, 58, 59, 60, 61, 63, 66–68, 69–71, 72, 73, 74, 75, 76, 77, 79, 84, 91, 92, 94, 96, 103, 104, 105, 107, 108, 111, 118–21, 125, 128, 137, 138, 141, 144, 146, 154, 155, 169, 172
missionaries: Christian, 23, 32–34, 36, 37, 59, 114, 116; Muslim, 29, 118
Mosque, 26, 36, 47, 53, 54, 67, 73, 87, 95, 96, 100, 101–6, 108–11, 135, 140, 148, 152, 155, 156, 168
Muslim, 1–6, 9–10, 13–18, 20–37, 39–54, 57–64, 67–77, 79, 83–84, 86, 87–112, 114–18, 121, 123, 125–32, 134, 136–49, 152–73

Nation of Islam, 23, 25, 26, 36, 152, 158, 162
Nixon, Richard, 70, 152

Ottoman Empire, 14, 23, 26, 28, 30, 35, 36, 41, 46, 47, 54, 57–60, 61, 74, 110, 114–17, 121–26

Pakistan, 14, 25, 26, 50, 69, 70, 71, 77, 102, 140, 141, 155
Pan-Islamism, 61, 62, 74, 75, 98, 100, 110, 116, 122, 126
Philby, St. John, 118–21, 124, 166
Prevent (Counter-terrorism Strategy), 51, 95, 144, 149–50, 154, 156, 158–60, 161, 162, 163, 164

Rawls, John, 5, 7, 8, 9, 18
Roosevelt, Theodore, 41, 42, 53, 112

Salafi(sm), 22, 26, 67, 160, 161, 168
Saudi Arabia, 63, 68–77, 83, 84, 86, 87, 105, 119, 137, 138, 140, 141, 142, 145
Sevres, Treaty of, 57, 58
sharia, 25, 51, 67, 115, 135–39, 144, 145; finance, 79, 82, 83–88, 91, 93, 171. *See also* 'Halal'
Special Relationship, 3, 17
Suez Crisis, 3, 82, 131, 144

terrorism, 2, 11, 13, 14, 15, 20, 44, 45, 48, 49, 51, 69, 73, 87, 88, 93, 95, 96, 140–64, 169; War on Terror, 14, 54, 57, 68–71, 73, 76, 77, 122, 163
Thatcher, Margaret, 12, 48–49, 54
Trump, Donald, 11, 45, 54, 72, 77, 144, 147, 155, 159, 160, 169

Webb, Alexander Russell, 120–22, 124, 126, 166

About the Author

Sean Oliver-Dee is a Research Associate at the Oxford Centre for Religion and Culture, Regents Park College, University of Oxford. He is the co-author of a number of government and parliamentary reports and has published articles, books, and chapters. Sean provides consultancy services for a number of government departments and NGOs.

www.ingramcontent.com/pod-product-compliance
Lightning Source LLC
Chambersburg PA
CBHW050906300426
44111CB00010B/1399